The First World War
in Africa

THE FIRST
WORLD WAR
IN AFRICA

HEW STRACHAN

OXFORD
UNIVERSITY PRESS

OXFORD

UNIVERSITY PRESS

Great Clarendon Street, Oxford OX2 6DP

Oxford University Press is a department of the University of Oxford.
It furthers the University's objective of excellence in research, scholarship,
and education by publishing worldwide in

Oxford New York

Auckland Cape Town Dar es Salaam Hong Kong Karachi
Kuala Lumpur Madrid Melbourne Mexico City Nairobi
New Delhi Shanghai Taipei Toronto

With Offices in

Argentina Austria Brazil Chile Czech Republic France Greece
Guatemala Hungary Italy Japan South Korea Poland Portugal
Singapore Switzerland Thailand Turkey Ukraine Vietnam

Oxford is a registered trade mark of Oxford University Press
in the UK and in certain other countries

Published in the United States
by Oxford University Press Inc., New York

© Hew Strachan 2004

British Library Cataloguing in Publication Data

Data available

Library of Congress Cataloging in Publication Data

Data available

ISBN 0-19-925728-0

3 5 7 9 10 8 6 4 2

Typeset by Kolam Information Services Pvt. Ltd, Pondicherry, India
Printed in Great Britain on acid-free paper by
Ashford Colour Press Ltd, Gosport, Hampshire

PREFACE

The First World War has not always gone under that title. For those who endured it at the time and who spoke English it was the Great War. In France, 'la Grande Guerre' still enjoys wide currency. In Germany, however, it was from the first a world war, 'Der Weltkrieg'. The use of the world 'Welt' did not necessarily carry precise geographic significance. It was as much an indication of the war's importance, of its likely implications for the future, and of the vast ideological and cultural baggage which accompanied it. Nonetheless, while recognising that point, we should not dismiss the incorporation of the world in the war's name as mere rhetoric. All of the original belligerents in 1914 possessed territories outside Europe; their decisions to go to war immediately implicated their colonies in the other continents. Britain was much more: it was the hub of the world's shipping, insurance, banking and trading networks. These were both its greatest asset in war and its principal vulnerability.

Germany committed its armed forces to the fighting within Europe, but it also recognised the opportunity which their colonies presented to strike at its enemies outside Europe. The British empire was the soft underbelly of the Entente. Germany's intention was what Britain in a later war would call a peripheral strategy, to target distant points to whose defence the enemy would be compelled to divert both forces and resources. In 1914 Germany had two major means by which it could develop such schemes. One was its alliance with the Ottoman empire, concluded on 2 August 1914, which brought the Turks into the war on the side of the Central Powers at the end of October. Germany hoped to precipitate revolution among the Muslim peoples subject to British, French, and Russian rule. There were reckoned to be about 50 million Muslims in Africa in 1914. The summons to Holy War, proclaimed on 14 November 1914, was heard in Nigeria, Uganda, the Sudan and the Congo; it was relayed as far south as Nyasaland. But few of those living south of the Sahara responded. Even in North Africa the threat of revolt was, ultimately, contained. These were territories which had once been under Ottoman rule, and the combination of temporal with religious authority which the Sultan in Constantinople claimed through the Caliphate made the threat that much greater. The story of what happened in Egypt and Libya to the east, and Algeria and Morocco to the west is contained in the first volume of my history of the war, *The First World War—To Arms*. This book focuses on sub-Saharan Africa.

German success, or the lack of it, in North Africa depended on its Turkish allies. In the rest of the world its principal arm, at least at the war's outbreak in 1914, was the cruisers of the German navy. The naval build-up driven by Alfred von Tirpitz was directed at the balance of power in the North Sea and focused on battleships. But the navy was also justified as an instrument of Bernhard von Bülow's *Weltpolitik*. It therefore had global aspirations, which its base in China, established at Tsingtao in 1897, demonstrated. The ships which showed the Kaiser's flag in peacetime were potentially the scourge of Britain's trade in wartime. The greatest constraint on their effectiveness was their need for supplies, ammunition and coal. A steamship was far less independent of support from the land than the sailing ship had been: it could only eke out its fuel over twenty days by keeping its speed down and in practice it might need to coal every eight days or so. In addition to its possessions in the Pacific, Germany had colonies in east, west, and south-west Africa. Each of them had harbours capable of equipping, victualling and bunkering warships. Duala, Swakopmund, and Lüderitz gave onto the Atlantic, Tanga and Dar es Salaam onto the Indian Ocean. British trade from the Far East and India, passing round the Cape of Good Hope or cutting north to the Suez canal was conveyed on routes close to these ports. The story of the German cruiser campaign is also told in *The First World War—To Arms*.

Britain's aim at the beginning of the First World War was the reverse of Germany's. Germany wanted to open the war up in order to divert Britain in particular from the war in Europe. Britain wanted to close it down so that it could concentrate its efforts in France and Belgium. Germany had anticipated the probability that in the event of war Britain would re-route the world's principal under-water cable links through London, so as to enable British intelligence to monitor signals traffic. It had therefore set about—and by 1914 had all but completed—the construction of a series of transmitters whose range spanned most of the world. In August 1914 Britain's attention was focused in Europe. Therefore, the task of its forces in Africa was minimal and tightly defined. On 5 August 1915 a sub-committee of the Committee of Imperial Defence stated that Britain's objectives outside Europe were to do no more than secure its maritime communications. It should do so by using only local forces to gain control of German harbours and to destroy the German wireless network which would enable the coordination of Germany's global strategy. Britain had no desire to add to the burdens of empire by acquiring fresh territory.

Britain's strategic aims did not, however, stand alone. First, they were influenced by what historians now call sub-imperialism—the ambitions not only of those on the spot but also of the semi-independent dominions of those on the spot. As what follows makes clear, South Africa harboured designs in southern Africa to which Britain had to pay court. The Afrikaner population had fought a bitter and protracted war against the British just over a decade before, and the revolt by die-hard Boers in 1914 reminded London that it could not take South Africa's loyalty for granted. The South Africans could—and did—do London's work for it in Africa, but in doing so were able to set their own agenda.

Secondly, the French, themselves a major African power, were worried by the prospect of their longest-standing imperial rival conducting campaigns in territories where they too had designs, while they themselves were perforce focusing their eyes and efforts on metropolitan France. Their sensitivities were compounded by their identification of west Africa in particular as a source of military manpower for deployment in Europe. As a result, Britain used its acquisition of German territory in Africa to regulate its relationships with its allies and supporters rather than to appease its own lust for empire. What followed can, with justice, be described as the last stage in the scramble for Africa. Moreover, unlike its first stage—the congress in Berlin in 1885, this was about more than drawing lines on the map. Men on the ground were testing those maps against reality, taking the penetration of colonial powers further into the interior. They did so in pursuit less of empire than of the enemy, but the local consequences were not very different, the opening of roads, the assessment of local resources and the development of the cash economy.

Much of that money was disbursed to pay for men, as well as for food. The war in Africa was fought largely by Africans. Its scale may have been dwarfed in absolute terms by the events unfolding at the same time in Europe, but the war's importance needs to be judged in its local context as well as its global one. The First World War ranks alongside the slave trade in terms of its impact on Africa. Its impact was felt across the entire continent, and throughout the war's length of four and more years. The fighting may have been confined to certain theatres but its needs drew on the economies of all the adjacent territories. The First World War removed men—and women and children—from their homes; it undermined traditional patterns of authority; it destroyed many of the economic and especially agricultural benefits which colonisation had brought; and in some rare cases it triggered the first demands for African independence.

The text of what follows remains largely as it was when it was first published in *The First World War—To Arms*. I have, however, taken the opportunity to correct misprints and I am most grateful to N. C. Palmer in particular for his careful reading of the text. I have modified what I said on the health of Germans in East Africa in the light of Ross Anderson's work, itself due to be published in 2004, and I am most grateful to Peter Yearwood for putting me right on aspects of the Cameroons campaign.

CONTENTS

LIST OF MAPS

1

INTRODUCTION

On 12 August 1914, in Togoland, Regimental Sergeant-Major Alhaji Grun-shi of the West African Frontier Force became the first soldier in British service to fire a round in the Great War. On 25 November 1918, two weeks after the signature of the armistice in Europe, at Abercorn in Northern Rhodesia Colonel Paul von Lettow-Vorbeck surrendered, the last German commander of the war to do so.

As much from its outset as beyond its formal conclusion, therefore, the First World War was far more than just a European conflict. In August 1914 British, French, Belgian, and German belligerence embraced the entire continent of Africa with the exception of Liberia, Ethiopia, and the relatively smaller colonies of Spain, Italy, and Portugal. Not even these would remain exempt from the war, at least in its indirect forms.

In the eighteenth century Britain and France had fought in North America and India for the possession of empire. Conflict between the great powers had as often originated in the colonies as in Europe itself. But in the course of the nineteenth century overseas expansion was conducted without such clashes: mercantilism gave way to free trade, and govern-ments did not see territorial possession as the key to exclusive commercial rights. In 1898 Marchand and Kitchener, soldiers both, staked rival claims at Fashoda, on the upper reaches of the Nile, but neither France nor Britain resorted to arms in pursuit of those ambitions. Wars were plenty, but they were conducted against the native populations, and their pur-poses were local and limited. In 1914 none of the central governments of the belligerent powers was harbouring notions of imperial aggrandize-ment at the expense of its European neighbours through the use of battle.

The Anglo-German antagonism had scant relevance to Africa. Britain encouraged the Germans to expand, possibly at the expense of Belgium and Portugal; Germany respected rather than reviled British rule. Thus, in 1914 the flow of major war was the reverse of that in the eighteenth century—from Europe to the colonies, rather than vice versa.

Moreover, when the news of the crisis of late July 1914 reached the white settlers of Africa it rarely provoked the popular manifestations of enthusiasm exhibited in the capitals of their parent countries. The duty of Europeans, opined the *East Africa Standard* of Mombasa on 22 August 1914, was not to fight each other but to keep control of the Africans.[1] The objective of colonial government was pacification. The advent of war was against the common interests of all whites, whatever their nationalities; their numbers were exiguous; their hold on the recently conquered African interior was precarious, and in many areas incomplete. The nominal title of government did not necessarily conform to the actual exercise of power, which often still lay with local chiefs and headmen. Economic penetration through the construction of ports and railways, through plantations and mining, had only just begun. Where mass meetings in support of the war did take place, for example in Salisbury in Southern Rhodesia, they emphasized the exceptional nature of such settlements—their urbanization and, in this case, their Englishness. But even in Rhodesia, German and Austrian reservists were able to leave for Europe in late August,[2] and in South Africa not until May 1915, after the sinking of the *Lusitania*, were there riots against German firms operating within the Union.[3]

The fear of the white settler was a dual one. First, the spectacle of white fighting white would reduce the status of the European. Secondly, war would either rekindle the warrior traditions of those tribes in whom they had only recently been crushed or train in the use of arms those to whom they were unfamiliar. Blacks would kill whites, and the forfeit would be white racial supremacy. In the event, the notion that the European hold on sub-Saharan Africa would be destabilized by the re-emergence of traditional forces proved misplaced; the impact of the war deepened collaboration, and its contribution to colonial decline was much

[1] Savage and Munro, *Journal of African History*, VII (1966), 314.
[2] McLaughlin, *Ragtime Soldiers*, 2, 5–7.
[3] Ticktin, *South African Historical Journal*, (Nov. 1969), 69–70.

longer-term—through the erosion of tribal loyalties and the broadening of new black elites that were urbanized, westernized, and politically aware.

For the Great War in Africa, although the product of European devices and desires, was fought principally by the Africans themselves. In all, somewhere over 2 million Africans served in the First World War as soldiers or labourers, and upwards of 200,000 of them died or were killed in action.[4] By comparison with Europe such figures are low—the first represents between 1 and 2 per cent of the total population of Africa. But in a local context a comparison with twentieth-century industrialized nation states is inappropriate; never before in the history of Africa had manpower been mobilized on such a scale.

Both during the war and after it, British and French propaganda accused the Germans of militarizing Africa: they had, said Lloyd George on 24 January 1919, 'raised native troops and encouraged these troops to behave in a manner that would even disgrace the Bolsheviks'.[5] Such rhetoric was fed by the ferocity with which the Germans suppressed the wave of resistance that struck their colonies with simultaneous force between 1904 and 1906. Genocide and famine were both deployed against the Herero in South-West Africa and the Maji-Maji in East Africa. Thereafter, however, German colonial administration became more liberal. Military responsibilities were circumscribed, commercial development promoted, and settlement doubled. As a result, the German colonial forces, the *Schütztruppen*, could draw in more whites: from 1913 conscripts were allowed to complete their reserve service overseas rather than remain liable for recall to Germany. But the settlers themselves became increasingly reluctant to meet the costs of an inflated military establishment, and order on a daily basis was handed over to an expanded police force. Admittedly their armament was similar to that of the *Schütztruppen*, and they could be, and were, incorporated with them.[6] Nonetheless, the point remains that it was not so much Germany as the Entente which was responsible for arming the African.

---

[4] These approximations are derived from M. E. Page, 'Black men in a white men's war', in Page (ed.) *Africa and the First World War*, 14; M. Crowder, 'First World War and its consequences', 283, 293.

[5] S. C. Davis, *Reservoirs of Men*, 160.

[6] Wolfgang Petter, 'Der Kampf um die deutschen Kolonien', in Michalka (ed.), *De Erste Weltkrieg*, 397–9.

The idea that the immense manpower pool of the African colonies might be harnessed for military purposes was given its most coherent and ambitious pre-war expression in France, by Charles Mangin in his book *La Force Noire*, published in 1910. Mangin predicted that French West Africa could raise 40,000 men, or 4 per cent of the total population of 10.65 million, and that enlistment in some areas could rise to 8 or 10 per cent. At the time such projections looked far-fetched, but by the end of the war France had enlisted 200,000 soldiers in West Africa.[7] When Britain declared war, the Africans involved, directly or indirectly, in hostilities totalled 50 million.[8] The actual burden of service was unevenly distributed. In West Africa Britain recruited about 25,000 soldiers[9]—a relatively large figure, but small by comparison with French efforts in the adjacent areas. Southern Rhodesia, influenced by the South African opposition to using blacks as soldiers in a white man's war, enlisted no Africans until 1916. But by then 40 per cent of the white adult male population was on active service, and sufficient fresh drafts for the Rhodesia Regiment could not be procured. The Rhodesia Native Regiment, formed in 1916, had embodied only 2,360 men by 1918, less than 1 per cent of the total African male population, and 75 per cent of them originated from outside the colony.[10]

The majority of those Africans enlisted during the war were not soldiers, or not primarily so. They were carriers.[11] The major problem of conducting operations in Africa, as it had been in all the small wars of European conquest in the nineteenth century, lay 'not in defeating, but in reaching the enemy'.[12] Lettow-Vorbeck likened the march and supply of a single company in East Africa to the movement of a division in Europe.[13]

[7] Michel, *L'Appel à l'Afrique*, 21–4, 404; Echenberg, *Colonial Conscripts*, 25–32.

[8] Osuntokun, *Nigeria in the First World War*, viii.

[9] Roger Thomas, *Cahiers d'études africaines*, XV (1975), 57.

[10] Peter McLaughlin, 'The legacy of conquest: African military manpower in Southern Rhodesia during the First World War', in Page (ed.), *Africa*, 121, 132; McLaughlin, *Ragtime Soldiers*, 75; id., *Small Wars and Insurgencies*, II (1991), 249–57.

[11] On carriers, see esp. Geoffrey Hodges, *Carrier Corps*; Hodges, 'Military labour in East Africa and its impact on Kenya', in Page (ed.), *Africa*; D. Killingray and J. Matthews, *Canadian Journal of African Studies*, XIII (1979), 5–23; D. Killingray, *Journal of Contemporary History*, XXIV, (1989), 483–501; D. C. Savage and J. F. Munro, *Journal of African History*, VII (1966), 313–42.

[12] *East African Standard*, 6 Apr. 1917, quoted by Savage and Munro, *Journal of African History*, VII (1966), 314.

[13] Lettow-Vorbeck, *Reminiscences*, 30.

Railway construction had only just begun to open up the hinterland; roads were few, and motorized vehicles fewer. Draught or pack animals, although usable in the highlands and savannah of some parts of Central Africa and in South Africa, fell prey to the tsetse fly in many tropical areas. For the campaigns in the Cameroons and East Africa, therefore, a human chain linked troops to their bases, and without it they could not move, feed, or fight.

None of the major belligerents had anticipated the numbers of carriers which major operations would demand. The pre-war colonial units of all three powers, Britain, France, and Germany, had been designed primarily for internal policing, employing limited numbers in each column, and projecting themselves over short distances. For these purposes some units, but not all, had their own enlisted carriers. However, in 1914–15 Britain and France launched offensive operations deep into German territory. In the Cameroons both the British and the Germans reckoned they needed between two and three porters for each soldier; the French tried to make do with less, but continually found their communications close to collapse.[14] Thus, in West Africa the forces of Britain and Germany in the Cameroons each employed a force of about 40,000 carriers.[15] In East Africa the distances were greater, and the numbers grew accordingly. The British recruited over a million labourers for the campaign.[16] They were drawn from a vast area, from the eastern Belgian Congo, Ruanda, Uganda, Kenya, German East Africa, Northern Rhodesia, Nyasaland, and the northern areas of Mozambique. The district commissioner of Tanganyika, an area where both sides had recruited labour, reported that a third of the taxable male population had been taken.[17] For the East African and other theatres, the British West African colonies provided over 57,500 carriers, twice as many as they did soldiers, and in 1917 Nigeria specifically had to procure 4,000 carriers a month.[18] British East Africa and Nyasaland each raised over 200,000 men (83 per cent of the total available manpower in the latter case), and Uganda 190,000. The

---

[14] Gorges, *Great War in West Africa*, 203; Purschel, *Kaiserliche Schutztruppe*, 28; Ministère de la guerre, *Armées françaises*, IX, 2ᵉ vol., 540–4.

[15] Mentzel, *Kämpfe in Kamerun*, 45; Gorges, *Great War in West Africa*, 203.

[16] Hodges in Page (ed.), *Africa*, 148.

[17] Killingray, *Journal of Contemporary History*, XXIV (1989), 489.

[18] Killingray and Matthews, *Canadian Journal of African Studies*, XIII (1979), 10; Osuntokun, *Nigeria*, 252.

Belgian Congo drew in 260,000 porters during the war, both for domestic and external needs; Portuguese East Africa contributed 30,000 porters to the British and 90,000 to its own forces.[19]

Such numbers could not be raised voluntarily. Most were impressed, either directly or indirectly. Chiefs would undertake to provide quotas. In British East Africa settler pressure to maximize the available labour supply led in 1915 to conscription. Desertion was therefore endemic. A convoy dispatched from Bangui in French Equatorial Africa in September 1914 had only forty-nine of its original complement of 298 porters left when it arrived at Boda.[20] One solution, adopted on this particular route but practicable only where the lines of communication were clear and local manpower abundant, was to fix the stages between villages so that the porters could return home each night. The alternative and more frequently applied check to desertion was to remove the porter from his native locality, and thus eliminate the temptation to abscond. But, once away from his own area, the carrier became prey to disease, the second major cause of high losses.

The carriers chosen by headmen were frequently those who were locally dispensable, and probably the less fit. Distant from their own homelands, they were often issued with rations with which they were unfamiliar. Many Europeans thought that mealie meal, made up of maize flour and cobs, was the standard African diet. In reality, maize was only just being introduced in inland areas. Ugandans subsisted on bananas, sweet potatoes, and beans. Fed on grain, they developed intestinal diseases and 40 per cent of the contingent raised in August 1914 were invalided within three months. In March 1917 Uganda focused its recruiting efforts on grain-eating tribes, but could pass only 5,763 of 41,706 called up as fit for service. Rice-eating tribes given maize fell victim to beri-beri. Even for those accustomed to mealie meal, the problems of its preparation undermined its nutritional value. In the porters' villages food was prepared by women. The men, therefore, lacked culinary skills. However, on the march they were expected to cook their own food. Mealie meal had to be boiled for one and a half hours, and the largest size of pot required six hours. The halts at night were too brief to allow

---

[19] Hodges, *Journal of African History*, XIX (1978), 101–16; Belgique, Ministère de la Défense Nationale, *Campagnes coloniales belges*, i. 34; Pélissier, *Mozambique*, ii. 684–5.

[20] Ministère de la Guerre, *Armées françaises*, IX, 2ᵉ vol., 141.

sufficient wood to be collected for the fire, and for the food to be dried and properly cooked. Dysentery was the consequence: it was responsible for half the porters' hospital admissions, and intestinal diseases of all sorts for half the fatalities.[21] Finally, the nutritional content of the porters' diet was often inadequate. Porters in British pay in the Cameroons received daily rations on two scales, either 2,702 or 1,741 calories: neither was sufficient for a man expected to carry up to 60 pounds for 24 kilometres a day. In East Africa in 1917 porters were getting less than 1,000 calories a day.[22]

Wastage levels were enormous. Among East and West Africans employed as carriers in the war the death rate (including those reported as missing) was—at about 20 per cent—similar to that of an army on a so-called major front.[23] Belgian porters succumbed in comparable numbers, which were five times those suffered by the native soldiers— or askaris—in Belgian service.[24] Many more were invalided, victims of ulcerated feet, malaria, and chest infections. Of 20,000 porters sent to the Cameroons by the British, 574 died and 8,219 were invalided.[25] The West African carriers in East Africa, after nine months service, could muster only 37 per cent effectives in the case of southern Nigerians and 8.3 per cent in that of northern Nigerians.[26]

Thus, a series of interlocking problems kept the lines of communication constantly on the verge of breakdown. Better provision for the care of carriers reduced death and disease, and so eased the demands for fresh recruitment. But it also threatened to place the personal needs of the porter ahead of those of the fighting troops. The longer the line of march, the more likely would the porters be to consume larger loads than they carried. Assuming an average ration of 3 pounds per day and a load of 60 pounds, a line of communication of ten daily marches needed as many porters as there were soldiers in the front line. A march of three weeks and the porter consumed his entire load himself.[27] Thus, there was a trade-off

[21] Hodges, *Carrier Corps*, 119–30; Lucas, *Empire at War*, iv. 236–8.
[22] Killingray and Matthews, *Canadian Journal of African Studies*, XIII (1979), 17–18.
[23] Hodges in Page (ed.), *Africa*, 143–4; Killingray, *Journal of Contemporary History*, XXIV (1979), 493; Lucas, *Empire at War*, iv. 214–15.
[24] Belgique, *Campagnes coloniales belges*, iii. 268.
[25] Moberly, *Togoland and Cameroons*, 427.
[26] Killingray and Matthews, *Canadian Journal of African Studies*, XIII (1979), 18.
[27] Lucas, *Empire at War*, iv. 269–70, 292–3; Fendall, *East African Force*, 206–7.

between the porter's own nutrition and the needs of the soldier, both in food and munitions.

Compromise had also to be sought in determining the European component of the forces engaged. Both sides were firmly convinced that the morale of their troops depended on the presence of white officers who were known to their men. But each British officer in East Africa needed between seven and nine porters. Such a ratio was not unusual: a Belgian officer had eight porters, and a German officer in West Africa had four to six porters, a servant, and a cook. The French scoffed at what they saw as luxurious over-provision. In the Cameroons two Frenchmen were reckoned to require three porters.[28] In reality such proportions were a reflection of the cavalier French approach to supply problems, not an indication of French immunity to the hazards of war in the tropics. Even in the final stages of their epic march through Portuguese East Africa, the Europeans in Lettow-Vorbeck's force were allowed three porters each.[29]

Disease, not battle, disabled armies in Africa. Thanks to the elimination of typhus and cholera, the armies fighting the war in Europe were the first to suffer more casualties through combat than through sickness. Outside Europe the old order prevailed. In East Africa 3,156 whites in British service died; 2,225 of these were victims of disease.[30] But the true scale of the problem is revealed by reference to non-fatalities: men fell sick rather than died. In West Africa the allied forces lost a total of 4,600 men through death or wounding in action or through death by disease; by contrast, over 35,000 cases were admitted to hospital.[31] Casualty evacuation was therefore another load for the hard-pressed carrier.

The conventional wisdom argued that not only was the European more reliant on the maintenance of the lines of communication, he was also less immune to local diseases. Of the vulnerability of whites, particularly in East Africa, there is abundant evidence. On 31 October 1915 one British battalion had 836 of its strength in hospital and only 278 in the field. By the end of 1916 12,000 out of 20,000 South Africans had been invalided home.[32] The 2nd Rhodesia Regiment, whose effective strength

[28] Charbonneau, *Revue militaire française*, 129 (mars 1932), 412–15; Student, *Kameruns Kampf*, 171; Belgique, *Campagnes coloniales belges*, i. 33.

[29] Deppe, *Mit Lettow-Vorbeck*, 108.

[30] War Office, *Statistics of the Military Effort*, 302.

[31] Gorges, *Great War in West Africa*, 261–2.

[32] Charles Miller, *Battle for the Bundu*, 139, 233.

was 800 men, was often reduced to 100, and had a wastage rate of 20 per cent per month.[33] Malaria was the principal cause of sickness: it resulted in 50,768 hospital admissions among the British forces in East Africa between June and December 1916. But it was not the most fatal of illnesses: only 263 deaths resulted, whereas 3,795 of the 8,902 admitted with dysentery succumbed.[34]

The argument that therefore campaigns in Africa should be fought by those native to the continent was not the straightforward solution it seemed. The health problems of the porters provide abundant evidence to the contrary. In the Cameroons, of the British forces 151 out of 864 white soldiers were invalided through sickness, and 434 out of 5,927 Africans; the French figures similarly showed only a marginal health advantage in favour of the native.[35] In East Africa African soldiers in British service suffered 1,377 deaths through combat as against 2,923 from disease.[36] In some respects the medical problems of the African were different from those of the European. His bare feet were vulnerable to jiggers, and 40 per cent of the West African Frontier Force were lame by the end of the Cameroons campaign.[37] One German doctor thought typhus, smallpox, meningitis, and sleeping sickness were all more dangerous to blacks than to whites.[38] The Europeans were convinced that the Africans enjoyed a relative immunity from malaria, or that they suffered it less acutely. But an African from a malaria-free region was no less vulnerable than a European if moved to an area where the illness was endemic. The migration of so many Africans out of their native localities exposed them to fresh infections, and the physical and psychological demands lowered their resistance to disease. By the same token, those fighting in or close to their own homelands proved more hardy. The health of the German forces in the Cameroons, most of them native to the area, held up remarkably well through eighteen months of campaigning. They were lucky, in that they had just taken delivery of a year's worth of medical supplies when war broke out. But the efforts to treat the sick as

---

[33] McLaughlin, *Ragtime Soldiers*, 41, 46.
[34] Mitchell and Smith, *Medical Services: Casualties*, 259.
[35] Moberly, *Togoland and Cameroons*, 427.
[36] War Office, *Statistics of the Military Effort*, 302.
[37] Lucas, *Empire at War*, iv. 66, 118.
[38] Deppe, *Mit Lettow-Vorbeck*, 154.

far as possible within their own companies showed the Germans' recognition of the value of familiarity in the morale of the patient.[39]

In aggregate, the fitness of the soldiers in Africa bore a direct relationship to the efficiency of the supply system and to the provision of satisfactory medical arrangements. The French were negligent in both respects, and paid the penalty. In the Cameroons expeditionary force, the French contingent had four medical officers; the comparably sized British contingent had twenty-seven. The French sickness rate was just over double that of the British.[40] The Germans were not slow to attribute their relatively good health in the West African campaign to their having sufficient doctors, allowing them to allocate one per company. To do less was false economy. A sick soldier undermined the efforts of the porters to supply that soldier; a sick porter starved the soldier and rendered him less robust; casualty evacuation consumed more labour; and manpower losses through preventable causes increased the demands on a fast-diminishing pool of available men.

The difficulties of supply, rather than the experiences of battle, did most to disseminate the impact of the Great War throughout the African continent. The numbers who experienced combat were few. The war in Africa was an affair not of 'big battalions' but of individual companies. A unit any larger than 100 to 120 men could not be readily supplied. Moreover, a company with its attendant porters mustered about 300 men and on the tracks of the equatorial rain forests of central Africa constituted a column 1,500 to 2,000 yards long; a formation any bigger was too large for effective, tactical control. The force-to-space ratio was, therefore, totally different from that of the western front. Small-scale actions in Africa settled the balance of power in territories as big as a whole theatre of operations in Europe.

One of the most striking differences was the almost total absence of artillery. Individually, heavy guns proved of value in the open grasslands of the northern Cameroons or northern Tanganyika. But collectively, guns had little opportunity. Even where draught animals were more readily available, in South-West Africa, the Germans were not able to turn a relative strength to advantage. Oxen moved slowly, and not at all in

---

[39] Purschel, *Kaiserliche Schutztruppe*, 81–3.

[40] Moberly, *Togoland and Cameroons*; Charbonneau, *Revue militaire française*, 129 (mars 1932), 419–20.

the midday heat. Mules were used for the transport of pack guns, but the lack of clear paths through the bush meant that they could take twice as long to cover the same distance as did the foot-soldier. Thus, the guns tended to arrive too late. In theatres where the tsetse fly ruled out animal draught, 300 porters could be required for a single field gun,[41] without considering its likely shell consumption. In the jungle, even a small-calibre mountain gun firing at a high trajectory needed a clearing of 100 yards, as well as good telephone communications with forward observers, for indirect fire.[42] Because none of the European powers had planned to fight each other, the guns possessed by each colony tended to be of varying calibres, obsolescent, and short of ammunition. In the Cameroons the Germans had fourteen guns of different types and 3,000 rounds.[43] When used, their moral impact, particularly on black troops unaccustomed to artillery fire however light, outstripped their destructive effect. Fighting in Africa was therefore predominantly an infantry affair, the machine-gun being the heaviest and most significant weapon regularly deployed.

Thus, the individual was not tyrannized, as he was on the western front, by the industrialization of warfare. The division between war and exploration, between the dangers of the bullet and the snakebite, was unclear in many of the pre-1914 imaginings of the war: both were antidotes to bourgeois decadence. In Africa, unlike Europe, the distinction could remain obscure. A single cruiser, SMS *Königsberg*, whose contribution to the balance of forces in the North Sea would have been negligible, acquired in East Africa a significance out of all proportion to her firepower. Her lair in the Rufiji delta was discovered by Pieter Pretorius, a big-game hunter whose skills and courage would have been, relatively speaking, nugatory in the trenches of Ypres or the Somme. Another big-game hunter, F. C. Selous, joined the 25th battalion, the Royal Fusiliers, the so-called Legion of Frontiersmen. His reputation as a naturalist and explorer was embroidered with stories that extended back to his schooldays at Rugby. His death in action in East Africa on

[41] Charbonneau, *Revue militaire française*, 129 (mars 1932), 404–5; Beadon, *Royal Army Service Corps*, ii. 296; Deppe, *Mit Lettow-Vorbeck*, 250–4.

[42] Haywood and Clarke, *Royal West African Frontier Force*, 272–3.

[43] Mentzel, *Kämpfe im Kamerun*, 18.

4 January 1917, at the age of 65, was of a piece with his entire life, not at odds with it; few other subalterns were as lucky.

The experience of Pretorius or of Selous was directly relevant. The major problems of the opposing sides were geographically determined. The Royal Navy knew that the *Königsberg* was at Salale from signals intercepts, but Salale was not marked on the navy's charts; eleven days elapsed in late October 1914 before it was identified as being on the Rufiji.[44] Cursed with inadequate maps, intelligence efforts were devoted as much to establishing the nature of the country and its resources as to learning the enemy's whereabouts and strength. Both the climate, with its switch from dry to rainy seasons, and the insect life, with its impact on the health of livestock and humans, were strategically decisive. East Africa was home to the anopheles mosquito, the tsetse fly, the jigger flea, the spirillum tick, the white ant, the scorpion, the poisonous spider, the wild bee, and the warrior ant. The range of larger fauna provided more than an exotic backdrop to the fighting. Soldiers, if sick or sleeping, were liable to be eaten by lions or hyenas; both elephants and rhinoceroses were known to attack patrols, with fatal consequences. On the other hand, game provided an important supplement to the diet, hippopotamuses and elephants in particular being shot for their fat.

Although fought between European powers for objectives that were also European, the African campaigns of the First World War bore more relationship to the nineteenth-century campaigns of colonial conquest than they did to the Great War itself. In relation to the outcome of the war they were, as is too often remarked, sideshows. But neither observation should be allowed to trivialize their importance. The first demonstrates the danger of characterizing the war in terms appropriate to only one theatre, even one not fitted to the entire geographical span of the war. The second judges Africa in terms of that one theatre, instead of recognizing that relatively the impact of the war on the dark continent was as great as that on Europe, that few black families were unaffected, and that at the end the transfer of territory completed the partition of Africa commenced four decades earlier.

[44] Yates, *Graf Spee's Raiders*, 249–59.

2

TOGOLAND

The first Entente victory of the war was the fruit, not of central staff planning, but of improvised action at the local level. The seizure of German Togoland was in perfect consonance with the objectives set out by the subcommittee of the Committee of Imperial Defence at its meeting in London on 5 August 1914—it employed only local forces, and it eliminated Germany's single most important overseas wireless station, that at Kamina, linking Nauen with Germany's other African colonies, with shipping in the South Atlantic, and with South America. However, both the initiation of the British attack and the rapidity of its execution were due primarily to Captain F. C. Bryant, temporarily commanding the Gold Coast Regiment in the absence on leave of both its senior officers.[1]

The main focus of the defensive plan for the Gold Coast was the protection of its north-eastern frontier, and of the navigation of the Lower Volta. Its offensive options included the possibility of pushing across the Volta into Togoland, isolating the north, and then swinging south, meeting a second and subsidiary thrust moving eastwards along the coast from Ada to Lome. The plan had been last revised in May 1913. It made no provision for French co-operation from Dahomey, to the east of Togoland, and, more importantly, it antedated the completion in June 1914 of the Kamina wireless station. That its basic thrust, the defence of the Gold Coast, should be abandoned in 1914 in favour of an attack on

---

[1] The best narratives of operations are Lucas, *Empire at War*, iv. 3; Moberly, *Togoland and Cameroons*, ch. 1; Sebald, *Togo 1884–1914*, 593–605; Haywood and Clarke, *Royal West African Frontier Force*, 97–104. On Bryant's role and plans, see Grove, *Army Quarterly*, CVI (1976), 308–23; Ekoko, *Journal of Strategic Studies*, VII (1984), 440–56.

Kamina was not in dispute. Brigadier-General C. M. Dobell, inspector-general of the West African Frontier Force, and fortuitously in London on leave, told the subcommittee of the Committee of Imperial Defence that Lome and Kamina were the only worthwhile objectives in Togoland. But Dobell was disposed to caution. Although Lome was just over a kilometre from Togoland's frontier with the Gold Coast, Dobell regarded that as a sufficient advance for the time being, and even made it conditional on the presence of a naval escort.

Events on the ground outstripped such calculations. The Gold Coast Regiment mobilized on 31 July, three days ahead of Britain's general mobilization. Bryant shifted the axis of its deployment from the north-eastern frontier to the south, concentrating three companies at Kumasi and two at Ada. On 4 August the French, on Togoland's other flank, prepared to implement their plan, also drawn up in ignorance both of their ally's intentions and of Kamina's existence, for a westward advance along the coast to Lome, beginning in the evening of 6 August. Bryant's energy was attributable as much to his desire to forestall any independent French initiatives as to a lust for battle.

The prospects confronting the Germans in Togoland were not encouraging. Their colony, a thin strip stretching inland from a coastline only 51 kilometres long, was bounded on all its frontiers by enemy territory. No regular soldiers were available for its defence; the garrison consisted of 152 paramilitary police, supplemented by 416 local police and 125 border guards; they had four machine-guns, only fourteen of the 1898-pattern rifles, and otherwise relied on the 1871-pattern *Jäger* carbine.[2] The governor was on leave. The first step, therefore, of his deputy, Major von Doering, was to propose neutrality to his British and French neighbours.

The Congo act, ratified by the Treaty of Berlin in 1885, allowed any power within the Congo basin to declare itself neutral. However, its provisions did not extend so far from the Congo itself. The basis for Doering's suggestion was not international law, but the self-interest of the white colonial powers of West Africa. The economic interdependence of the three belligerents was obvious. For the British colonies, Germany was the major purchaser of their palm kernels, and was strongly represented

---

[2] Reichsarchiv, *Weltkrieg*, ix. 466. German strengths are variously given; Schwarte, *Weltkampf*, iv. 360, has 400 effectives; Sebald, *Togo*, has 500, rising to 1,000 on mobilization; Haywood and Clarke, *Royal West African Frontier Force*, 98, manage to find 1,500.

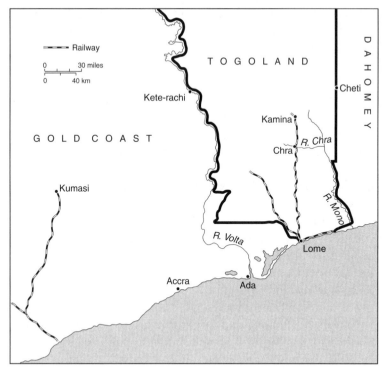

MAP 1. TOGOLAND

in the trading houses and shipping arrangements of Nigeria and of the Gold Coast; for French West Africa, Germany had become between 1910 and 1914 its fastest-growing export market, and was particularly strong in Togoland's neighbour, Dahomey.[3] But von Doering's bid rested less on common commercial grounds than on German worries about the loyalty of their black subjects. Thus, instead of playing to the Entente's weakness, he highlighted its strength. Britain's local reputation as a benevolent colonial administration was a powerful incentive to Entente belligerence, not to neutrality. Bryant, although restrained by W. C. F. Robertson, the acting governor of the Gold Coast (another whose superior was on

---

[3] Killingray, *Journal of African History*, XIX (1978), 43, 54; Osuntokun, *Nigeria*, 22–4; Crowder, 'The 1914–1918 European war and West Africa', 503; Lucas, *Empire at War*, iv. 21; Michel, *L'Appel à l'Afrique*, 147–8.

leave), even wanted to arm the Ashanti and foment insurrection on the Gold Coast–Togoland border. Thus, appeals on the basis of white supremacy were not calculated to restrain the British or the French. Von Doering's bid for neutrality was seen for what it was—a reflection of German weakness.

Bryant's response to the French initiatives and to the German plea was unequivocal. Without consulting Robertson, let alone London, he sent an emissary to Lome on 6 August to demand the surrender of Togoland. Von Doering signalled to Berlin that he planned to abandon the defenceless Lome and the territory 110 kilometres to its north, and to fall back inland to Kamina. Dispatched by wireless in clear, the intercepted German message justified Bryant's impetuosity. On 9 August the Colonial Office, assured of French co-operation, allowed Bryant to attack Kamina. On 12 August two companies of the Gold Coast Regiment took possession of Lome. It was the decisive step of the campaign. The harbour at Lome enabled Bryant to concentrate fourteen days sooner than if he had been confined to land routes.

The railway and the road which linked Lome and Kamina were 'parallel but not always adjacent',[4] and the Germans had made some rather half-hearted efforts to destroy the former. Advance off the road was impeded by swamp and bush. Furthermore, the Gold Coast Regiment, in meeting the requirements of Bryant's revised concentration, had already marched considerable distances. Nonetheless, the British encountered no serious resistance until 22 August. The Germans withdrew across the Chra river, blowing the railway bridge and taking up strong positions on its northern bank. In the subsequent attack the British columns lost contact with each other in the bush, and the courage of the Gold Coast forces wilted under their first exposure to machine-gun fire: the British suffered 17 per cent casualties. However, the Germans, although their losses were light, fell back once more under cover of dark. The action on the Chra marked the end of any serious resistance. On the night of 24/5 August the Germans destroyed the Kamina wireless station, smashing its nine huge masts and burning its switchboard and batteries with oil. On the following day von Doering surrendered. The war in the German colonies continued for over

---

[4] Lucas, *Empire at War*, iv. 29.

four years, but its principal strategic objective was accomplished in its first month.

In the first three weeks of August Kamina had handled 229 messages, linking Nauen not only to German colonies elsewhere but also to German shipping. Every day gained in its defence, therefore, had wider operational effects. But, confronted with a choice between the needs of Germany at war and the narrowly defined interests of the colony itself, von Doering opted for the latter. No effort was made to protract resistance. Six out of the seven provinces of Togoland were abandoned without a fight. Bridges were not destroyed. The Chra was the only river line out of three which the Germans defended. Von Doering interpreted the instructions to protect Kamina in the most literal terms: he held its perimeter, not its outworks. And even then the British captured there three machine-guns, 1,000 rifles, and 320,000 rounds, enough for several days' continued resistance.[5]

Manpower was a problem. The wireless operators, newly arrived and quartered inland, constituted an enclave with which the settler population did not identify. Over the three weeks of hostilities von Doering's strength had probably doubled from its peacetime establishment; he had 300 German residents available, including 200 who were reservists, and he had compulsorily recruited native levies during the course of his retreat from Lome. However, the Kamina position was still too extensive for the number of troops available. Furthermore, the Germans' military commander, Captain Georg Pfähler, had been killed in action on 16 August. Von Doering took counsel of his fears. He almost certainly exaggerated the strength of Bryant's force, whose only marked advantage in relation to his own lay in its possession of three 2.95-inch mountain guns. But, having failed to strike Bryant early, von Doering was confronted with converging forces of greater numbers. To the west a British force was moving on Kamina from Kete-Krachi, and to the east a French column from Cheti. Further Entente forces, mostly French irregulars, were pushing into northern Togoland. Thus, the defence of Kamina could only have been protracted for a matter of days. The maintenance of resistance in the bush, the primary objective having been lost, held no appeal for the deputy-governor; he could not be sure of native support, and its effects would be

---

[5] Klein-Arendt, *Kamina ruft Nauen*, 265–74.

likely to set back the economic benefits of colonialism. Von Doering's less-than-vigorous defence and his expeditious surrender were thus of a piece with his initial hopes for neutrality.

3

THE CAMEROONS

Germany's second West African colony, the Cameroons, was, like Togoland, bounded by the possessions of its enemies. Along the length of its north-western border, from the Atlantic to Lake Chad, lay British Nigeria. From Chad southward to the Congo, and then back westwards to the ocean, stretched the expanses of French Equatorial Africa. Only the rectangular slab of Muni or Spanish Guinea, stuck like a postage stamp in the bottom left-hand corner of German territory, and the offshore island of Fernando Po, also a Spanish possession, broke the German sense of isolation. Spanish neutrality was to prove a major boon to German defences.

The bulk of German development lay in the west, on the Atlantic littoral, with the hill-station of Buea, and the ports and wireless masts of Victoria and, above all, Duala. In 1914 two major railway lines were under construction; one to the north-east, destined for Lake Chad, had reached Nkongsamba, and the other south and east, bound for Jaunde, was complete as far as Eseka. But if the bulk of European infrastructure lay on the coast, the heart of the Cameroons itself was inland. In the north a line of mountains, parallel with the Nigerian frontier, formed a plateau, covered in tall elephant grass, free of the tsetse fly, and favourable to livestock; its major feature, Mount Cameroon, lay some 5,000 metres above sea level as a symbolic barrier to the west. To the south the highlands fell away to the central rivers, the Sanga and the Njong. Below them, and as far as the French border, lay jungle and swamp, an area whose rivers, notably the Sanaga, fed the Congo. In 1911 French concessions after the second Moroccan crisis had extended Germany's frontiers to the south-east, at one point to the Ubangi, at Singa, and at another to the Congo itself, at Bonga. Thus, of the 480,000 square kilometres of German territory, the coastal strip was but a small fraction, and effectively as isolated from the interior to its east as it itself was by the sea to its west.

Germany's pre-war thinking about the defence of its colony had shifted focus in accordance with its own advance. The recent settlement of its inland frontiers—1911 with France, and (in matters of detail) 1913 with Britain—had been accompanied by the problems of pacification (barely completed in some areas) and incorporation (still under way in the Congo territory in 1914). The navy, although happy to have Duala as a base for cruiser operations in the South Atlantic, was prepared neither to produce the funds to fortify it nor provide the ships to protect it. The general view in the Colonial Office was that international agreement would provide no better defence. The Congo act embraced the eastern and south-eastern Cameroons, but for the French and British to remain neutral on one front, so allowing the Germans to concentrate on the north, seemed improbable. The logical conclusion, to rest the defence of the colony on its own forces, the *Schütztruppen*, and to conduct it from the interior of the country, was not, however, an easy step. The governor, Ebermaier, was averse to using black troops in a white man's war; his military commander thought that, given the vulnerability of the Cameroons' extended frontiers, sustained resistance would be impossible if the colony's link with Germany through Duala was not kept open. Therefore, only reluctantly, with a renewal in 1913 of the decision not to spend money fortifying Duala, did the local authorities begin to reckon on defending the colony from the interior.[1]

---

[1] The basic premises of German strategy, which have almost entirely eluded English-language authors, are spelt out by Mentzel, *Die Kämpfe in Kamerun* (1936), 25–34, and are also to be found in Reichsarchiv, *Weltkrieg*, ix. 470–2. Mentzel's is the most sensible overview of the campaign in any language; his earlier survey (1932) is also suggestive, but brief. The fullest (as well as most critical) operational account is the French official history, Ministère de la Guerre, *Les Armées françaises*, IX, 2ᵉ vol.; the British official history, Moberly, *Togoland and Cameroons*, focuses on British operations but fails to provide a wider context; Student, *Kameruns Kampf*, the most detailed German account, has the same defect. On the tactics of bush war, see Purschel, *Kaiserliche Schutztruppe für Kamerun*, and Charbonneau, *Revue militaire française*, 129 (mars 1932), 397–420, and 130 (avril 1932), 80–99. Memoirs, helpful but posing as more objective accounts, include Aymérich, *Conquête du Cameroun*, and Gorges, *Great War in West Africa*. Haywood and Clarke, *Royal West African Frontier Force*, ch. 4, and Osuntokun, *Nigeria*, ch. 6, are both valuable. The only recent English-language survey, Farwell, *Great War in Africa*, is bounded by the Anglocentric concerns of Moberly and Gorges. Michel,

The plan, drawn up on 24 November 1913, and to provide the basis of German operations until mid-1915, chose as its focus not Duala but Ngaundere, in the centre of the northern highlands. The south, however impenetrable to the invader, was not considered because its climate was poor and it lacked the agricultural resources of the northern plateau. Four of the twelve companies of *Schütztruppen* were to be based on Ngaundere, three at Bertua to the east of Jaunde, two (plus the police training company) at Jaunde, and three at Bamenda in the north-west. Thus the central and northern plateau of the Cameroons, naturally defended by mountains to the north, by jungle and swamp to the south, was to become an inner bastion. The loss of the coastal strip or France's reconquest of the territories forfeited in 1911 would not represent setbacks of strategic significance. The Germans in the Cameroons intended to conduct a defence sufficiently protracted to ensure that when the hostilities in Europe came to an end Germany's claim to the colony would, at the peace talks, still be bolstered by possession. Thus, the stubborn resistance of the Cameroons was motivated not by any German desire to draw Entente troops from Europe, not by a wish to use a sideshow for a wider strategic purpose, but by the fact that colonization mattered as an end in itself.

The major implication of the 1913 plan was that the *Schütztruppen* were to defend the Cameroons against an external enemy. This was not a task for which they were either equipped or trained. The stated role of the *Schütztruppen* was to protect the white settlers, to maintain order, and to suppress slavery. Their total establishment was 205 white officers and NCOs and 1,650 blacks. When first formed, they had recruited from outside the Cameroons and from the coastal areas; by 1914, although 13 per cent of the askaris were still drawn from outside, the major recruiting area had become the central Cameroons, and in particular the district of Jaunde. Enlistment was voluntary, and the minimum term of service fixed at three years. In reality, most served for an average of five years, and some for much longer; the Germans feared that if warriors trained in the arts of war returned to their tribes when they were still militarily effective, any insurrection would benefit from their skills. The consequence of this concern was a body of men that, by the standards of

Guerres mondiales et conflits contemporains, 168 (1992), 13–29, is helpful; Nouzille, *Revue internationale d'histoire militaire*, 63 (1985), 9–20, is disappointing.

its potential foes, was homogeneous and well-trained. The askari was accustomed to fighting superior numbers and winning by virtue of his discipline and his firepower. But the *Schütztruppen* also suffered from the weaknesses of regular, professional armies. The families of the men became part of the military establishment and accompanied those of more than two years' service on campaign. Morale was closely identified with the leadership of individual officers, bonds forged over time and not easy to replace in the event of casualties. And although the mobilization of reservists was allowed for in 1913, no reserve organization was in place in 1914.

Indeed, little had been done by 1914 to follow through the implications of the 1913 plan. Quality sustained the *Schütztruppen* in their domestic tasks; quantity would be at issue when facing the comparable forces of their European neighbours. France had 20,000 black troops in its West African and Equatorial colonies in August 1914;[2] Britain's West African Frontier Force (which encompassed Nigeria, the Gold Coast, Sierra Leone, and the Gambia) mustered 7,552 of all ranks.[3] Many of these formations were, like the Germans', committed to peacetime tasks, and would not be available for an expeditionary force to the Cameroons. Nonetheless, the most urgent need of the German government was to procure more men. The idea of the nation in arms became reality far sooner for the 2,000 white settlers than it did for their fellow-nationals at home; the incorporation of the police immediately doubled the Germans' strength to 3,200 black troops; the reservists were under arms by January 1915; and the maximum force achieved at any one time was 1,460 whites and 6,550 blacks, a total of thirty-four companies.

Two strains were generated by this quintupling of the armed forces. The first was persistent, but not ultimately decisive. Fully sixty-five of the *Schutztruppe*'s German officers and NCOs were at home on leave in August 1914. The deficit was never made good. The addition of the police worsened it; for a peacetime strength comparable with that of the *Schütztruppen*, they had only thirty Germans. The European reservists did little to improve it. On mobilization they were formed into separate companies. The supply problems of purely European units robbed these

[2] Michel, *L'Appel à l'Afrique*, 42–3.
[3] War Office, *Statistics of the Military Effort*, 383.

companies of mobility, and thus of any utility after the loss of the coastal areas, and they were disbanded in 1915. But the dispersion of their members to other formations did not ease the demand for trained German officers. Most field companies in 1915 had only one or two European officers each, plus a medical officer and a couple more Europeans for each of the machine-guns (of which each company had three to four). Combat experience suggested an optimum would have been twelve to fifteen Germans per company.[4] In these circumstances the loss of a single German officer could have considerable repercussions.

The second strain was both persistent and decisive. Some effort was made to increase the firepower of the *Schütztruppen* in the light of the 1913 plan. The number of machine-guns, forty-three initially, rising to sixty, was probably sufficient given the limited fields of fire available in the enclosed territory of the equatorial rain forests. The issue of the 1898-pattern rifle, to replace the 1871 *Jäger* carbine, was expedited. But the process was not complete in 1914. The colony possessed 3,861 1898-pattern rifles and carbines, and 2,920 of the older patterns; there were 2.25 million rounds available for the former and for the machine-guns, and 500,000 rounds for the latter.[5] Therefore, only nine-tenths of the available men could be armed. By 1915 supplies of the 1898-pattern ammunition were having to be restricted to the use of machine-guns. The colony put in hand the manufacture of its own rifles and ammunition, but the performance of the latter served to undermine the askaris' faith in the former. The munitions factories established at Jaunde and Ebolowa were a tribute to German ingenuity, not least in view of the fact that all but one of the five munitions artificers in the colony had been captured by the end of September 1914.[6] Spent cases were collected from the battlefield; percussion caps were manufactured from the brass plates worn by the inhabitants of the grasslands; black powder was made from sulphur, saltpetre, and charcoal, and when the saltpetre was exhausted nitroglycerine was extracted from stocks of dynamite: 800,000 rounds were produced in this way. But such ammunition could not be stored for long periods; frequently it would not enter the breech or got stuck in the

[4] Purschel, *Kaiserliche Schutztruppe*, 118–19; also 54–60.
[5] Ibid. 60–2; Mentzel, *Kämpfe in Kamerun* (1936), 18–19, and Student, *Kameruns Kampf*, 23, adopt these figures but Mentzel, *Kämpfe in Kamerun* (1932), 44, has different totals.
[6] Schoen, *Deutschen Feuerwerkswesens*, 1395–6.

barrel; when fired, the smoke identified the position of the firer, and the bullet itself rarely ranged more than twenty yards.[7]

Limited in men and munitions, restricted in objective to protracted defence, the Germans were constrained to adopt manners of fighting very different from those used either by the *Schütztruppen* in the past or by the armies of Europe on the western front. In essence, the askari now had to wage war as his tribal opponents had done. Before 1914 his task had been to bring a reluctant foe to battle; after 1914 his main endeavours were to avoid intense fighting, to limit his own casualties while inflicting losses on the enemy, and to give up ground rather than hold it. Close-order tactics based on the 1906 German infantry regulations were replaced by open order, frontal attack by all-round defence. Munitions shortages put a heavy emphasis on fire discipline and short-range combat, on surprise rather than fire-effect. The terrain, the force-to-space ratio, and the extended lines of communication of the British and French forces all suited the tactics of guerrilla warfare. The opportunities for outflanking the enemy or for threatening his rear were abundant, and envelopment was the normal mode of attack. Thus the defence was active, not static. But though the style of small wars became the means of fighting, position war remained at its core. The *Schütztruppen* were still committed to the protection of specific areas and their points of entry; river crossings, jungle clearings, and—in the north—the forts guarding the highland plateau were the scenes chosen by the Germans for their encounters with the enemy.

Ebermaier, however reluctant he may in origin have been to embrace this form of operations, became the heart and soul of its effective execution. The split between purely military exploitation of the colony's resources for the purposes of war, and the civilian defence of its peace-time advances and infrastructure, evident in East Africa and implicit in Togoland, never surfaced in the Cameroons. The overall strategy, to hold as much of the Cameroons for as long as possible, was one that harnessed military priorities to the objectives of German colonialism. Ebermaier's powers were enhanced, after the destruction of Kamina, by his isolation from Berlin. He was able to impose a centralized and interventionist control of the economy virtually from the outset, and far earlier than was

---

[7] Student, *Kameruns Kampf*, 154–6, 286–7, is particularly graphic on these difficulties.

deemed necessary in Germany itself. Its battlefield manifestations were in the mobilization of manpower and the manufacture of munitions. Their achievement was the product of a total revision in the attitude of the German authorities, albeit one consonant with the shift in operational focus from coast to interior. White settlers had regarded themselves in particular and the Cameroons in general as dependent on imports from Germany. It required the war, the loss of Duala, and the removal of those imports to break their dependence, and to demonstrate the fertility and self-sufficiency of the colony. On 7 August 1914 Ebermaier assumed power over all supplies and property in the Cameroons. In the subsequent week all food in the hands of commercial firms was collected, rationing was introduced, and prices were controlled. On 14 August it was reckoned that stocks were sufficient to last four months. In reality, starvation never became an issue. Cultivation was intensified, and the Cameroons proved itself able to supply a reasonably sized force for an indefinite period. Ebermaier ensured that markets remained open by paying the white population primarily in bank drafts and the askaris in silver. Circulation was maintained by taxing the askaris in cash, and thus the supply of silver—the only currency acceptable to the native population, but limited in quantity as it was delivered from Germany—remained sufficient to keep the economy active.[8]

Ebermaier's authority was further enhanced by the relative weakness of the centralized military command. The grouping of companies proposed in the plan of 1913 had not been implemented during peace for fear of provoking the British and the French. Instead, the companies were strengthened individually in order to enable them to operate independently. There were good military arguments in favour of dispersion rather than concentration—the supply problems of a force larger than a company was one, and the extent of the territory to be covered was another. But most pressing were the difficulties of communication and of intelligence-collection, both powerful inducements in favour of delegating command.

The main internal links in the Cameroons radiated from Duala and followed the railway lines. In peace, communications with the outposts in the north were relayed via Lagos and Yola, and those in the east via

---

[8] Purschel, *Kaiserliche Schutztruppe*, 30–1, 76–80; Student, *Kameruns kampf,* 153–9.

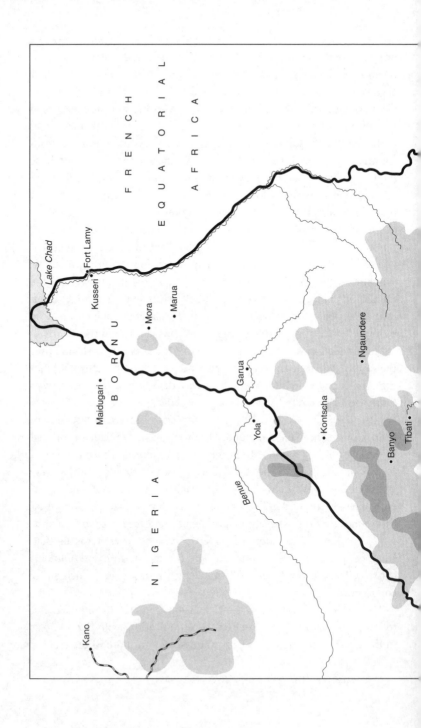

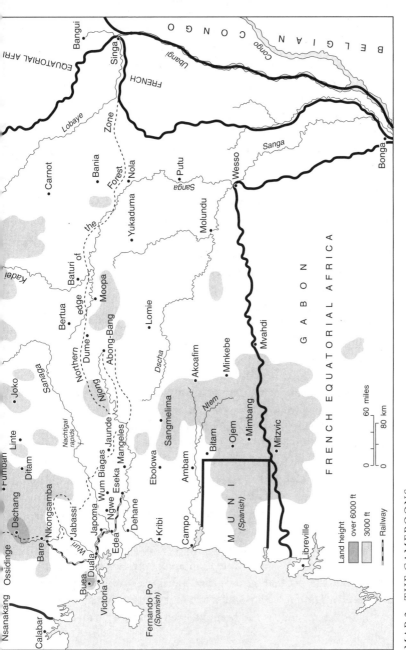

MAP 2. THE CAMEROONS

Libreville and Fort Lamy. Both were cut on the outbreak of war, and
Duala's capture disrupted the western network. The *Schütztruppen* had
no integral signals organization to replace what was lost. The equipment
available, heliographs and field telephones, was not even sufficient for full
unit contact at the local level; improvised links using chicken wire or
barbed wire were disrupted by the weather or by wild animals. By January
1916 a total of 2,435 kilometres of line had been created, and the equipment was salvaged and re-erected as the Germans withdrew.[9] But the
main signals system was a series of posts communicating by flag. Messages travelled slowly—about 50 kilometres a day—and without security.

Intelligence was hard to gather, and when obtained tended to be of
immediate relevance only. The terrain was too enclosed to make reconnaissance easy. The problems in assessing information provided by the
local population—that they saw all bodies of troops as enemies, that they
often could not count, and that they tended to say what they thought the
hearer wanted them to say—applied also to reports from the askaris
themselves. Therefore Europeans were used to reconnoitre, but their
inability to move as discreetly as the natives meant that fighting patrols
were the norm. Thus, the Germans knew if the British and French
planned to attack; what they could not so easily do was form an overall
idea of their purposes or of the distribution of their forces.

Without adequate communications or sufficient up-to-date intelligence command from the centre was impossible. Furthermore, the
maps were poor and on too small a scale (1 : 300,000) to enable detailed
orders to be based upon them alone. Zimmerman, who had succeeded to
the command of the *Schütztruppen* in April 1914, was condemned to being
a frustrated spectator. He had no chief of staff, and therefore he could not
abandon his headquarters for a visit to one of the fronts. The problems
diminished as the Germans were pushed inwards and their front con-
tracted. But even then Zimmerman could not direct the operations in the
north, the defence of the forts of Mora, Garua, and Banyo, which
screened Ngaundere. And so a tension arose between the pivot of his
strategy and the fact that his own effectiveness was greater in the centre
and the east. The only easement open to him was to create an intermediate level of command, as had been intended in 1913. Six battalion-sized

---

[9] Klein-Arendt, *Kamina ruft Nauen*, 274.

formations (*Abteilungsverbande*) were established—one each in the north, the west (covering the southern Nigerian frontier), the south, the south-east, and the east, and one placed centrally at Jaunde. Significantly, this distribution put the weight in the east and not in the west. However, for all his problems, Zimmerman had two major advantages over his opponents. First, he was operating on interior lines, and thus could switch companies between each *Abteilung* and, as became necessary in 1915, merge those in the north and west and those in the south and south-east. Secondly, his command structure was nationally homogeneous.

The key to understanding the course of the Cameroons campaign is to appreciate how imperfectly the British and French understood these intentions of the Germans. Neither power had anticipated offensive operations in West Africa, neither power had formed a plan for the conquest of the Cameroons, and thus neither power had set about building up the intelligence necessary to the conduct of a campaign there. A major windfall for the British was the capture of a large stock of German maps of the Cameroons from a liner in the Atlantic.[10] The French in the south-east had to wait until the fall of Molundu on 22 December 1914 for a similar stroke of luck.[11] But in general the problems of acquiring intelligence during the campaign were as great as, if not greater than, they were for the Germans. The ignorance of the German strengths, dispositions, and strategy was still virtually complete when the official histories came to be written.[12] Moreover, the strategy of each of the Entente powers was determined by its own national considerations. Thus, particularly for the first year of the war, the three major belligerents in the Cameroons provided an extraordinary spectacle, the French and British pursuing divergent objectives, and neither of them striking the Germans sufficiently hard at the points where they could be hurt.

The priorities of Joseph Aymérich, the military commander of French Equatorial Africa, were defensive. But French plans had been thrown into confusion in the south-east Cameroons, where additional territory had been ceded to Germany in settlement of the second Moroccan crisis in 1911. The two prongs of the German New Cameroons, extending to Singa

---

[10] Gorges, *Great War in West Africa*, 136.   [11] Aymérich, *Conquête*, 63.
[12] The only German source referred to by Moberly or Gorges is Schwarte, *Weltkampf*, iv. 377–85; Entente intelligence during the war had clearly provided little.

and Bonga, split the French colony in three, and sat on the main means of internal communication, the Ubangi and Congo rivers. At Singa the French telegraph line between Brazzaville and Bangui passed over German territory for 12 kilometres. The length of the frontier (3,000 kilometres), and the dispersed and isolated nature of the French posts put a premium on efficient communications in order to enable French concentration and an effective defence. On 6 August, therefore, the French seized Singa and Bonga. Simultaneously Aymérich set about the formation of four columns designed to take the war into German territory. From the east, Morisson's column was to follow the course of the Lobaye river from its confluence with the Ubangi at Singa; the second, Hutin's, was to move from the south-east along the Sanga; the third, Le Meillour's, with its base in Gabon, was to push up from the south; and the fourth, Miquelard's, was to do the same, cutting the Cameroons from Muni.

War, therefore, arrived in the Cameroons as a result of local French initiatives. No orders to attack had been received from Paris; the Germans, their signals intercepted by the French, had heard from neither Duala nor Berlin, and frequently had no forewarning that hostilities had begun.

The confusion was prolonged by the desire of Belgium, master of all the eastern bank of the Congo and of its estuary with the sea, to preserve the neutrality of the Congo act. The British had no intention of observing the act,[13] the Germans had no expectation that it would be. The Belgian initiative did not reflect the local interests of colonial government but was prompted from Europe, based on a desire to enforce Belgian neutrality there rather than in the Congo.[14] The effect was to hamstring French movements, and in particular to isolate Gabon from the rest of Equatorial Africa. The French noted that the Belgian governor had a German name, Fuchs. His replacement by a 'veritable Belge', Henry, coincided with a German attack on the Belgian Congo from East Africa.[15] On 28 August the reliance of Belgium on France in Europe was at last reciprocated by France's ability to rely on Belgium in Africa. Thereafter France's use of Belgian railways, rivers, and telegraph lines, as well as

---

[13] Osuntokun, *Nigeria*, 173; Moberly, *Togoland and Cameroons*, 16.
[14] Belgique, *Campaignes coloniales belges*, i. 17–23; Aymérich, *Conquête*, 26–7.
[15] Michel, *Guerres mondiales et conflits contemporains*, 168 (1992), 13, 16.

600 Belgian troops with Hutin's column, proved vital to Aymérich's movements.

French operations against the Cameroons had thus assumed a momentum before they received a direction. In Paris the general staff had no plans for an offensive in West Africa. But M. Merlin, the governor-general of Equatorial Africa, home on leave like the other senior colonial administrators of the day, took the opportunity to concert his thinking with that of Gaston Doumergue, foreign minister until 26 August 1914 and colonial minister thereafter.

Both Merlin and Doumergue were convinced of the desirability of recovering the territory ceded in 1911. The war provided the opportunity not only to do so, but to go further—to eject the Germans from West Africa with British co-operation. The instructions which Merlin, therefore, delivered to Aymérich on his return to Africa on 15 September specified two objectives—one operational, to mount an offensive in the south and east, and so give indirect support to the British who would land at Duala; and the second political, to recover the ceded territory. However, the apparent congruity of these tasks, both with each other and with what Aymérich had already done, was unsustainable. The French offensive had already been commenced as an independent operation, and the impossibility of rapid communication with the British in the west would maintain that independence. Secondly, the fulfilment of the political objective gave the French attack an aim which was not secondary but primary.

While France's concerns were territorial, Britain's were maritime. The Admiralty wanted to deny the use of Duala's wireless station and port facilities to German cruisers. The irrelevance of territorial conquest was confirmed by Dobell, who in a memorandum of 3 August advised the Committee of Imperial Defence's subcommittee that the seizure of Buea, Victoria, and Duala would be sufficient to strangle the enemy. The attractiveness of Duala as the focus for British operations was confirmed by the Colonial Office's reports of black disaffection in the Cameroons. Although exaggerated, they were not without foundation for the coastal region, where British influence had dominated until 1884 and was still far from extinguished in 1914.[16] A plan to develop Duala as a white settlement by forcibly removing the black population had aroused the

---

[16] Osuntokun, *Nigeria*, 177–8.

ire of Rudolf Bell, the German-educated paramount chief of the Duala. Bell was charged with high treason in May. Then a message to the French from Martin-Paul Samba of Ebolowa, announcing his intention to lead a revolt, was intercepted by the Germans. Both Bell and Samba were executed on 8 August. The Germans in Duala expended as much military effort in controlling the local population as in preparing to meet a British landing.[17]

The formation of the Cameroons expeditionary force took a month. A landward thrust from Nigeria towards Duala was rendered inadvisable by the nature of the intervening country. Therefore troops had to be collected along the West African coast, and the shipping assembled for a seaborne invasion. The interval allowed the completion of Togoland's conquest, and the consequent isolation of Duala from Germany by the destruction of the Kamina wireless.

On one level the Cameroons expeditionary force met Merlin's and Doumergue's objectives. It included a French contribution of 2,000 Senegalese from Dakar under the command of Colonel Mayer. Thus, of the total of 13,000 Entente forces deployed in the Cameroons, the majority (7,000) were French. The expeditionary force, therefore, served France's political objectives by enhancing its claim to be the dominant voice in the eventual partition of the Cameroons. But it did not serve the operational purposes relayed to Aymérich. The orders given to Dobell, who was to command the force, were to seize Buea, Victoria, and Duala. He had no instructions to undertake the further conquest of the colony, and thus Merlin's idea of a reciprocating effect between Dobell's advance and Aymérich's was, at this stage, complete fantasy. From the outset of the war the War Office had recognized that the Germans were likely to continue their defence from the interior,[18] but not until 29 September did the CID subcommittee ask itself how Dobell could break off his attack at the coast. It concluded that he could not: to secure Duala, the conquest of the colony must be completed and more men would be required. But its recommendation to that effect was ignored by the government, both then and thereafter.[19] The original British strategy, to secure German ports and

---

[17] Digre, *Imperialism's New Clothes*, 23; Andreas Eckert, '"Verdammt seien die Deutschen!"', *Die Zeit*, 5 Aug. 1994, 58; Stoecker, *German Imperialism*, 275.

[18] Osuntokun, *Nigeria*, 176–7.

[19] Moberly, *Togoland and Cameroons*, 71–2, 145, 215–16.

wireless stations, and to use only minimal local ground forces, remained valid well into 1915.

The contribution of the West African Frontier Force to the Duala expedition was limited to 2,500 men, because the primary concern of Britain's local forces in relation to the Cameroons was, like that of France, defensive. Furthermore, again like France although for different reasons, those defensive arrangements were in disarray.

On 1 January 1914 a new administrative structure, amalgamating the emir-dominated north and the largely acephalous south, had been imposed on Nigeria. The Nigeria Regiment contributed 70 per cent of the West African Frontier Force. When war broke out, the defensive scheme for Nigeria, revised in the light of the administrative and regimental amalgamation, was still in draft. The confusion was compounded by the fact that Sir Frederick Lugard, the colony's governor-general, had taken the only available copy home on leave. Moreover, neither it nor the regiment's primary tasks had prepared the latter for what it was now expected to do. Training, on Lugard's insistence, had been kept to company level; the main attention in dealing with an external threat had been to coastal defence, and the troops were therefore more adept at entrenching than at mobile operations. Like the *Schütztruppen*, they had no indigenous staff organization or technical services. It had been assumed that operations would be conducted within Nigeria, and that consequently these would be provided by the local infrastructure.[20]

Nigeria's defensive scheme allowed for the formation of five columns on the Cameroons border, two in the north at Maidugari opposite Mora, one at Yola on the Benue river opposite Garua, one at Ikom on the River Cross facing Nsanakang, and one near the coast at Calabar. On 6 August the Colonial Office, anxious for the internal security of Nigeria, ordered the columns not to advance into the Cameroons without further instructions.[21] However, Lugard's absence and the uncertainties about the offensive-defensive implications of the new plan helped to create a vagueness about what was intended. The cause of clarity was not served by communication difficulties between Lagos and Kaduna, the headquarters of Colonel C. H. P. Carter, commanding the Nigeria Regiment.

---

[20] Ibid. 8–9; Haywood and Clarke, *Royal West Africa Frontier Force*, 104; Osuntokun, *Nigeria*, 169–72; Gorges, *Great War in West Africa*, 40–4, 47.
[21] Gorges, *Great War in Africa*, 79; Moberly, *Togoland and Cameroons*, 59–60.

On 15 August a retired British officer told Carter that the German garrison at Garua had on 11 August known nothing about the outbreak of war. A day previously London had authorized reconnaissances by the northern and southern columns. Carter now requested permission to attack Garua, and when this was granted extended his order to include an attack on Mora. Thus in late August all five columns were advancing into enemy territory.[22]

Carter's advance was of course unwittingly directed at the guts of the German defences. Both Mora and Garua were the main northern guardians of Ngaundere and the highland plateau. Garua's specific task was to support the *Schütztruppen* deployed further north in Mora and Bornu, and to provide a rallying point in the event of their retreat.[23] Its defences consisted of five self-contained circular works, positioned to give each other supporting fire, and whose approaches were broken up with barbed wire and traps; their trenches, 7 metres deep, with overhead protection and deep dugouts, represented the techniques of modern war. Those at Mora were similarly well-constructed, and rose to 500 metres, atop precipitous and intersected slopes. Both would require heavy artillery for their reduction. Carter had only 2.95-inch mountain guns. Moreover, the French garrison at Fort Lamy, under Colonel Largeau, could not assist in the attack on Mora. Its efforts were concentrated on suppressing the German post at Kusseri, whence it was repulsed in August, and which it did not take till 25 September. By the end of August the British attack on Mora had fallen back to the south, adopting a position designed to block Mora's links with Garua. At Garua itself the rebuff was more severe. Von Crailsheim, the German commander, had picked up sufficient from the unusual movements on the Nigerian frontier to increase his garrison to three companies. The British attack, undertaken with insufficient reconnaissance over open ground, was a complete failure, the Nigerians breaking under a German counter-attack, and the commanding officer being killed. The Cross river column took Nsanakang, but on 6 September was surprised by the Germans and suffered 50 per cent casualties as well as losing eight of its eleven British officers. Thus, all along the Nigerian frontier the British were forced onto the defensive. The effect on the

---

[22] Osuntokun, *Nigeria*, 181–2; Haywood and Clarke, *Royal West Africa Frontier Force*, 106–11.
[23] Suren, *Kameruns Kampf*, 109, 114.

German askaris' morale was of crucial significance; never before had they fought the enemies of other European powers, and yet in all the initial engagements in the north they had proved victorious. Almost as impressed were the tribes of the Benue valley. In September and October the ambitions of the northern *Abteilung* at Garua had grown sufficiently for it to push strong patrols into Nigeria itself, to Yola, and also northwards towards Marua and its links with Mora.

Carter's attacks, however misconceived, did at least serve one broader purpose—they confirmed the Germans in their neglect of Duala. Dobell, who left Lagos on 20 September, instructed the frontier columns in the south to remain on the defensive, and those in the north and centre to concentrate against Garua. Carter was replaced in command by Colonel F. Cunliffe. Cunliffe's task was to support the main thrust on Duala.

By early September a flotilla of small craft had clustered around the British cruiser HMS *Cumberland*, and on 5 and 6 September anchored in Ambas Bay, off Victoria. The original intention was to land here and cut across Cape Cameroon to Duala. However, the rainy season rendered the intervening rivers impassable. By the time the convoy had changed plans and proceeded round the cape into the Cameroon estuary the converse pressure had begun to apply. Although the Germans had not mined the rivermouth, they had sunk mine ships across its main channel. A direct advance on Duala along the shore was impossible. Therefore, the only means of ingress was up the rivers and creeks leading off the bays of the Cameroon estuary, using the smaller boats in the shallow waters. When the rainy season ended the water would fall and further advance become impossible. Thus, the middle weeks of September were passed in a series of navigational thrusts and in running battles between British and German light craft. On 16 September the German gunboat *Nachtigal* was sunk, and by the 22nd the survey was complete and a channel 19 feet deep cleared to within 5,000 yards of Duala.

On 25 September Dobell, his command now assembled at the entrance to the channel, issued an ultimatum calling on Duala to surrender. His plan was to push his main force up the Lungasi river to Japoma, where the river was bridged by the railway to Eseka. Thus he would cut off the town and its garrison from the south and east. But the Lungasi was blocked by a boom, and on 27 September Dobell readied himself for a frontal attack on Duala. The Germans, meanwhile, had no intention of fighting for Duala.

Realizing from Dobell's ultimatum that attack was imminent, they fell back inland on 26 September, taking what they could in transport and destroying what they could not. On 27 September Dobell captured Duala without a shot being fired. On 6 October the Senegalese, this time in the face of stiffer opposition, took the Japoma bridge.

The immediate British objectives, certainly in the eyes of the Admiralty, had been gained. However, the Germans had not withdrawn far. Some had followed the northern line towards Bare and Dschang; most had gone east along the Wuri river to Jabassi or south-east on the midland line to Edea. All three concentrations had to be cleared in order to render Duala safe from German attack.

While the rains lasted Jabassi was the most accessible. Using the river, and mounting a 6-pounder gun on a dredger, a British force attacked on 7 October. However, its movements lost unity in the thick bush, and once into open ground the West Africans wilted under the concentrated fire of machine-guns. The waters of the Wuri then fell, and the attackers re-treated to Duala. On 13 October the water-level rose again. The attack on the following day was directed up both banks of the river, and was better co-ordinated by Gorges, the British commander, as he stayed afloat to be able to observe the progress of operations. He was rewarded with success.

The value of riverine transport was even more graphically illustrated in the capture of Edea. The obvious route followed the railway line. But the British established that the Sanaga and Njong rivers, both issuing into the bight of Biafra, the former from Edea, and the latter linked to Edea by a track from Dehane, were navigable by small craft. Using the vessels released by the fall of Jabassi, British and French columns pushed up on Edea from the south, while a third column followed the railway. Again the Germans fell back without fighting, and Edea was taken on 26 October.

The advance up the northern railway, being less dependent on water navigation, was left until December. On 2 January 1915 the British took Dschang. However, having advanced beyond the railhead they destroyed the fort of Dschang, and then fell back onto securer lines of communication at Bare and Nkongsamba. Similarly, when the Wuri fell Jabassi was abandoned for a post further downstream which could be more readily supplied.

By the end of 1914 Dobell had achieved all his immediate objectives. The obstacles he had overcome had been almost entirely navigational and logistical; at no point, except at the Japoma bridge, had the Germans mounted a sustained defence. Even Dobell himself recognized that he had encountered at best only two of the twelve regular *Schütztruppen* companies;[24] most of his opposition had been provided by the police or by European reservists, and it had not been their job to mount major operations in the coastal areas.

In part, the ease of his task was attributable to Cunliffe's columns on the Nigerian frontier. But the major contribution in 1914 was made by Aymérich's attack in the south and east. It would be wrong to say that Cunliffe and Aymérich cleared the path for Dobell at Duala, because the Germans had never proposed to block the latter's advance in the first place. But Merlin's strategy succeeded to the extent that it was defence of the New Cameroons that caused most worry for Zimmerman in 1914.

Since its acquisition in 1911 the Germans had had little opportunity to survey the new territory or to incorporate it within the original colony. They had stationed no troops on the River Sanga south of Nola. The three companies of *Schütztruppen* on the upper Sanga, both east of the river and west as far as Dume, had an area of 200,000 square kilometres and a front of 1,700 kilometres to defend. The easternmost company, having initially planned an offensive from Carnot towards Singa, was recalled by Eymael, commanding the *Ostabteilung*. Thus, throughout August the only German troops east of the Sanga and south of Nola were police detachments.

The tempo of Morisson's and Hutin's advances was therefore dictated by the constraints of supply rather than by enemy action. None of the French columns had the lines of communication or the forward stocks necessary for immediate offensive operations. The navigability of the Sanga compensated for the pre-war deficiencies as far as Hutin was concerned. His most vulnerable point was Wesso, on the confluence of the Sanga and the Dscha, and just inside French territory. But an attack mounted by the Germans from Yukaduma miscarried because of the swollen state of the rivers. Morisson's initial difficulties were far greater. The Lobaye was not navigable, and therefore forward movement was impossible until porters were organized.

---

[24] Haywood and Clarke, *Royal West Africa Frontier Force*, 125–6.

Aymérich's intention was that both columns should converge on Nola, and he anticipated a joint attack on 16 or 17 October. But the co-ordination of the two columns was impossible. Lateral communications took eight to thirteen days. When Morisson was first apprised of the plan to take Nola (the order was received on 21 September), he reported his supply problems as so great that Aymérich revised his instructions, suggesting a defensive role on the Lobaye. This second set of orders was dispatched by Aymérich on 30 September and reached Morisson on 7 October. In the interim, however, Morisson had resolved his logistical difficulties, and on 2 October had begun his advance on the line Carnot–Bania (north of Nola) as originally instructed. On 17 October Morisson entered Carnot without opposition. Hutin, meanwhile, acting in accordance with his orders from Aymérich to take Nola in conjunction with Morisson (orders given on 29 September), arrived there the day after Morisson entered Carnot. The news of Nola's capture did not reach Morisson until 24 October, and Aymérich (who, understandably uncertain where he could best position himself, had moved to Wesso) two days later. But by now the information was out of date. Hutin became worried about the supply of so many troops so far forward, and feared that the Germans on the Dscha would try to cut his communications at Putu. Leaving a single company at Nola to link with Morisson, he withdrew his main body back to Wesso.

On 29 October Morisson, perplexed as to his next move, asked Aymérich for further guidance. However, what Morisson could not afford to do was to stay still while he awaited Aymérich's reply. For much of October the Africans had been on half rations and on the 21st the Europeans were put on two-thirds. So he advanced. By the end of the month the problems were resolved as he was into territory fertile enough to enable him to requisition. But, as his troops ate off the surrounding land, so they needed to move to find fresh sources of supply. Therefore he continued to advance. He captured Baturi on 9 December. But the further he went, the remoter became his contact with Aymérich. From Baturi to Brazza-ville, telegrams took between thirty and thirty-five days, and replies a further twenty to twenty-eight days. While Morisson pushed westwards, in obedience to one scheme of operations, Aymérich developed another.[25]

[25] Ministère de la Guerre, *Armées françaises*, IX, 2ᵉ vol., 206–31.

The collection of porters and the co-ordination of command for Le Meillour's and the Miquelard's columns proved even more complex than it had been for Morisson's. Orders from Libreville to Miquelard's base at Mitzvic took between nine and twenty-seven days, and then a further nine days elapsed before they reached Le Meillour at Mvahdi. One letter from Brazzaville to Mitzvic took fifty days, and another, from Mvahdi to Libreville, forty-four days. Aymérich's decision to go forward from Brazzaville to Wesso left the two Gabon columns to their own devices. The original intention was to put the weight on Miquelard's, directing it along the southern border to Muni, and then north to Ojem, so cutting the German links with neutral Spanish territory. However, in mid-September, at Mimbang, midway between Ojem and the border, the French column ran into the Germans; its officers suffered heavy casualties, and its three companies broke and ran. In October the Germans advanced up to and across the border. Their victory was a major one. The decision not to defend Duala heightened the value of Muni as the Germans' point of contact with Europe and the wider world: supplies, including ammunition, continued to enter the Cameroons via Muni at least until early 1915.[26]

Not until November were the Gabon columns ready for forward movement once more. Now the weight was placed on Le Meillour, not on Miquelard, and the former was given overall command. His objective was Akoafim. Facing him were eight German companies, both regular and reservist. The obvious way to ease Le Meillour's path, at least from the perspective of Merlin, now in Libreville, was to get Hutin's column to act in conjunction with Le Meillour's right flank. Zimmerman, in order to reinforce Eymael and bring the strength facing Morisson in the Bertua–Dume area to five companies, had reduced the troops holding the Molundu–Lomie–Yukaduma sector to 750 policemen and reservists.

Aymérich's orders of 1 December, therefore, reflected the movements of Le Meillour's column and not those of Morisson's. Ignoring the facts that Hutin was held up at Molundu, and that his column's advance would be slowed once it left the line of the Sanga, Aymérich instructed Hutin to take Molundu, and then to move south-west to aid Le Meillour's advance from Gabon. Hutin's and Le Meillour's columns were now to have the major

[26] Aymérich, *Conquête*, 94.

role, with Lomie as a joint objective. Only when they had reached that point was Morisson to resume his advance. Morisson was indeed dealt severe blows by Eymael at Bertua on 25, 27, and 28 December 1914. But Eymael still abandoned Bertua, and soon thereafter he lost to the north the two additional companies with which he had been reinforced. Moreover, in late November Morisson's supply problems were eased once more, as the route up the River Sanga became available to him.

Hutin meanwhile had not one but two sets of orders. Those given him on 17 November told him to take Yukaduma, and clearly intended him to retain contact with his detached company at Nola; they had not been cancelled by those of 1 December. Molundu fell on 22 December; thereafter, part of Hutin's column pushed north to Yukaduma and part west to aid Le Meillour.

At the close of 1914 the Germans could be reasonably satisfied with their position. In the north and south German defences still rested, broadly speaking, on the frontiers. The losses of territory to Dobell's force in the west and to Aymérich's columns in the south-east had been anticipated; the defensive core in the northern highlands remained intact; to the south-west communications with Muni were secure. German casualties had been more than compensated for by new recruitment. Zimmerman had two major worries. The first was the rapid progress of Morisson's column, which he feared would advance on Ngaundere from the south, converging with the French from Chad and the British from Nigeria. He was prepared to weaken his forces facing Le Meillour to check Morisson, thus illustrating how different from French strategy was the Germans' sense of their own vulnerability.[27] His second concern was Dobell's next step. If Dobell elected to persevere beyond the head of the northern railway and Dschang, he would enter the northern plateau. Alternatively, he might choose to reinforce the French at Edea, on the midland railway, and push on to Jaunde between the Sanaga and Njong rivers, so threatening the link between Ngaundere and the south-west coast.

The Germans mounted two attacks in January and February 1915 designed to bring relief from the threats to east and west. Zimmerman could not easily concentrate forces against the British column at Dschang, but he did have companies around Edea. On 5 January Mayer's

---

[27] Student, *Kameruns Kampf*, 104–5.

Senegalese held Edea against a determined German assault. Tactically, French fire superiority prevailed; strategically, Zimmerman achieved his objectives—the British became alarmed for their rear and fell back from Dschang, and talk of Mayer's column co-operating with Miquelard's advance from the south was quashed.[28] In the east, von der Marwitz's *Südostabteilung*—relieved on its southern flank by Hutin's move to the west—co-operated with Eymael's *Ostabteilung* to threaten the flank and rear of Morisson's extended, and now unsupported, advance. On 24 February the Germans retook Bertua, and by the end of the month Morisson had fallen back 100 kilometres to the line of the Kadei.

Dobell was in a quandary. The ease of his initial operations, up until December 1914, had opened up the prospects of a more extensive advance than that so far authorized by the Colonial Office. He asked for more troops, and on 26 December 1914 justified his request by alluding to 'the possibility, by constant activity of effecting the surrender of the whole of the Cameroons'.[29] But the reinforcements approved, 400 men from Sierra Leone, did no more than make good his losses. On 5 March 1915 he reported that he had only two battalions fit, and demanded reliefs, deeming six months' campaigning in the Cameroons sufficient for any man.[30] But he had strained the resources of British West Africa to their limit. Lugard argued that the security of Nigeria was being undermined by the demands of the Cameroons campaign; a revolt in Warri province gave force to his resistance to Dobell's needs.[31] Dobell suggested that the Indian army contribute. The battalion which he was eventually given was of low quality, and in February 1915 had mutinied in Singapore. His other expedients, to recruit native levies, and to establish a local police force at Duala so as to release troops for the front, were no more than palliatives.[32] The French component of Dobell's command was in an equally poor state. Although Dobell was responsible for Mayer's orders, Dakar was responsible for his supply. But Senegal had no stocks from which it could provision an expeditionary force. Mayer was left to find most of his porters within the Cameroons. At the end of October, despite Mayer's proximity to the coast, the rice to which the Senegalese

---

[28] Haywood and Clarke, *Royal West African Frontier Force*, 127, 133–6.

[29] Moberly, *Togoland and Cameroons*, 216.   [30] Ibid. 246.

[31] Osuntokun, *Nigeria*, 110–14, 222–4.

[32] Lucas, *Empire at War*, iv. 86.

were accustomed was replaced by locally requisitioned root crops. Health declined, and the problems compounded themselves as the French had too few doctors. By mid-December only one officer and a maximum of three NCOs were fit to march in each company.[33] On 10 March 1915 London signalled to Dobell that he was to make the best defensive arrangements possible and that no further offensive was anticipated. The basic CID strategy remained unchanged.

But that strategy had never been in accord with the grand schemes, both political and operational, of Merlin. The French experience of 1914 showed that effective command was exercised by the column commanders, and that the orders issued from Brazzaville bore little relation to the situation pertaining on the ground. The consequence was a series of separate advances whose effects in combination were the result of chance rather than design. Aymérich's direct influence was restricted principally to Hutin's column, and then only by virtue of his abandoning Brazzaville for points further forward. Aymérich's absences created Merlin's opportunity. Merlin had failed to achieve the co-ordination in operations which he had anticipated in September 1914. Command was divided over three governments (including the Belgians), four governors-general, six independent commanders-in-chief, and eight column commanders.[34] Dobell had the major responsibility, but liaison between him and the French was effected via London and Paris; Cunliffe in the north was not in direct contact with Dobell; the status of Brisset's column from Chad, now acting with Cunliffe and outside Aymérich's control, was unclear. By February 1915 Aymérich at least had begun to recognize that the solution was greater delegation. But Aymérich had lost the initiative to Merlin. Merlin's ambition, despite all the practical difficulties, was to achieve the centralization of strategy which had so far eluded him.

On 6 February 1915 Merlin convened a conference in Brazzaville to discuss the next moves. Its central idea was an advance from the south and south-east towards Lomie and Dume, with the object of cutting off Jaunde. Morisson would have to take Dume, or run the risk of being exposed and isolated. Miquelard's column should advance to the Ntem in order to complete Jaunde's separation from the south-west. To the

---

[33] Ministère de la Guerre, *Armées françaises*, IX, 2e vol., 195–205.
[34] Charbonneau, *Revue militaire française*, 130 (avril 1932), 89.

north Brisset was to be placed under Cunliffe's command, and the two should take Barua, and possibly then link up with Morisson.

An advance on Jaunde was therefore the concept that would unite the advancing columns in reciprocating action. On 11 February Aymérich left Brazzaville in order to attend to the supply and communication problems of Hutin's column, which were worsening as it extended to the west. Merlin set off for Duala, to convince Dobell that he too should adopt Jaunde as his objective.

Dobell was in no state to fall in with Merlin's schemes. His inclination was to put the weight on attrition and on seapower. By tightening the blockade of the Spanish coast the Germans would be exhausted, and at the same time the limited Entente forces would not be overextended. Furthermore, on 4 February a captured message from Zimmerman to the Garua garrison revealed that Ngaundere, not Jaunde, was the centre of the German defensive scheme. This intelligence was relayed to the Entente commanders on 26 February, and was taken with particular seriousness by Largeau in Chad, who acquired further information to corroborate its thrust. Merlin dismissed it.[35] Dobell was sufficiently won over by Merlin to abandon his own instincts, to accept that the attack on Garua—instead of being the major thrust demanded if Ngaundere was the hub of German resistance—should be supportive, and to agree that he himself could lead a direct advance on Jaunde. Merlin's representation of the French advance in the south and east was what convinced Dobell. The line Dume–Lomie–Akoafim–the River Ntem, the objective set at Brazzaville on 6 February, would be reached, Merlin said, by the end of March. As he spoke to Dobell, Merlin—freed from the embarrassment of Aymérich's presence or intervention—placed the French columns where he imagined or desired them to be, not where they were. Furthermore, in the plan finally agreed on 12 March Merlin committed the French to a timetable and an advance of which neither Aymérich nor his column commander had cognizance, and to a degree of co-ordination and lateral communication which experience had proved was impossible to achieve.[36]

Two routes led from Edea in the direction of Jaunde. The southern was the railway line, but it was complete only as far as Eseka. The northern

---

[35] Ministère de la Guerre, *Armées françaises*, IX, 2ᵉ vol., 368–9.   [36] Ibid. 395–8.

was a forest track passing through Wum Biagas. Dobell formed two columns, the British under Gorges to take the track, the French under Mayer the railway; when the French reached Eseka they were to join the British at Wum Biagas, and the two would then proceed together. Forest and swamp, until just short of Jaunde, made the ground ideally suited to defence. With 300 rifles on the track and 275 on the railway,[37] the Germans forced Dobell's troops into fighting for every day's advance. The British took Wum Biagas on 4 May, and the French captured Eseka on 11 May. On 25 May Mayer's troops led the way out of Wum Biagas towards Jaunde. His command, weakened by malnutrition and disease before he started, was now taking heavy casualties. When attacked, his men were slow to deploy off the track into the bush. Twenty-five per cent of those engaged in the advance were killed or wounded. The Germans harried the French flanks and rear. The carriers, mostly local men pressed into service, disappeared as soon as shots were exchanged. By 5 June Mayer had only progressed 19 kilometres beyond Wum Biagas, a rate of a 1.5 kilometres a day. At that speed Dobell could not reach Jaunde before the rainy season halted all movement. On 11 June he approved Mayer's request for permission to retreat. The following day a German attack against Mayer's rear, scattering his carriers, wreaked havoc with his lines of communication. By 28 June Dobell was back at Ngwe. Both his Nigerian battalions were reduced to half their strength;[38] sickness and supply difficulties ruled out any immediate resumption of the offensive. The advent of the rains provided confirmation. Until October, therefore, action in the west was confined to a tightening of the blockade of Muni. Dobell used the respite to repair his shattered forces, to give leave, to let his sick recuperate.

The degree to which Dobell's first advance on Jaunde was a failure depends on the object which it was trying to fulfil. For Merlin, it was the major stroke to ensure total victory in the Cameroons. For Dobell, it was—at least initially—a supporting move to relieve pressure on Aymérich; not his own but the French advance from the south and east promised, particularly given the optimistic account of its progress from Merlin, to be the decisive blow against German resistance. Dobell had, after all, received no authorization from London to move beyond the

---

[37] Student, *Kameruns Kampf*, 180.
[38] Haywood and Clarke, *Royal West African Frontier Force*, 150.

coastal area, and France, not Britain, desired to complete the conquest of the German colony. But, whatever the views of the War Office (which on 3 April took over military responsibility for the campaign from the Colonial Office), Dobell himself began to be attracted by Merlin's ambitions. On 12 April the setbacks to the progress of their columns led the French to ask Dobell for a postponement until 1 May. Dobell could have cancelled the offensive—justifying his decision by reference to his own instructions from London, to the state of his command, to his doubts about whether Jaunde was even the right objective, and to the proximity of the rainy season. Buoyed by his own initial good progress, he did not.

Aymérich, absent from Duala in March, remained committed to the fulfilment, not of the programme conceived then but of that to which he had been privy in Brazzaville on 6 February. Like Merlin he saw Jaunde as the heart of the German defence; unlike Merlin he had few illusions about the pace of his columns' advance. He anticipated their reaching the objectives set on 6 February not in late March or early April, but in June. Finding himself committed by the Duala conference to a plan in whose formulation he had had no share, his first response had been to seek its postponement.

In April none of the French columns was in a position to give effective support to each other, let alone to Dobell. Morisson was not yet fit to move after his retreat to the Kadei. The effect of his falling back was to force Hutin to reorientate himself to the north, and thus away from Le Meillour and the lines of advance fixed at Brazzaville and Duala. Moreover, Hutin's movements remained ponderous and painful. His supply problems, although ameliorated by local resources, were still not fully resolved. On 16 April he calculated he would need 1,512 porters; Aymérich thought a figure double that would be nearer the mark. The supply officers at Brazzaville and Molundu reckoned 12,000 porters were needed to transport three months' supplies to both Morisson's and Hutin's columns. But they were uncertain how many porters were actually present with Hutin's column, given the rate at which they were deserting and falling sick. They therefore did not know how many effectives they were trying to feed. Overestimating the number of porters in line with their own expectations, they created loads that were beyond the capacity of the porterage available. Moreover, the further Hutin advanced the more reliant he became on land rather than on riverine communications, and the more porters were carrying food to feed other porters, not to feed fighting men.[39]

More serious than Hutin's problems were those of the southern offensive, adumbrated at Brazzaville and at Duala as the principal French offensive, but which had collapsed into a series of uncoordinated and feeble sallies. Le Meillour had planned to begin his advance on 1 March, but had brought it forward to late January in order to aid Hutin. He therefore set off before his supply arrangements were complete. Like Hutin, he was naively optimistic about his needs. In December 1914 he reckoned that both his and Miquelard's columns would require 400 porters; in March 1915 he announced he would need more than double that number for his column alone; in fact he had only forty. On 13 February he learnt that Miquelard, whose line of march had been fixed as Ojem and then Akoafim in order to support Le Meillour's own advance, had encountered strong German forces. Miquelard therefore called on Le Meillour to support him by attacking Akoafim. The latter did so, but his efforts were half-hearted, publicly because of his supply problems, privately because of his own lack of drive. On 17 March Le Meillour received the results of the conference at Brazzaville on 6 February, but he was now back at Minkebe, not advancing on Lomie. Furthermore, the Brazzaville conclusions did not make clear whether his task was to act in conjunction with Miquelard on his left or Hutin on his right. Communications with either took at least twenty days. Le Meillour decided to support neither, but to push between Ojem and Akoafim. The German forces, up to 75 per cent of them at any one time racked with dysentery or blackwater fever, were able to check an attack that lacked either administrative coherence or strategic direction. Thus Aymérich, whose communications with the Gabon columns were further lengthened by his leaving Molundu on 25 April for Yukaduma, learnt on 14 May that Le Meillour was neither attacking Akoafim nor conforming to the February programme.[40]

In June the failure of the French offensive in the south began to be offset by the recovery of that in the east. On 7 May Aymérich, succumbing to Merlin's pressure for progress, instructed his columns to take such

---

[39] Ministère de la Guerre, *Armées françaises*, IX, 2ᵉ vol., 540–4.
[40] Ibid. 323–32, 351–5, 562–70; Student, *Kameruns Kampf*, 216–17.

offensive opportunities as presented themselves. Their objectives were still limited, their tasks to fix the enemy, not to pursue him *au fond*. On 22 May he brought coherence to Hutin's movements by directing his column and Morisson's to aim at their eventual convergence. The pause on the Kadei, the support of the local population, and the fact that he was on the edge of more fertile territory enabled Morisson's column to rebuild. Morisson resumed his advance, reaching Moopa on 23 May, Bertua a month later, and finally entering Dume on 25 July. Hutin's supply problems were countered by weakening German resistance. Only those *Schütztruppen* companies still issued with peacetime ammunition could be used in major operations. In mid-June all but ninety men in *Südostabteilung* mutinied, a reflection of the inadequate ammunition supply, of the death of their respected commanding officer von der Marwitz, and of the fear of capture.[41] Although Hutin was not in a state to exploit the opportunity—most of the mutineers returned to the ranks in late June—he finally entered Lomie on 24 June; Hutin was now able to recruit locally, even drawing in former askaris.[42] In August the two columns were united under Morisson's command, and together formed a joint front facing west and running from Bertua and Dume to Abong-Bang and Lomie. At last, therefore, the French were beginning to meet the commitments entered into by Merlin. But by now Dobell's advance and retreat were done.

Nonetheless, a strategic breakthrough was achieved between March and October 1915. It came on the front where neither Merlin nor Dobell had sought it. Its significance was therefore more evident to the Germans than it was to the Entente powers.

On 24 January 1915 Lugard wrote to Dobell, asking for heavy guns in order to enable the British to make good the setbacks suffered early in the war in the northern Cameroons by capturing the stronghold of Garua. Speed was essential, as the waters of the river Benue were falling and the opportunity to get the guns up the river would be missed. But on 10 April a German thrust to the Benue on 10 April caused the Emir of Yola and his native administration to flee, so threatening to undermine the British hold in northern Nigeria. Lugard, therefore, wanted Garua taken to

---

[41] Student, *Kameruns Kampf*, 219; Purschel, *Kaiserliche Schutztruppe*, 67–8.
[42] Aymérich, *Conquête*, 127.

restore British prestige in northern Nigeria, not to give Britain control of the Cameroons. The purpose, however, of the German attack was to ensure that Cunliffe's forces did not simply mask Garua in an advance into the highland plateau. Zimmerman had told von Crailsheim in January that the task of the Garua garrison was to protect Ngaundere. Provided the Germans held Ngaundere, they could exploit their interior lines in order to concentrate sufficient men against individual enemy columns scattered over all fronts. If Garua fell then Ngaundere would follow, and, in Zimmerman's words, 'the whole war plan would collapse'.[43]

Crailsheim's faith in his chief's analysis was confirmed by the capture of a letter from Morisson, saying that the French forces in the south could not advance any further until Cunliffe's column in the north had captured Garua. But Zimmerman changed his mind. In fresh orders, dated 13 April 1915, Zimmerman now warned against the dangers of locking up all available forces in a fort. He feared that Cunliffe might mask Garua, and fall on Ngaundere and Banyo. In such circumstances the defence of Garua, however heroic and protracted, would be useless. Garua's garrison was cut to one-and-a-half companies, a total of 250 rifles, so as to create a mobile force to cover the flanks of Ngaundere and Banyo. To add insult to injury, Zimmerman also took two officers and 60,000 rounds (although the Garua garrison was convinced that the total was twice that) to reinforce the *Südabteilung*. Crailsheim protested that in the rainy season the high water meant that Garua could not be bypassed; he argued in vain.[44]

Cunliffe, with fourteen companies in all, plus supporting arms, now enjoyed an overwhelming superiority. But he continued to treat Garua with the respect its fortifications deserved. He supplemented his mountain guns with two heavy artillery pieces. Although the waters were falling, a naval 12-pounder was navigated up the rivers Niger and Benue. The French insisted on contributing a 95 mm piece, brought from Dakar, so delaying the operation yet further. But as a result the British enjoyed a preponderance of fire which took Crailsheim totally by surprise. By 9 June Cunliffe's infantry had worked forward to within a

[43] Student, *Kameruns Kampf*, 147; see also Osuntokun, *Nigeria*, 189–90. Peter Yearwood has provided important additional information on the capture of Garua.
[44] Suren, *Kampf um Kamerun*, 197–228, 326.

kilometre of the German positions, the British to the south and south-east and the French under Brisset to the east. He hoped to cut off Crailsheim's retreat, but the askaris were alarmed by their first experience of heavy artillery fire. Half the garrison escaped by swimming down the Benue, and thence to Banyo; the balance, 300 men, surrendered without an assault having taken place, on 10 June.

Cunliffe was oblivious to the enormity of the blow which he had delivered the Germans. He was convinced that Jaunde, not Ngaundere, was the centre of their defensive effort, and that his role was, as the Duala conference had specified, to support Dobell. Dobell, however, was in retreat, and could not resume his advance until the rains ceased. Therefore, Cunliffe concluded, the sensible thing for him to do was not to push south but go north, and reduce the now-isolated Mora with his heavy artillery.

Brisset, technically his subordinate, disagreed. Of all the allied commanders, both Brisset and his immediate superior, Largeau, the military governor of Chad, had been the most impressed by the intelligence pointing to the German reliance on Ngaundere. The fertility of the highland region, the support of neighbouring Chad, and the relative lack of rain made rapid movement easier in the north than in any other area of operations. On 28 June a British column took Ngaundere. Brisset then moved south-west on Tibati, and pushed a company south to Kunde to link with Morisson's right. By late July Brisset's thoughts and actions aimed at a total inversion of allied planning, placing the initiative on a general offensive with the North Cameroons force.

For the British, Brisset's independence was not a manifestation of a different strategic view but of insubordination and French bloody-mindedness. Cunliffe concluded that the rainy season would preclude immediate operations south of the line Kontscha–Banyo–Bamenda, and that those positions should therefore be consolidated, whereas the lack of rain in the north created the ideal opportunity to take Mora. Largeau's ambivalence—recognizing the military need for obedience, while being in sympathy with Brisset's objectives—gave Brisset continuing leeway. That leeway was consolidated by delays in communication with Merlin, Dobell, or Aymérich. The subordinate status of Brisset's command, in reality clear enough since February, was not reaffirmed until the end of August. However, Brisset lacked the men to achieve the objectives which he had set himself without Cunliffe's aid. Thus the Germans had time to regroup.[45]

With the fall of Garua the *Schwerpunkt* of German defences did at last shift to Jaunde. Thus, for the first time in the war German strategy and allied objectives were brought into line. Zimmerman's lifeline could no longer be the northern plateau; it had now to be the resources of neutral Spanish Muni, and therefore the axis of his operations became Jaunde and Ebolowa, both of them supply dumps and manufacturing centres. In the north he created a new *Nordabteilung* by drawing troops from Banyo and Dschang, and sending them east. Too late to hold Ngaundere, they centred their defences on Tibati and Banyo, forming an arc that ran west to Ossindinge through Dschang to the Sanaga, a front of 1,000 kilometres. Equipment was pulled back south of the Njong. Allied confusion gave Zimmerman sufficient respite to plug the gaps in the north, at least for the time being.[46]

Dobell's retreat and the coming of the rains brought a pause in the west which allowed Zimmerman to improvise an attack in the east against Morisson's communications between Bertua and Dume, the aim being to drive the French once again beyond the Kadei. The Germans' intention was to reinforce their left in order to lap round Morisson's northern flank. But the command structure was confused; the troops drawn from the west and from Banyo were still formally part of the *Nordabteilung*; and Duisberg, the officer in charge of the attack, was pulled south by his concerns for the dangers from that quarter. Thus, by 13–16 September the German offensive, their last major effort of the campaign, had stalled. Even as it did so, Zimmerman drew off two companies to the south and one to the north, thus blocking any hopes of its renewal.

Broadly speaking, therefore, the major German concentrations between July and September were pointed north and south, not east and west. The latter were, however, the points from which the British and the French proposed to press their advance. The fall of Ngaundere had convinced Dobell that Jaunde was now his proper objective in a way it had not been in March, and thus only its reduction, not the blockade of

---

[45] The British sources all see Brisset's actions as evidence of French Anglophobia and not of a different strategic appreciation. Ministère de la Guerre, *Armées françaises*, IX, 2ᵉ vol., 363–4, 387–92, 458–61, 586–98, provides a corrective.

[46] Student, *Kameruns Kampf*, 207–9.

the coast, would force the Germans to surrender. Moreover, he was determined to create a force sufficiently strong to enable his columns to take Jaunde even if Aymérich could not give them effective support. The French were equally decided that Aymérich should be enabled to advance on Jaunde from the east even if British action in the west remained limited. On 25 and 26 August Merlin and Dobell, this time with Aymérich also present, conferred once again at Duala and a joint thrust on Jaunde was fixed to begin after the rains were over, on 15 October in the east and on 15 November in the west. The problems of communication with Cunliffe's command reinforced the decision that, as before, opportunities in the north should be subsidiary and supportive.

The second Duala conference also discussed an attack from the south. Merlin and Aymérich favoured a thrust from Campo on the coast, designed to combine with the French columns coming up from Gabon. They had been prodded in this direction by Doumergue, who, with one eye cocked towards French territorial ambitions and the other to the German line of communications to Spanish territory, wanted to give the French companies at Campo a role more significant than that of 'frontier guards and customs officers'. But Doumergue was in Paris and had to defer to Dobell in Duala. The latter was the de facto allied commander in the Cameroons, and he preferred to concentrate his forces. He was supported by Mayer, who was anxious that he, rather than the Campo contingent, should secure any available reinforcements. Britain's material superiority meant that Mayer was struggling to keep France's end up in the advance from the west; only two months previously Doumergue himself had reminded him that, although he was Dobell's military subordinate, he was also 'the representative of the Republic in the Cameroons'.[47]

Such grandiloquent language might have surprised Aymérich, whose role in the campaign now became direct. With Morisson's and Hutin's columns adjacent to each other, but with the two column commanders at loggerheads, Aymérich could assume personal control of the eastern advance. His left, under Hutin, moved along the Njong, its task being to protect the major thrust by Morisson, whose right rested on the Sanaga, feeling north in the hope of linking with Brisset. In practice,

[47] Michel, *Guerres mondiales et conflits contemporains*, 168 (1992), 20, 26.

the balance in Aymérich's advance was reversed. Hutin's column encountered the heavier German resistance, while Morisson's progress on the
Sanaga was comparably easier. Moreover, the link with Brisset proved
elusive. Not until 6–8 December did news filter in of Brisset's position,
and he was then still 150 kilometres from the Sanaga. Of Dobell's movements Aymérich knew nothing; in going forward to exercise command
himself, he lost contact with the other columns. By late December his
isolation and his lengthening communications forced him onwards, the
choices confronting him being the rapid seizure of Jaunde or retreat. On
2 January 1916 his gamble began to pay off. He learnt that Brisset was just
north of the Nachtigal rapids, above Jaunde on the Sanaga. Two days later
he heard that Dobell's British column had reached Jaunde. The co-
ordination of the columns, even if not their communication, had been
achieved, and thus their individual movements had had reciprocating
effects.

In the west Dobell's British column had retaken Wum Biagas on
9 October and his French column Eseka on 30 October. Both places were
prepared as forward bases, linked by motorized transport to Edea, so that
the final assault on Jaunde could proceed without a halt. A force of 9,700
men was assembled. Their advance in late November avoided the tactical
failings of the first attempt: a strong column on the forest road was flanked
on either side by detachments on as wide a front as possible, so checking
German sallies against the rear. By mid-December the British were out of
the jungle and into open country. The French reached a comparable point
a week later, at Mangeles. The British pressed on without waiting for the
French, and entered Jaunde on New Year's Day 1916.

To the north, converging forces from Bare and Ossindinge had cleared
Dschang by 6 November. Cunliffe, recalled from Mora without capturing
it, directed Brisset on Tibati, and most of the rest of his force on Banyo.
Banyo was a strong-point as formidable as Mora and Garua. The position
rose to a height of 400 metres, and was formed of a network of 300 stone
breastworks or sangars. The advance of Cunliffe's troops up its steep
slopes on 4 November was protected by mist; holding the ground gained
the following day, they assaulted the summit on 6 November. On
2 December the Ossindinge column took Fumban, and by 18 December
Cunliffe's command was arrayed on the front Joko–Linte–Ditam. On
8 January 1916 his and Aymérich's troops linked at the Nachtigal rapids.

The allied advances from east, west, and north had encountered little sustained German resistance. In part, this was the product of superior numbers, and (at last) efficiently organized supply columns and better-protected lines of march. The Germans, as they were boxed in, should have profited from a shortening of their lines of communication to put up a more vigorous defence. In reality this was impossible. None of Zimmerman's units had sufficient ammunition to allow itself to be drawn into a sustained firefight. Most of the rounds issued to askaris were the ersatz manufactures of Jaunde and Ebolowa. One company facing Morisson's column fired eight rounds per man on 29 November; by the end of the following day each soldier had only twelve rounds, and then only four after further fighting on 1 December. An effort by Zimmerman to counter-attack against Dobell on 16 December lasted forty minutes, until his men ran out of ammunition.[48] Retreat was therefore unavoidable, and as they fell back the Germans could neither plunder the ammunition of their enemies nor, increasingly, rescue their own spent cases for recycling.

But the softness of the German defences had another cause. The sources of ammunition lay to the south of the Njong—ersatz production was based at Ebolowa, and the only route for communication from Europe lay via Spanish Muni. And yet the thrust of the allies' advance on Jaunde was directed north of the Njong. Aymérich's efforts had emphasized not his left but his right, Morisson's column and the link with Brisset. Dobell was similarly resistant to being drawn south. He was told by the War Office on 2 August of the importance of the axes between Jaunde and Muni and Jaunde and Kribi, and of the road from Ebolowa to Ambam.[49] But in his desire to take Jaunde without having to rely on Aymérich, Dobell concentrated his forces further north, on the direct route to Jaunde, and made clear to the French that he could not support Le Meillour.

The task of cutting the Germans' line of retreat, therefore, lay with the Gabon columns. Both the Brazzaville conference in February and the second Duala conference in August had paid lip-service to the need to block the Germans off from Muni. But in the allocation of manpower this

[48] Student, *Kameruns Kampf*, 286–7, 298
[49] Moberly, *Togoland and Cameroons*, 314–15.

objective never received sufficient priority. In July Le Meillour's efforts to clear the eastern side of the Muni border were rewarded with the capture of Ojem and Bitam, but were halted by the Germans on the River Ntem. Merlin and Aymérich hoped to support Le Meillour by reinforcing a column landed on the coast at Campo, and intended to stop traffic on Muni's northern border. But Dobell refused to favour the Campo column at the expense of the advance on Jaunde, and even withdrew the troops which he had provisionally allocated to it. Merlin appealed to Paris for six companies from French West Africa. On 20 October 1915 two companies landed at Campo from Dakar, but without maps, interpreters, or guides. On 15 December two further companies and a proper complement of supporting arms made the Campo column a going concern. But it was too late. Le Meillour's efforts to cross the Ntem in late October and again in late November were checked, not least because for two months part of his command was diverted to Akoafim. Le Meillour finally got beyond the Ntem in mid-December. Even then his progress towards Ambam remained slow.[50]

Thus, in December the Spanish frontier still remained open for 200 kilometres. Zimmerman determined that he would take his command through this gap and into neutral territory. The German decision to retreat was therefore not prompted by the fall of Jaunde. As at Duala, the Germans preferred not to sacrifice the investments and developments of peacetime colonialism in a short-term defensive action, but instead to evacuate the town before Dobell's arrival. What proved decisive was Le Meillour's crossing of the Ntem, which made the cutting of German communications only a matter of time.[51] On 28 December, four days before the British arrival in Jaunde, Zimmerman issued orders for the retreat of the German forces to the south-west. The axis Jaunde–Ebolowa–Ambam now became the corridor whose collapsing walls must be kept open long enough to allow the evacuation of the Schütztruppen still in the north and west. The gap on the frontier closed to 50 kilometres, but by 15 February a great exodus had been accomplished. About 15,000 people—and possibly more—had crossed into Spanish territory, including 1,000 Germans, 6,000 askaris, and 7,000 family and followers. The

[50] Aymérich, Conquête, 103, 109–10, 158–66.
[51] Student, Kameruns Kampf, 318–19.

loyalty of the Beti of Jaunde to the Germans was the major factor in ensuring that, even in defeat, the *Schütztruppen* retained their integrity and their cohesion as a fighting force. Thus was the German policy of integrating the wives and children of the askaris vindicated; thus too was evidence provided that many in the Cameroons saw the German defeat as no more than temporary.[52]

The failure of the Campo and Gabon columns to cut off the German retreat was complemented by the delay in the allied pursuit from Jaunde. Dobell was slow to recognize the direction the Germans had followed. Some anticipated that the *Schütztruppen* would break into small units to continue guerrilla operations within the colony. Dobell himself reckoned that major units still lay north and west of Jaunde. When he did finally realize that his efforts should be bent to the south, he was anxious not to press the pursuit too hard for fear of driving the Germans across the frontier before the Campo and Gabon columns had been able to form a cordon to block their path.

Aymérich was put in command of the pursuit. But his eastern columns were exhausted, and their lines of communication extended. Not until 14 January was he ready to leave Jaunde. Hutin's column moved south and south-east to Sangmelima, to mop up any pockets of German resistance in that direction, and to be ready to outflank Ebolowa. Two columns, one under Haywood and another under Faucon, moved directly against Ebolowa, Faucon entering the town on 19 January. The supply problem was now acute. Hutin's column was left to live off the land. But the area between Jaunde and Ebolowa had been stripped of supplies by the retreating Germans, and the Beti had abandoned their villages in deference to German wishes. Dobell therefore argued that forces the size of Aymérich's could not be sustained in the south-western Cameroons. Moreover, for him the fall of Ebolowa marked the end of German resistance. Haywood and the British forces in the pursuit were directed towards Kribi. Not until 28 January did Dobell reverse his decision, and by then Haywood's resumption of the march to the south was too late.

Dobell's decisions, however misguided in terms of the reality of Zimmerman's movements, were justified by logistic realities. Aymérich's

[52] Frederick Quinn, 'The impact of the First World War and its aftermath on the Beti of Cameroun', in Page (ed.), *Africa*, 175–6.

force was advancing too fast for its lines of communications; already extended at Jaunde, which lay 700 kilometres from its intermediate base at Nola on the Sanga, they were increased by 200 kilometres in ten days in the advance on Ebolowa. Beyond Ebolowa supply could no longer be maintained. The Germans having just been through the area, the villages were empty, and few porters could be found; those that were recruited did not stay. Faucon reduced the supplies carried by his column from six days' to four, and increased the load carried by each soldier from two days' to three, so saving on porters. Switching the lines of communication from Jaunde and Nola to Eseka and Duala took time. Aymérich's columns did not finally link with Le Meillour's until 14 February.[53]

The final act of the Germans' defeat in the Cameroons was accomplished not on the Muni frontier but at the opposite extreme. The *Schütztruppen* at Mora, undefeated but apprised of the retreat into Spanish territory, surrendered on 18 February. The garrison of 155 soldiers still had 37,000 rounds of ammunition.[54]

For all their abundance at Mora, the lack of munitions became the major German explanation as to why their defence of the Cameroons had not been more protracted. The companies facing Dobell and Aymérich had been unable to sustain combat since September 1915. And without ammunition the idea of continuing operations from the jungle fastnesses of the south, or of raiding across the French border into Gabon or Equatorial Africa became absurd.

Yet, although real enough, the munitions' deficiency gained importance only in the light of von Lettow-Vorbeck's campaign in East Africa. When, after 1918, it became apparent that von Lettow-Vorbeck had fought on after German territory had been all but overrun, and had kept his forces intact until the end of the war, the question—implicit but nonetheless real—arose as to why Zimmerman had not done the same. Thus, rather than celebrate the achievement of a defence far longer and far more successful, against considerably superior forces, than had ever been anticipated, the Germans tended to ask why it had not been even better sustained.

---

[53] Aymérich, *Conquête*, 169–86; Ministère de la Guerre, *Armées françaises*, IX, 2ᵉ vol., 756–807.
[54] Osuntokun, *Nigeria*, 193.

The true answer lay less in the munitions supply than in the higher direction of the campaign. In East Africa the overall conduct of the defence was assumed by the *Schütztruppen* commander, and his objective became not the preservation of a German colony, but the use of that colony to distract the British from concentrating all their efforts in Europe. In West Africa the civilian governor, Ebermaier, became the inspiration of German defence. His objective was to maintain Germany as a colonial power in the Cameroons. At no stage was heavy fighting allowed to do damage to the principal settlements, in particular Duala and Jaunde. Moreover, despite their continuous retreat, and despite their belief that the local tribes would follow the power that exercised the greater strength, the Germans continued to have a lien on local loyalties. There were major exceptions. In the west older contacts with the British resurfaced, and the disruption of the commercial life of the coastal areas produced dissatisfaction with German rule. In the south-east the territory had been too recently French for Aymérich's men not to have some leverage, even if at times they threatened to forfeit it by their own brutality. But in the central heartlands, and particularly of course among the Beti, loyalty to the Germans lasted even beyond defeat.

The retreat into Spanish Muni, although it condemned the *Schütztruppen* to military inutility, was thus of a piece with their political purposes. A German enclave persisted in West Africa. The Spanish authorities, with only 180 militiamen, had neither the inclination nor the power to intern the *Schütztruppen*. In April 1916 the Germans moved to Fernando Po. Aymérich received reports that there ammunition was reaching Ebermaier's men, that he had 500,000 rounds, and that his troops were drilling and training, awaiting the day of German victory in Europe before re-establishing themselves as a major West African power.[55]

French fears were exaggerated; the British blockade made Muni and Fernando Po poor bases for the Germans. But it remains true that the final settlement of the Cameroons was the product more of affairs in Europe than of the outcome of the campaign in the Cameroons. If Germany had won the war in 1918 it might still have re-established its authority in the Cameroons. Neither Britain nor France managed

---

[55] Ibid. 193–4; Aymérich, *Conquête*, 198–9.

adequately to fill the administrative vacuum created by Germany's withdrawal.

As the conquest of the Cameroons proceeded, its de facto occupation developed three separate enclaves—to the west, to the north, and to the south-east. Confronted by what seemed to be the total absence of state administration, the column commanders had to assume civil, financial, and technical responsibilities, as well as military. Dobell enjoyed a staff of British colonial officers specifically trained for such functions; moreover, he had the medical equipment and logistical support to sustain at least some of them. As early as December 1914 it seemed likely that a partition which followed the lines of spheres of influence as well as the preferences of the population would divide the Cameroons centrally, along the line of the Sanaga. This was much further south than the growth of Doumergue's territorial ambitions could now countenance.[56] The French therefore proposed that the south-east, the territory that had belonged to them until 1911 and which they had conquered by dint of their own efforts, should be administered by them; the remainder, including Duala, should be a condominium pending a final partition at the end of the war.

Britain's responses to condominium were divided. The Foreign Office, anxious to concede to the French where it could in order to gain elsewhere, was happy to accommodate France's wishes. By early 1916 the Cabinet's war committee too saw France's immersion in West Africa as a way of keeping it out of East Africa. But other departments were more annexationist. The Admiralty wanted Duala, and if Britain had Duala, then it held the economic key to all of the Cameroons except the south. The Colonial Office assumed that most of the Cameroons would go to France, but was more annexationist with regard to the frontier with northern Nigeria than its key official on the spot. Lugard's policy of 'indirect rule' in Nigeria had been deepened by the outbreak of war. The withdrawal of district officers and their supporting troops increased Britain's reliance on the loyalty of the emirs. In Bussa, where administrative reorganization failed to respect traditional authority, rebellion flared in June 1915. Elsewhere the authority of the chiefs often lacked deep roots and was vitiated by corruption; the manpower and fiscal demands of the war cast them in the roles of British agents. On the Gold Coast

---

[56] Michel, *Guerres mondiales et conflits contemporains*, 168 (1992), 24, 27.

resistance to chiefly direction was evident as soon as the troops departed for Togoland in August 1914, and in 1916 fuelled the Bongo riots.[57] Lugard therefore wanted to bolster the chiefs of northern Nigeria by the restoration of what he deemed to be their traditional lands. In doing so, he simplified the fluidities of the political relationships within the emirates, and tended to define them in terms of geographical boundaries rather than of more subtle influences. Although he was hazy as to what it might mean on the map, his aim was to ensure the integrity of the emirates of Bornu and Yola.

At a meeting on 23 February 1916 Georges Picot for France, 'who knew nothing of the lands and peoples he was dividing', drew a line 'with a heavy pencil' which Sir Charles Strachey, the representative of the Colonial Office, was constrained to accept. As one of Strachey's colleagues later observed: 'If only you had not had a pencil in your hand at the time.'[58] The provisional partition followed the main north–south road, not the distribution of tribal affiliations. It gave the northern Cameroons to the line Garua–Ngaundere–Tibati–Joko–Nachtigal to the British and the rest to France. The Foreign Office had prevailed. The Admiralty did not get Duala. The traditional territories of the major British loyalist on the northern Nigerian frontier, the Emir of Yola, remained split. The zones of occupation created in 1916 ran across the boundaries formed by right of conquest, especially in the west.

Administratively, neither power was up to the task of resettlement and reconstruction. The British zone was incorporated as part of Nigeria, but the Nigerian administration was already weakened by the departure of its staff for military service, and was therefore not equal to an extension of its territorial responsibilities. In the French zone, the territories originally ceded in 1911 were reincorporated with French Equatorial Africa, and the remainder was governed by the army and answerable directly to Paris.[59]

---

[57] Crowder, *Revolt in Bussa*; Thomas, *Journal of African History*, XXIV (1983), 57–75; also Afigbo, *Warrant Chief*, 118–57.

[58] Yearwood, *Canadian Journal of African Studies*, XXVI (1993), 235; see also Yearwood, *Borno Museum Society Newsletter*, XXV (1995), 32–44.

[59] Elango, *International Journal of African Historical Studies*, XVIII (1985), 657–731; Louis, *Great Britain and Germany's Lost Colonies*, 57–62; Andrew and Kanya-Forstner, *France Overseas*, 97–9; Osuntokun, *Nigeria*, 206–32; Aymérich, *Conquête*, 200–9; Digre, *Imperialism's New Clothes*, 37–48.

The casualties were the tribes of the Cameroons. Where there had been fifty Germans there were now five or six Frenchmen. Education fell victim to the internment and evacuation of German Catholic pastors. German doctors left with the *Schütztruppen*. In their stead witchcraft and magic regained dominance. Feuds and thefts multiplied, evidence of the loss of order and of the violence already legitimized by the war.[60] Ultimately, the post-war settlement did confirm the French hold on three-quarters of the Cameroons, but it was a grip that reflected the realities of diplomacy more than the realities of French rule in the period 1916–18.

[60] Quinn, in Page (ed.), *Africa*, 177–8; Quinn, *Cahiers d'études africaines*, XIII (1973), 728–30.

4

SOUTH-WEST
AFRICA

The replacement of domestic discord by renewed national purpose, a sense of union that conquered class and even ethnic divisions—these are the themes seen as characteristic of the early months of the war for most of its belligerents. South Africa was an exception. Furthermore, the splits which sundered the newly formed Union were a direct reflection of pre-war tensions. South Africa is therefore the exception that proves the rule—not the rule that powers went to war as a flight from domestic crisis, a creation of hindsight, but the rule that the fear that war would provoke revolution inhibited the move to war while not in the end preventing it. Admittedly, the pressures to which South Africa was exposed were unusually severe. Its internal conflicts were at once social, racial, and national; it was only on the third that the Union foundered.[1]

In August 1913, and again in January 1914, troops were deployed on the Rand to suppress strikes among white miners. The effect of martial law was to boost the status and membership of the South African Labour party, to fuse the English skilled worker and the landless Afrikaner in joint action. In 1911 the party affiliated with the International. But when war broke out this link proved brittle. The party's executive committee remained loyal to its principles, and resolutions opposing war were

---

[1] On South Africa in the period of the First World War, see Garson, *Journal of Imperial and Commonwealth History*, VIII (1979), 68–85; Hancock, *Smuts 1870–1919*; Katzenellenbogen, 'Southern Africa and the war of 1914–18'; Meintjes, *Botha*; Walker, *History of Southern Africa*, ch. 14.

passed at conferences in December 1914 and January 1915. However, many of the party's branches supported the war, and so did its principal organ *The Worker*, edited by F. H. R. Creswell, a major in the Rand Rifle Corps. In parliament the Labour party backed the Unionist party, while outside it the pacifists began to break away, setting up the War on War League in September. The popular responses to the sinking of the *Lusitania* in May 1915 made this split overt: in August the English members ensured that the party declared its loyal support for the war, while in September the leaders of the left formed the International Socialist League. The Marxists found that their fellow-travellers included at least some Afrikaners, driven by nationalism to reject a war undertaken by the British empire.[2]

One of the principal planks around which the pre-war Labour party had coalesced was its advocacy of the industrial colour bar. The dependence of the mines on the skills of white workers became a means to protect the employment of all whites against black competition. Socialism stood cheek-by-jowl with racism. Civil rights discrimination against coloureds, and particularly against Indian immigration, countered by Gandhi's tactics of passive resistance, provoked a strike by 130,000 Indians in Natal in 1913. Some amelioration of the Indians' plight was effected in June 1914, and when war broke out the colour bar was eased by shortages of skilled white labour. Both coloureds and blacks used the opportunity to stress their loyalty, at least to the British empire if not to South Africa. Persuaded by London's propaganda that this was a war for liberalism and self-determination, the less radical and more middle-class elements argued that co-operation could be the path to full citizenship. The South African Native National Congress, the future African National Congress, declared its support for Louis Botha, the prime minister, and Walter Rubusana, its leader in the Cape, offered to raise 5,000 infantry. The coloureds' association, the Africa Peoples' Organization, issued its own attestation forms in a bid to form a Cape Coloured Corps in August: by September it had mustered 10,000 volunteers, and in 1915 the unit was approved by the government.

---

[2] Ticktin, *South African Historical Journal*, I (1969), 59–80, on the Labour party; on popular responses in general, see Nasson, *Journal of Imperial and Commonwealth History*, XXII (1995), 248–76; also Nasson, *War & Society*, XII (1994), 47–64.

Thus the war quietened agitation in two of the major areas of domestic division. But for Afrikaner nationalism war provided fuel to flames only recently rekindled. In 1907 the Treaty of Vereeniging had promised unity for Boer and Briton within South Africa, and in 1910 the creation of the Union gave Afrikaners an effective measure of self-government. But the Boers themselves were divided. In 1902 some had left South Africa for German South-West Africa or for Portuguese Mozambique rather than be subject to British rule. Many more, then or later, effected a compromise—to live within the empire for the time being while still harbouring as ultimate goals both independence and republicanism. Thus, the collaboration of Louis Botha, the Boer general and the Union's prime minister, could be deemed temporarily expedient. But Botha's policy of conciliation was shattered by the speeches and actions of J. B. M. Hertzog of the Orange Free State. Hertzog accepted English and Dutch equality within South Africa, but argued that equality should be expressed through separation, both linguistic and cultural; fusion would be a cloak for Anglicization. Botha's first efforts to meet Hertzog's challenges included his incorporation within the Union cabinet. But in 1912 Hertzog's criticisms were too overt for any fiction of unity to be sustainable. Following his exclusion from the cabinet, Hertzog seceded from Botha's South Africa party, and in January 1914 formed the Nationalist party. Thus Botha had already lost a large section of Afrikaner support when war broke out.

In August 1914 Hertzog did not disagree with Botha's assumption that British entry to the war automatically involved South Africa. Botha's immediate release of imperial troops from South Africa for Europe was therefore uncontroversial. It was the move from passive participation to active involvement that made specific the doubts of Afrikaner nationalists.

On 7 August, in pursuit of the objectives laid down by the CID subcommittee, London asked Pretoria whether it could seize the harbours and wireless stations of German South-West Africa. In this case, however, the immediate naval priorities chimed with echoes of pre-war annexationism. The German presence in southern Africa had provided a haven for diehard Boer rebels; it had also, in its ruthless suppression of the Herero rebellion in 1904, triggered fears of a native uprising within the Union. Thus, for London, the conquest of South-West Africa would ease the long-term security considerations of South Africa, and would tie the Union more closely to the empire.[3] For Botha himself it opened even grander visions—the incorporation of all southern Africa, including Bechuanaland, Rhodesia, and Nyasaland, within the Union.[4] He was therefore anxious that South Africa itself, and specifically its troops and not those from elsewhere in the empire, should respond to London's request.

Botha's cabinet was less convinced. At its meeting on 7 August four members supported him and four opposed. Much of the discussion focused on the practical difficulties of mounting the campaign. But the fundamental concern was Afrikaner reaction. The Boers of the Union could well end up fighting the Boers of South-West Africa. Principle was also at issue: Britain justified its engagement in the war by reference to the rights of small nations, and yet such scruples had not restrained it from crushing the Boer republics fourteen years earlier. For Boers to become the agents of British imperialism, particularly when the empire itself might be forfeit if Germany proved victorious in Europe, was to the Nationalists both morally unacceptable and politically inexpedient.

Nonetheless, by 10 August the cabinet had convinced itself that, rather than become a source of increasing division among Afrikaners, the conquest of German South-West Africa could be a means for a new-found unity between English and Dutch. London had renewed its request on 9 August. The cabinet agreed to meet it on two conditions, both designed to ensure domestic unity. Parliament was to be asked to approve the campaign, and only volunteers were to be called upon to serve. Botha mentioned neither condition in his reply to London.[5] Nor was the prime minister alone in his underestimation of Boer opposition. J. C. Smuts, the minister of defence, reckoned that, 'when all is over and German South-West Africa again forms a part of our Afrikaaner heritage, feeling will quickly swing round and our action be generally approved'.[6] His inner conviction overrode his acceptance of mounting evidence to the

---

[3] Louis, *Great Britain and Germany's Lost Colonies*, 31.

[4] Meintjes, *Botha*, 205–6; M. W. Swanson, 'South West Africa in Trust 1915–1939', in Gifford and Louis (eds.), *Britain and Germany in Africa*, 632; Hyam, *Failure of South African Expansion*, 26.

[5] Spies, *South African Historical Journal*, I (1969), 47–57.

[6] Hancock and Poel, *Smuts Papers*, iii. 201.

contrary; it generated a mishandling of South Africa's mobilization that fell only just short of disaster.

A month elapsed before the South African parliament was called. On 10 September the assembly dutifully approved Botha's policy by ninety-one votes to ten, and on the 12th the Senate followed suit by twenty-four votes to five. On 14 September parliament was prorogued, and did not reconvene until 26 February 1915. Formally, the decision to invade South-West Africa was hallowed by popular approval. In reality, the inauguration of military preparations had preceded their ratification; the commencement of operations was postponed until late September, not because of constitutional nicety but because of the problem of naval co-operation. Most telling of all, the public justification for the campaign was no longer conquest but defence. The theme on which Botha and Smuts harped in their parliamentary speeches was the possibility of a German takeover of South Africa. Such improbabilities were buttressed by reference to border incidents, duly dressed up as a German invasion. The annexation of German territory and the cabinet's hope that this would fuel domestic conciliation were never mentioned.

The parliamentary session was the first open acknowledgement of South Africa's plan to invade South-West Africa. But speculation had begun on 11 August, when Smuts published the government's intention to organize adequate forces 'to provide for contingencies'.[7] Smuts specifically mentioned four volunteer regiments, thus reflecting the cabinet's condition of the previous day. But the 1912 Defence act, which created an army for South Africa, made all European males aged 17 to 60 liable for military service in time of war, and committed all those aged 17 to 25 to compulsory training. South Africa's forces had four main elements: a small body of permanent troops, either mounted rifles or artillery; an 'active citizen force', largely English in composition, based on pre-1912 volunteer regiments, but completed to a strength of 25,000 if insufficient volunteers were forthcoming; rifle associations for older men, predominantly Boer burghers liable to be commandeered as they had been in the war with the British; and a cadet corps for those aged 13 to 17. The declared aim was Anglo-Boer integration but for many Boers the effects smacked of British imperialism. Khaki uniforms, clean-shaven faces and

---

[7] Hancock, *Smuts 1870–1919*, 379.

hierarchical rather than patriarchal and elective command structures were the military tools of the Boers' enemies not of the former Boer republics. The establishment of a cadet corps confirmed that the ultimate objective was Anglicization.

Moreover, the dualities of the Defence act carried a further threat. The act embodied both voluntarism and conscription. The intention to rely on the former could not be effected without providing expectations as to the latter. Botha declared in 1912 that he wanted 'a real Army, not only capable of coping with a little Kaffir war, but also able to defend South Africa against any odds, wherever they came from'.[8] His readiness in 1914 to dispense with the imperial troops stationed in South Africa displayed his resolve—an ambition which suggested that Smuts's four volunteer regiments would not be enough.

The ambiguity in Smuts's actions may have been the product of genuine confusion. The South African forces had no central staff and no command organization; Smuts and the civilian officials in the ministry of defence did everything. The minister's own command experience in the Boer War, although distinguished, was restricted: he had handled only small bodies of troops, with limited logistical needs. Furthermore, the outbreak of war found him without contingency plans, either for the defence of the Union or for the seizure of German territory.

On 14 August Smuts held a meeting of senior officers to make good some of these deficiencies. He endeavoured not to reveal the objective of the proposed arrangements, a manoeuvre that displayed his naivety about military planning as much as his sensitivity as to what he intended. However, C. F. Beyers, the commandant-general of the defence forces, having elicited that an invasion of South-West Africa was proposed, expressed his opposition. Beyers was not alone; many of the commandants had been appointed on his recommendation, not Smuts's, and two in particular, J. C. G. Kemp (the district staff officer of Western Transvaal) and S. G. Maritz (the district staff officer of the northern Cape, adjacent to the German frontier) made no secret of their sympathy for Beyers. Nobody resigned; nobody was dismissed. Smuts reasoned that to have such men in the service, and under oath, was better than to have them out.

---

[8] Swart, *Journal of South African Studies*, XXIV (1998), 746; for what follows see also Collyer, *Campaign in German South West Africa*, 15–20.

Without an effective planning organization, and with what there was split as to what to do, the weakness of Pretoria's initial proposals for offensive action is unsurprising. But the major cause of confusion in fact arose from the difficulties of co-ordination with the Royal Navy.

The spine of German South-West Africa, running through the relatively fertile tableland in the north and centre of the colony, was the main railway. Beginning in the north, with spurs from Tsumeb and Grootfontein, it ran south-west to Karibib, and then south to the capital and main wireless station at Windhoek. From Windhoek it progressed through Keetmanshoop as far as Kalkfontein, about 95 kilometres short of the Orange river. Two lines ran to the coast, one in the north from Karibib to Swakopmund, and the other in the south from Keetmanshoop to Lüderitz. These two breaches apart, the perimeter of the colony was well-endowed with natural defensive barriers. The Atlantic coastline was bordered by a waterless strip, between 65 and 95 kilometres wide. The eastern frontier was bounded by the Kalahari desert. The obvious landward route for invasion, therefore, lay to the south, from the Cape across the Orange river. But the supply problems presented by this approach were considerable. The South African railhead at Prieska was about 225 kilometres from Upington, the base for offensive operations across the frontier. The territory north of the Orange river was arid. Furthermore, any advance from this direction would simply push the Germans back up their railway line, onto their own resources and lines of communication. It would not strike directly at the maritime objectives so important to the CID subcommittee.

By contrast, control of Swakopmund promised to bring decisive results in short order. Britain owned a small slab of territory alongside it, at Walvis Bay. It gave onto the most direct route to Windhoek, and seizure of these points would cut off any German troops facing south. Swakopmund was therefore Smuts's initial preference for a landing. But it was abandoned for lack of sufficient shipping to transport and escort expeditionary forces to both Swakopmund and Lüderitz. The fact that, given the choice, Lüderitz was selected over Swakopmund reveals how muddled the thinking had become. An offensive from Lüderitz carried many of the disadvantages present in the advance across the Cape frontier. The idea that it could be co-ordinated with the latter was far-fetched: the forces so deployed would describe an arc of up to 950 kilometres, without lateral

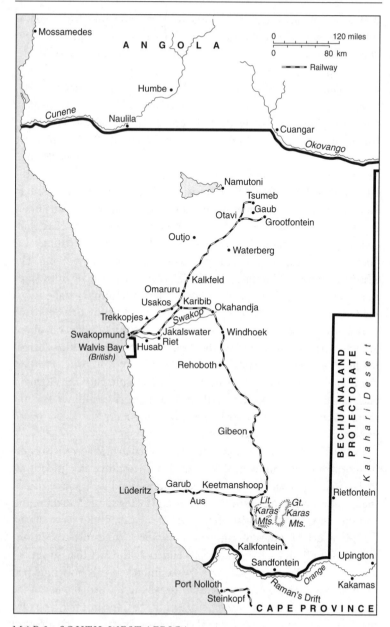

MAP 3. SOUTH-WEST AFRICA

communications, and would be attacking an enemy that would enjoy the advantage of the central position and the use of the railways in order to effect local concentrations.[9]

This, nonetheless, was the scheme adopted by Smuts on 21 August. Naval bombardment was to account for the wireless station and jetty at Swakopmund. The land forces were divided into three groups: Force A at Port Nolloth, on the Atlantic coast south of the Orange river; Force B at Upington; and Force C at Lüderitz. The total strength of all three groups was 5,000 rifles and fourteen guns, and in isolation each was insufficiently strong for offensive operations.

On 19 September Force C landed at Lüderitz. With three aircraft to their opponents' none, the Germans were able to track the movements of the South Africans. They decided not to defend the harbour, concluding that the guns of the Royal Navy would give the British artillery superiority. Instead, they concentrated their defensive efforts on the Orange. The river, although fordable in a number of places, was a sufficient obstacle to provide good opportunities for local counter-attacks before the South Africans could establish bridgeheads. Force A pushed north-eastwards from Port Nolloth, reaching Raman's Drift on the Orange by 14 September. On 24 September Pretoria knew that the Germans were moving south to Kalkfontein, not west to Lüderitz, but they relayed this information to Force A by post, with the result that it did not reach the force commander, Henry Lukin, till 7 October. Lukin's problems at Raman's Drift were considerable. The strength of his column was 1,800 rifles; he reckoned he had sufficient transport for 800. He pushed an advance guard of about 300 men and two guns forward of the Orange, but unsupported and without the wagons to carry their reserve ammunition. On 26 September the Germans, with 1,200 men and three batteries, encircled Lukin's advance guard at Sandfontein and killed or captured the entire command.

Both Lukin and Smuts shared a measure of responsibility for the Sandfontein disaster. Moreover, neither the conduct of the reconnaissance nor the resilience of the fighting (when they surrendered, the South Africans' ammunition stocks were far from exhausted)[10] reflected well on the new Defence Force. But the reputations of both commanders and

[9] Collyer, *Campaign in German South West Africa*, 28; Corbett, *Naval Operations*, i. 316; Hancock and Poel, *Smuts Papers*, iii. 201–2.

[10] Hennig, *Deutsch-Südwest im Weltkriege*, 98.

commanded were saved by the action—or lack of it—on the part of S. G. Maritz, commanding Force B.

Lukin argued that the success of his advance was vitally dependent on the support of Force B progressing from Upington. But Maritz had refused to move, pleading that his forces were insufficiently trained, that some of them were conscripts and therefore could not be obliged to cross the frontier, and that many of his officers would refuse to obey. By failing to act against such dissent earlier, Smuts had now left it too late to act at all. If Maritz resigned or was dismissed, Lukin's column would be even more exposed. Smuts asked Maritz to come to Pretoria. He refused, and on 2/3 October instead moved his command out of Upington to Kakamas. Smuts, under pretence of reinforcing Maritz, moved fresh units to Upington on 4 October and gave the overall command to Coen Brits. The latter's loyalty was unthinking: he was alleged to have told Botha (in Afrikans, for he spoke no English), 'My men are ready; who[m] do we fight—the English or the Germans?'[11] On 7 October Maritz made contact with the Germans along the border, and on the 9th went into open rebellion, promoting himself to general and declaring South Africa's independence and war on Britain. He threatened to attack Upington unless he could speak to Christiaan De Wet, Beyers, Kemp, and Hertzog.[12]

Maritz's summons to the Afrikaner nationalists for support confirms that, from his perspective, the rebellion was a planned coup against Botha's government and not a spontaneous uprising by diehard Boers still carrying on the war of 1899–1902. After the commandants' meeting with Smuts on 14 August Maritz had initiated a plot to install Beyers as president of a provisional government, J. H. De La Rey as commandant-general of the defence force, Christiaan De Wet as head of the Orange Free State, and himself as head of the Cape. The rebellion was timed for 15 September. But in reality the uprising collapsed into a series of ill-co-ordinated movements, with diverse objectives, its execution characterized by compromise and indecisiveness.

Maritz himself was relatively junior, an unpleasant personality, and—in his station at Upington—remote from the centres of power within the

---

[11] L'Ange, *Urgent Imperial Service*, 4; this is the most recent account of the campaign.

[12] Davenport, *English Historical Review*, LXXVIII (1963), 73–94, is the major scholarly account of the rebellion; both Hancock, *Smuts*, 379–91, and Meintjes, *Botha*, chs. 14 and 15, are helpful; Lucas, *Empire at War*, 377–432, is full but partisan.

Union. Potentially far more influential was De La Rey, a venerable hero of the Boer War and a close friend of both Botha and Smuts. De La Rey, fired by the apocalyptic visions of a crazed seer, was convinced that the return of the republic was imminent and that the outbreak of the war provided the opportunity to act; he also seems to have believed that Botha remained wedded to a declaration of Afrikaner independence if the opportunity arose. At any rate, De La Rey was persuaded by Botha and Smuts not to go into open rebellion on 13 August, and at a meeting on 15 August told his followers to disperse. At the Nationalists' first congress, held in Pretoria on 26 August, De La Rey's public position was akin to that of Hertzog: his loyalty was to South Africa, not to Britain or Germany. For Hertzog, neutrality promised success for South Africa whoever won in Europe; commitment to one side could prove fatal if the other proved victorious.

On 15 September, the day appointed for the rebellion and the day after parliament had been prorogued, Beyers, Kemp, and others resigned their commissions, protesting their opposition to the proposed invasion of South-West Africa. But Maritz was not ready. Moreover, that same afternoon Beyers and De La Rey failed to stop at a police roadblock, and the latter, mistaken for a member of a murderous gang, was shot dead. Beyers and Kemp felt that the opportunity to rebel had passed. At a meeting following De La Rey's funeral they confined themselves to protests against the invasion of South-West Africa, and to the organization of further meetings. When Botha, who had replaced Beyers as commandant-general, asked the commandants to volunteer for service in South-West Africa they did so without exception.[13]

But for Maritz's move to open defiance, therefore, Boer discontent might have fizzled and crackled without explosion. Maritz's declaration prompted Beyers, De Wet, and Kemp to renew contact with each other on 13 October. Even now they tried to cajole Botha rather than to topple him. Botha refused to listen. Moreover, on 11 October, in response to Maritz's rebellion, Smuts declared martial law, thus definitively moving from voluntarism to conscription for the recruitment of the defence force and so forcing Boers to decide where they stood. On 22 October the rebel leaders took a rather lukewarm decision to act, leaving the initiative

---

[13] Meintjes, *Botha*, 230.

to Beyers in the Transvaal and to De Wet in the Orange Free State. The fact that they did so hardened Maritz's resolve as he began to consider surrender after suffering defeat at Brits's hands at Kakamas on 24 October. Thus a series of ill-co-ordinated risings gained an outward appearance of cohesion and conspiracy. Thus too, 'strong speech and rash action went hand in hand with compromise'.[14]

Most rebels saw their action in a Boer tradition of 'armed protest' against a government policy of which they disapproved. Their motivations embraced opposition to conscription, resistance to the invasion of South-West Africa, and a sense of betrayal by Botha and Smuts. But they tapped into other grievances as well. Their strength was greatest in the regions which drought had ravaged and where indebtedness had increased, and among the landless, ousted by the farmers' preference for cheaper black labour. Landless Afrikaners were confronted by 'encroaching urban proletarianization'.[15] It was a process which threatened the familial and familiar values engendered by a society of pastoralists; their political values were egalitarian and republican. Into these they injected millenarianism, foretelling not only the end of British rule but also of capitalism. The Dutch Reformed Church, which at the outset supported the war, refused to decide whether the rebellion was treasonable or not. The fact that Hertzog, though appealed to by Maritz, stayed silent throughout—neither condoning nor repudiating the rebellion—increased the ambiguity as to the rebels' main aims. But it also ensured that, although Hertzog was its major beneficiary, the rebellion never assumed an exclusively national character. Opposition to the British, although present, took second place to the domestic dispute among the Boers.

To avoid Boer killing Boer in South-West Africa, Boer proposed to kill Boer within the Union. For Botha this was a better outcome than for either British or (as was offered by London) Australian troops to suppress the rebellion. By using Afrikaners rather than Englishmen, Botha hoped to preserve his policy of conciliation between the white races. Manoeuvre and negotiation, not battle and bloodletting, were the key features of the conduct of the rebellion on both sides. The total government casualties

---

[14] Lucas, *Empire at War*, iv. 396.
[15] Nasson, *Journal of Imperial and Commonwealth History*, XXIII (1995), 264. See also Swart, *Journal of South African Studies*, XXIV (1998), 738–43.

were 101 killed and wounded for 30,000 engaged. The rebels, whose maximum numbers may have reached 10,000, had 124 killed and 229 wounded.[16]

De Wet's personal dominance of the Orange Free State, allied to the central position of the province, gave his rising the greatest significance. Furthermore, his son's death in action envenomed his motives more than those of the others. With a following of about 5,000 men, he was attacked by Botha in Mushroom Valley, south of Winburg, on 12 November. Botha's plan miscarried: he hoped to have Lukin's and Brits's forces from the west in position to encircle De Wet. Nonetheless, the rebel force was broken and De Wet himself forced to flee into the desert, where he was captured on 2 December.

Botha's influence in Eastern Transvaal limited the dangers in that quarter. In Western Transvaal Beyers's efforts to negotiate with the government while still resisting it were an open confession of the weakness of his following and of his own uncertainty as to the correct course of action. Efforts to link with De Wet came to nought after Mushroom Valley, and on 16 November Beyers's own force was broken in an attack near Bultfontein. Beyers fled, first east, then west, and finally north. On 8 December he was drowned in the Vaal river while trying to escape capture by government forces.

Only Kemp was still in the field, and he—together with 500 men—had been dispatched by Beyers across the Kalahari to link with Maritz. After an epic trek, that defied the elements as well as the government, Kemp entered German territory to effect a junction with Maritz on 2 December. Kemp's report on the state of the rebellion within the Union was optimistic. But the exhausted condition of his men and horses prevented immediate offensive action. He himself was sick. Maritz did not inspire the confidence of the Germans. Conflicts between Maritz and the commander of the 'free corps' formed by the Germans from Boers within South-West Africa deepened the distrust. A thrust across the Orange river on 22 December that achieved both surprise and envelopment failed owing to the problems of Boer command. Kemp refused to subordinate himself to Maritz, and wanted to cut back to the Transvaal. Maritz in his

---

[16] Hancock, *Smuts 1870–1919*, 391; Lucas, *Empire at War*, iv. 425–6, gives much higher losses, totalling about 1,000 for both sides; Meintjes, *Botha*, 249, says 374 government troops were killed and wounded, and 190 rebels were killed and 350 wounded.

turn felt he could not be seen to attack in direct co-operation with the Germans. When the Boers crossed the frontier once again, on 13 January 1915, with 1,000 men, they were only accompanied by four German guns; the main German thrust was intended to be over 160 kilometres away to the west, on Steinkopf via Raman's Drift. Maritz's attack was directed at Upington but was not delivered until 24 January, and even then scattered its efforts over an 8-kilometre front. Reports of the rebellion's defeat increased the bickering. In a bid to revive the rebellion, the Germans abandoned their attack on Steinkopf for one closer to Upington, at Kakamas, on 31 January. But the attack miscarried, and they were in any case too late. The Boer rebels, including Kemp, had surrendered on the previous day. Only Maritz, the 'free corps', and the artillery which the Germans had allocated to the rebels returned across the frontier.[17]

Botha's policy of conciliation, begun during the course of the rebellion with an amnesty, continued after its conclusion with clemency. Only one rebel was executed: an officer who had not taken the precaution of resigning his commission before turning against the government. Of the leaders, 281 were put on trial, but by 24 March 1916 only fifty were still serving sentences and by the end of that year all had been released. Nonetheless, Botha had failed. The split between his South Africa party and Hertzog's Nationalists, between self-government within the empire and republicanism without, was confirmed. The threat of Boer rebellion persisted throughout the war. In the elections of October 1915 the Nationalists made a net gain of twenty seats, pulling in Afrikaner support from the South Africa party and the Labour party. Botha's power rested on the votes of English Unionists.

What had not prompted the rebellion was a pre-war German conspiracy to destabilize the British empire. Superficially the connections existed to confirm such a theory. The Kaiser had rattled his sabre in support of the Boers in 1896; Hertzog had been educated in Europe and not in Britain; Beyers had visited Germany just before the outbreak of war; Maritz had served in the campaign against the Hereros and was alleged to have been negotiating with the Germans since 1912. But not until the outbreak of war itself, and Britain's entry to it, did the Germans see the

[17] Hennig, *Deutsch-Südwest in Weltkriege*, 102–5, 123–4, 129–32, 155–9; Oelhafen, *Feldzug in Südwest*, 98.

exploitation of British vulnerabilities at the Cape as an appropriate means of warfare. Furthermore, even then the perspective in Windhoek differed from that in Berlin. On 2 August Moltke included a Boer rebellion in a catalogue of indirect means by which Britain might be distracted from Europe.[18] But Dr Theodor Seitz, the governor of South-West Africa, realized that his support for rebellion must be measured and limited if its effects were not to backfire on Germany. Anything that smacked of a German-sponsored invasion of the Union from South-West Africa was in danger of reuniting South Africa's fractured peoples in a war of national defence. Contacts with the rebels were initiated on 26 August 1914, but because of the practical difficulties of communication could only be sustained with Maritz. On 17 October the Germans were prepared to recognize the formation of an independent South African republic in exchange for Walvis Bay, but left its achievement in the hands of the Boers themselves. Seitz was therefore punctilious in limiting German aid to the Boers to food and equipment. In this he was supported by the commander of the *Schütztruppen*, von Heydebreck, who shied away from the problems of direct co-operation in the field.[19]

At no stage, therefore, did the Germans mount a major attack across the Orange into South African territory. Pre-war instructions from the Colonial Office in Berlin, to remain on the defensive, were reiterated by Heydebreck on 4 August. The Germans were unable to exploit Botha's moment of maximum weakness, in November 1914, for fear that offensive action on their part would undermine the bases of rebel support. When in late January they did plan an attack, it miscarried owing to the Boers' failure at Upington and their subsequent surrender. By February 1915, when the rebellion was over, the Germans' moment to launch limited attacks against weak and scattered South African forces had passed. The only real advantage which the rebellion brought the Germans was a stay of execution. Botha was forced to postpone his invasion of the German colony, and thus was boosted the German hope that victory in Europe would come in time to settle Germany's position in South-West Africa.

The delay was not, however, a period in which the Germans' capacity for protracted defence waxed noticeably stronger. Seitz's consciousness of

---

[18] Kautsky (ed.), *Die deutschen Dokumente zum Kriegsausbruch*, iii. 133.
[19] Seitz, *Südafrika in Weltkriege*, 29–32, 35–9; Hennig, *Deutsch-Südwest*, 74–5; Oelhafen, *Feldzug in Südwest*, 8–9, 31–2; Zirkel, 'Military power in German Colonial Policy', 104–7.

his vulnerability was accentuated by the fact that the forces available to him were considerably less than they had been a decade earlier. In August 1905, during the Herero rebellion, the Germans had 21,000 troops in South-West Africa. In August 1914 they numbered 2,000. Of the German population of 15,000, about 3,000 were mobilizable reservists. Thus, the Germans' total strength hovered around 5,000 men. The South Africans consistently exaggerated it, and even after the war put it at 7,000. Such a figure could not have been reached except by including auxiliaries of little military value. The major manpower resource, the native population of 80,000, was deliberately neglected, in the firm expectation that war with an external enemy would provoke at least the Hereros, and perhaps other tribes, to insurrection. The same argument kept the police force, in any case only 482 men, tied to its peacetime role except in the frontier areas. The Boer 'free corps' raised just over 100 men from a population of 1,600, and was disbanded after the fiasco before Upington at the end of January 1915.

In addition to numerical weakness, the Germans suffered from a lack of tactical and operational cohesion. This was not, as it was in the Cameroons, the product of inadequate communications. The completion of the railway in 1910 had been used to justify the reduction of the colony's garrison. So efficient were the internal wireless links that the Germans used them to excess, feeding the South Africans a flow of valuable intelligence in the form of intercepts. But the *Schütztruppen* had not, as a consequence, been grouped in larger formations. Instead, they were scattered in squads throughout the country, so as to provide local protection to the German settlers. As late as 10 February 1915, 132 separate units could still be counted. Thus, the senior officers had no experience of higher command. Moreover, in a war of low casualties it was ironic that those with staff training proved particularly vulnerable. Von Heydebreck fell victim to a premature explosion from a rifle grenade on 12 November 1914; his obvious successor had been killed at Sandfontein; and on 31 March 1915 the chief of staff to Viktor Franke, the new commander, died as a result of a fall from his horse. For the major stages of the campaign the Germans had as their chief of staff a reservist without staff training, and they had no officer to run the railway on military lines. They did organize three, and later four, battalions, each of three to four companies. They gave these the title of regiment in a bid to deceive the

South Africans, not to reflect their actual strength, which at 450 men was equivalent to about half of a normal battalion.

The German forces in South-West Africa were therefore small both in aggregate and in their component parts. But South-West Africa could not have sustained forces of any larger size on a war footing. The colony had about 7 million marks in circulation; Seitz reckoned a further 5 million were needed to cover the costs of mobilization and defensive preparations. On 8 August, disregarding the colonial office's instructions to the contrary, Seitz printed his own note issue, and then introduced a savings scheme to keep gold in circulation.[20] With this cover he was able to accumulate sufficient food stocks to provide for the *Schütztruppen's* peacetime strength in men and horses for fourteen months. But Seitz reckoned that, for the population as a whole, there was food for five months, and in some areas, including Windhoek, barely enough for three. In October the private purchase of food was forbidden. Only the Ovambo in the north cultivated enough to produce a surplus, and that only in years of heavy rain. The 1915 harvest was bad, and the Ovambo themselves starved. The Herero and Hottentot to the south had been hunters until the arrival of the Germans, and had become dependent on imports of maize and rice. The German farmers concentrated on cattle farming rather than on arable. On one level, therefore, the postponement of the South Africans' attack worked against the Germans. Oxen and mules were requisitioned to meet the *Schütztruppen's* transport needs. Consequently, the livestock normally available for cultivation consumed existing stocks of fodder without contributing to its replacement.[21]

The military impact of virtual famine in 1915 was considerable. Units could not remain either concentrated or stationary for long, as they had to disperse to forage and to water. Apart from a camel-mounted company for service in the Kalahari desert, the regular *Schütztruppen* were organized as mounted infantry with Cape ponies. The loads which they carried were heavier than those borne by the South African commandos; the latter, by riding lighter, put less strain on their mounts and proved far more mobile than their opponents. Moreover, the lack of fodder deprived

---

[20] Solf, the colonial minister, said he had authorized governors to issue promissory notes, or 'weissen Schuldscheine', as wages for employees, 10 August 1914; see Wolff, *Tagebücher*, i. 69.

[21] Reichsarchiv, *Weltkrieg*, ix. 475; Seitz, *Südafrika in Weltkrieg*, 15–17; Oelhafen, *Feldzug in Südwest*, 15–16 takes a more positive line on food.

the Germans of their ability to exploit their one area of real military strength. The *Schütztruppen* had forty-six guns, in addition to eleven machine cannons and nine light mountain guns; furthermore, they possessed, in dumps at Windhoek and Keetmanshoop, sufficient shells.[22] But the guns went short of ammunition for want of food for the oxen to draw the wagons.

The obvious route by which the Germans could relieve their economic plight lay to the north, through Portuguese Angola and its main southern port Mossamedes. German officials had already prospected across the frontier before the war. Ideas for linking the Portuguese and German railways had been adumbrated. But such talk was not congenial to the Portuguese. Their hold on Angola was incomplete, about a fifth of the colony enjoying effective independence in 1914, and was sustained only by continuous and brutal campaigning. Indeed, so notorious was Portuguese colonialism, so damaging to the cause of European civilization, that Britain and Germany had considered the partition of Portugal's African colonies in 1913.[23]

Anglo-German hostility in Africa both deepened and eased Portuguese fears for their colonies. German rhetoric about a central African empire gained credibility, and threatened Portugal's two major possessions, Angola and Mozambique. On the other hand, worries about British designs were abated by virtue of the Anglo-Portuguese alliance. The alliance, which dated back to 1386, did not require Portugal to become a belligerent. Indeed, the disorganized state of the armed services, the volatile political position after the fall of the monarchy in 1910, and the lack of any immediate war aim determined the contrary. Nor was there pressure from Britain. Portugal seemed likely to be a liability, not an asset; on 3 August Sir Edward Grey asked it to be neither neutral nor belligerent. But such an undignified stand, with Portugal obliged to Britain but not equal with it, rankled. Little by little, the belief that Portuguese self-respect demanded active belligerence, and that

[22] Reichsarchiv, *Weltkrieg*, ix. 475; Seitz, *Südafrika in Weltkrieg*, 11–12, gives 70 in all; Hennig, *Deutsch-Südwest*, 30, says 30 guns, but he may be referring to field guns only. Oelhafen, *Feldzug in Südwest*, 13, gives 12 mountain guns, 8 field guns, and 50 antiquated pieces of eight different calibres. Seitz and Hennig are the two principal sources used to describe the German aspects of the campaign. Oelhafen is less analytical than either, and often differs from Hennig on numbers and even dates.

[23] Langhorne, *Historical Journal*, XVI (1973), 361–87.

Portugal's African colonies would thereby be assured of British guarantees, gained credibility.[24]

The combined effect of these responses was to move Angola onto a war footing. On 11 September 1,500 troops left Lisbon for Portugal's West African colony, with a similar contingent bound for Mozambique. In Angola itself the governor-general ordered a state of siege on 8 September. His public intention was to check the banditry of the Ovambo in southern Angola; his true purpose was to stop the Germans' traffic from Mossamedes, via Humbe, and across the frontier. The troops from Europe, which boosted the total Portuguese strength in southern Angola to between 6,000 and 7,000 men, were to make this barrier effective. On 19 October 1914 a German patrol (according to the Portuguese) or mission (according to the Germans), fifteen strong, was arrested at the Portuguese border fort of Naulila. The Germans' interpreter, a Dane, deepened the confusion rather than elucidated it. In the ensuing mêlée the German administrator from Outjo and two reservist lieutenants were killed, apparently while making their escape.

When the news of Naulila reached Seitz he was uncertain whether or not Germany and Portugal were at war. The destruction of the Kamina wireless station precluded regular and direct contact with Germany; transmissions from Windhoek were interrupted by electric storms, and reception (Windhoek could listen to messages between Nauen and the United States) did not necessarily answer specific questions. In reality, as Seitz discovered in July 1915, Germany and Portugal were not at war. But the evidence on the ground—the build-up of Portuguese troops in southern Angola, the closing of the frontier to commerce, and now the murders of German officials—suggested the contrary. Seitz could not afford to have large bodies posted on his northern frontier. But the Boer rebellion gave him sufficient respite to organize punitive actions with a view to negating any Portuguese threat at the outset.

On 31 October a Portuguese post at Cuangar, its garrison oblivious of the events at Naulila, was surprised and massacred by a small German detachment operating out of Grootfontein. Four adjacent posts were then abandoned by their men rather than face the Germans. Meanwhile a much larger force, about 500 Germans, aided (as the Grootfontein force

---

[24] Vincent-Smith, *European Studies Review*, IV (1974), 207–14.

had been) by local Africans, and commanded by Franke, temporarily quitted the south for an attack on Naulila itself. Franke's advance beyond the railhead was slow, his column needed 2,000 oxen to move, and the Portuguese were alerted to his approach by mid-November. Franke attacked Naulila on 18 December. The two sides were approximately equal in strength, but the Naulila fortifications had been designed to deal with native insurrection, not the Germans' six artillery pieces. A lucky shell detonated the Portuguese munitions dump. The Portuguese, poorly commanded and not acclimatized to African service, broke and fled; their losses totalled 182.

The defeat, though severe, was local. But Alves Roçadas, the Portuguese commander, fell victim to exaggerated notions of German military brilliance. Anticipating a German envelopment, he fell back to Humbe, abandoning all the Ovambo region between the Cunene river and the Rhodesian frontier. Equipped with the arms (including 1,000 rifles and four machine-guns) left by the Portuguese in their panic, the tribes of the entire area rose in revolt, spurred by their hatred of Roçadas, by the evident military weakness of Portugal, and by famine. The Portuguese, now commanded by Pereira d'Eça, confronted a long campaign, punctuated with major battles and conducted with fearful brutality. Pereira d'Eça was alleged to have ordered the killing of all natives aged over 10: some were hanged with barbed wire, others crucified. Franke, meanwhile, retired southwards. Throughout the rest of the South-West African campaign Germany's northern frontier would be neutralized by a buffer of insurrectionary Ovambo.[25]

Franke's reputation as a fighting soldier, evidenced by his being awarded the *pour le mérite* for his services in the Herero rebellion, was confirmed by the Naulila attack. He returned to Windhoek to find himself appointed commander of all German forces in South-West Africa. But his tenure of that command suggested that courage and initiative on the battlefield were not allied to strategic or operational resourcefulness. The conduct of the German defence, which in 1914 had

---

[25] Pélissier, *Guerres grises*, 482–8; Pélissier, *Cahiers d'études africaines*, IX (1969), 97–100; Hennig, *Deutsch-Südwest*, 108–22; Seitz, *Südafrika in Weltkrieg*, 39–41; Ribeiro de Meneses, *Journal of Contemporary History*, XXXIII (1998), 91. Oelhafen, *Feldzug in Südwest*, 76–92, gives different figures from those adopted here.

not been without its rewards, was in 1915 to be marked by an almost total lack of fighting spirit.[26]

Heydebreck, Franke's predecessor, had correctly identified the main routes by which the South Africans might advance. But the lack of German fortifications at Swakopmund and Lüderitz, and the problems for an invader of crossing the coastal desert strip, had decided him to concentrate his western defences inland at Usakos and Aus. In a plan drawn up in 1911 he had identified the major danger as lying in the south, and had proposed to conduct his principal operations on the Orange river. The course of events in 1914 reinforced his pre-war thinking.[27] No landing had taken place at Swakopmund. That at Lüderitz was advancing on Aus, rebuilding the railway which the Germans had destroyed in their retreat, but its progress was slow and easily observed.

Franke's strategy followed Heydebreck's—to fall back into the interior and to the north, forcing the enemy to expend both time and effort in coping with the inhospitable border regions. While Franke was at Windhoek with two companies, two were left at Swakopmund, four were positioned at Aus, and seven were distributed in the south. Franke's intention to withdraw and Windhoek's central position in relation to the colony's railway and wireless communications made sense of his dispositions, provided he remained responsive to enemy movements. But the bulk of the *Schütztruppen* lay outside the orbit of his direct command, facing south, and not ready to guard the Germans' line of retreat to the more productive areas of the north.

On 25 December 1914 the South Africans landed at Walvis Bay. The destruction of Spee's East Asiatic Squadron on 8 December had removed the major threat to British amphibious operations in the South Atlantic, as well as German hopes of naval success. The German response was extraordinarily lackadaisical. Major Ritter, temporarily commanding in Franke's absence in Angola, and determined to mount an offensive in the south, reckoned that any advance from Walvis Bay could be pinched out round Windhoek by redeployment from Aus and by Franke's troops returning from the north. Franke took over from Ritter on 20 January, but even he, though much less optimistic, averred that the operations in

---

[26] Botha suggested his nerve had gone, 25 May 1915: Hancock and Poel, *Smuts Papers*, iii. 283.
[27] On Heydebreck's 1911 plan, see Reichsarchiv *Weltkrieg*, ix. 476; Schwarte, *Weltkampf*, iv. 364, makes related points.

the north were no more than a demonstration. The South Africans occupied Swakopmund without opposition on 13 January. The Germans fell back to defensive positions between Riet and Jakalswater. Throughout January most of their efforts were put into reinforcing Aus, and planning the abortive thrusts across the Orange. On 25 February the German command finally acknowledged that the major South African advance might develop from Swakopmund. Offensive and counter-offensive operations south of Kalkfontein were abandoned. But only one company was diverted to the north. Aus remained the largest single concentration, and the troops at Kalkfontein were given the task of protecting it from the south and east.

With hindsight, the Germans would have been better advised to abandon the south of the colony and to concentrate all their forces against Swakopmund. Such decisiveness, however, would have presumed a greater clarity and urgency in the movements of the South Africans.

By early 1915 South Africa had at least 70,000 men under arms, of which 43,000 were employed in the campaign in South-West Africa. Such abundance of manpower apparently freed Pretoria from the compulsion to concentrate. Thrusts from Swakopmund, Lüderitz, the Cape, and even across the Kalahari were all possible, and all undertaken. Botha, who on 22 February landed at Walvis Bay to take over command of the northern force, was convinced that the advance from Swakopmund on Windhoek would be the blow that proved strategically decisive. It would sever the Germans' main axis of communications at its centre and wrongfoot the German strategy of a fighting withdrawal from south to north. He was also persuaded, both by common sense and by the intercepts of German communications, that the Germans would recognize this and withdraw to the north of the colony. He wished, therefore, to co-ordinate the offensives from Lüderitz and across the Orange river in the light of this appreciation. But Botha was not able, at least at first, to give the Swakopmund landing the priority which his status suggested.

Throughout 1914 the landing at Lüderitz had assumed a primacy which could not now be easily set aside. Progress there was slow: the railway had to be restored, and horses died of thirst or sank knee-deep in the soft sand. The force commander, Sir Duncan McKenzie, proceeded with excessive deliberation. But Botha feared that if he pushed him too hard he would resign, and that his Natal commandos would take offence, thus bringing English–Afrikaner tensions into play. To the south Smuts, although nominally defence minister in Pretoria, was planning his own campaign, combining three brigades in a push on Keetmanshoop from the south, and a further column coming across the Kalahari from the east. Botha told Smuts that his advance would be redundant if McKenzie took Aus, as all points to the south and east would then fall automatically. In April he prevailed on Smuts to go to Lüderitz, to direct the southern operations both there and on the Orange river. The penalty, however, was further confusion in Pretoria, where the defence ministry was robbed of its head and therefore could not issue orders on its own responsibility.

If the manpower superiority available on paper had translated directly into fighting power these frustrations would not have mattered. But Botha's concept of operations rested on the mobility and horsemanship of the Boer commandos. Manoeuvre, envelopment, and speed were the essentials with which he planned to dislodge the Germans. To do this, the mounted brigades need their own integrated transport. The only alternative or additional means of supply was the railway line from Swakopmund inland. But this had been destroyed by the Germans and had first to be reconstructed. Moreover, the decision was taken to convert it from narrow gauge to the South African standard gauge. Although the earthworks and embankments were intact, progress was sluggish: 42 kilometres in two months, up until the end of February, and 1–5 kilometres a day thereafter. At that rate Boer mobility would be forfeit, and the Germans would have ample opportunity to fall back on their own communications, fighting a series of defensive actions in prepared positions.

Pretoria nonetheless assumed that Botha's advance would follow the pace and direction set by the railway line. Troops left the Cape assured that their transport needs would be met at Swakopmund. On arrival they found nothing. The brackish water on the coast rendered horses ill for the first few days. Inland, the Germans had poisoned the wells with sheep-dip. Fresh wells were dug, but their capacity was limited to a maximum of 8,000 gallons a day. Water was therefore shipped from the Cape. The remount position remained desperate. Wagons had teams of ten mules, when they needed twelve to cross the sandy terrain. A round trip of 95 kilometres, to the front and back, rendered the beasts unserviceable for a week. In theory each regiment's transport carried sufficient supplies for two days, and each brigade's for a further three; in practice the regiment's bore half a day's, and the brigade's one. Thus, the loss of weapons and mules under McKenzie and Smuts whittled away Botha's striking power. Eight thousand mounted troops were deployed in the south, but only 5,000 in the north.

Friction between Pretoria and Swakopmund and between Swakopmund and Lüderitz flared. Within the northern force, the engineers building the line and the remount officers allocating the mules and horses were predominantly English; the frustrations they engendered exacerbated Boer animosity. For British staff officers, Boer independence—manifested tactically by a failure to report back progress or to co-ordinate actions—proved equally infuriating.[28]

Botha's advance on Windhoek was therefore a staccato affair. Unusually heavy rain flooded the bed of the Swakop river, and reports of sufficient grazing inland decided Botha to abandon the railway route to Usakos in favour of the more direct approach along the Swakop. On 19 March he struck out from Husab towards Riet and Jakalswater. The Germans had rested their defences on an arc of hills west of Jakalswater and Riet and curving round to the south. The whole position extended over 48 kilometres and was held by four under-strength companies, with minimal artillery support and only thirty rifles in reserve at Jakalswater. On 20 March the South Africans enveloped the Germans with mounted brigades to north and south. The infantry in the centre engaged the Germans frontally at a range of 1,000 yards. The Germans on the right were pulled northwards towards the Swakopmund–Jakalswater light railway, opening the gaps in the centre; their retreat to the east lay across open ground now flanked by enemy cavalry. Virtually the entire German command on the central heights, about 200 men, was captured. But Botha's hopes of sufficient grass for his horses proved misplaced. On 24 March he had no choice but to pull them back to Swakopmund. Riet was established as a forward base for the accumulation of supplies. Deprived of transport, Botha could not move on either Usakos or

---

[28] Collyer, *German South West Africa*, 58–61, 73, 77, 85–6, 156–7, is blunt on most of these issues; Collyer was Botha's chief of staff and his account is incisive, if didactic. See also Botha's letters to Smuts, Hancock, and Poel, *Smuts Papers*, iii. 242–70. Other English-language accounts: Lucas, *Empire at War*, iv. 433–58; Farwell, *Great War in Africa*, 72–104. Reitz, *Trekking On*, is the memoir of a participant.

Windhoek. Thus, during late March and early April, as the southern offensives developed, the Germans' line of retreat to the north lay open.

Jakalswater–Riet proved to be the only major defensive action fought by the Germans in the entire campaign; it finally convinced Franke of the seriousness of the threat from Swakopmund. Furthermore, an intercepted message from Botha to McKenzie revealed that a major advance from Lüderitz was also in hand. Aus was directly threatened from the west, but also increasingly from the south and east. All the river crossings on the Orange were in South African hands by the end of March, and with the capture of Kalkfontein on 5 April Jacob van Deventer's southern force gained a foothold on the German railway: the South Africans' own railhead was pushed forward from Prieska with the aim of linking the two networks. On 31 March 3,000 men under Berrangé breached South-West Africa's eastern frontier near Rietfontein. By pushing motor vehicles carrying water ahead of the main column, they had traversed 400 kilometres of the Kalahari desert in two weeks. With Deventer's and Berrangé's columns converging on Keetmanshoop from south and east, the potentially strong defensive postion of the Karas mountains was enveloped from both sides.

McKenzie had halted at Garub to muster sufficient supplies to sustain the large forces which he calculated would be required to take Aus. But when he entered the town on 30 March he was unopposed. Despite its strong defences, Aus was evacuated on 27 March and most of its garrison directed north.

The German withdrawal from the south was conducted by Hauptmann von Kleist, a strong-willed officer of fighting temperament and outdated tactical views. Franke was too distant or too confused to impose his will. Kleist's principal task was to get his command and as much livestock as possible intact to the north. But, like many of the Germans whose only direct experience of Afrikaners had been Maritz's rebels or the diehard Boer émigrés, he underestimated the military qualities—and above all the speed of manoeuvre—of his opponents. He concluded that McKenzie's force would halt at Aus, and that the southern columns would aim to converge on Keetmanshoop, not encircle his own units. Kleist therefore allowed small fractions of his forces to become engaged in minor actions, and failed to press his retreat with sufficient expedition. He abandoned Keetmanshoop on 19 April, but then halted at Gibeon, concluding that he had sufficient distance between himself and his opponents. However, on 14 April McKenzie's horsemen had quitted Aus and the line of the railway, striking north-east towards Gibeon. The South Africans covered 335 kilometres in eleven days, and on the night of 25/6 April hit the railway line just north of Gibeon. Kleist's command, 800 men and two field guns, was completely unprepared. McKenzie's men blew the line north of Gibeon during the night, but the enveloping force was deployed too close to the site of the explosion, in exposed positions, and the bright moonlight enabled the Germans to counter-attack and drive the South Africans back. When daylight came, McKenzie's handling of the main assault from the south did much to recover the situation, but the Germans were able to escape to the north in the direction of Rehoboth, albeit at the cost of 241 casualties.

So far, much to the Germans' surprise and relief, the native population had remained quiet. But Kleist's defeat at Gibeon, combined with the German evacuation of the south, spurred the Bastards to rise in revolt. The Germans felt aggrieved. The Bastards, or Basters, émigrés of mixed blood from the Cape, had been treated with relative generosity, granted their own lands and the formation of their own police company. But the company, intended for use within the Bastards' own territory, was employed first on German lines of communications and then in guarding white prisoners of war. In performing these duties it released Germans for the front line. Furthermore, the Bastards did not escape the requisitioning of oxen and wagons. On 1 April Neels van Wyck, a Bastard chief, contacted Botha, offering to co-operate against the Germans. Although himself reliant on at least 30,000 blacks and coloureds as labourers and drivers, Botha remained keen that this should be a white man's war and told van Wyck not to get involved. But ten days later the Bastards began seizing weapons and oxen from German settlers, killing three who opposed them. On 18 April Bastard police attacked Rehoboth. By 25 April three German companies were engaged in a punitive expedition into Bastard territory, west of the railway line and south of Rehoboth. But the collapse of the Germans' hold on the south forced them to break off their action on 8 May, and to carve out a line of retreat to the north, skirting Windhoek to its east.

The combination of Kleist's slow withdrawal and then the Bastard rebellion prevented the rapid formation of a large German concentration to face Botha. On 25/6 April the Germans tried to use their control of the main Swakopmund–Usakos railway line to attack the South African infantry at Trekkopjes. The aim was to blow the railway to the South Africans' rear so that the forward formations could be isolated and defeated in detail. German pilots had revealed that the South Africans had withdrawn their artillery but had mistaken a dozen armoured cars for water trucks. The Germans lost their way in the dark, failed to destroy the railway, and so allowed the South Africans to be reinforced.

Until now Botha's supply problems had prevented him taking advantage of the Germans' dispersion; the chance of cutting off the forces to the south by mastering the railway line at Karibib evaporated, as his men slaughtered and ate the draught oxen for his artillery and the goats intended to trigger the mines which the Germans had laid in his path. On 18 April he had only 125 of the 400 wagons he reckoned he needed to maintain two to three days' supply with his troops. However, at the end of the month Pretoria promised 300 wagons and sufficient mules. Confident he would soon be able to sustain his advance, Botha now felt able to exploit the five days' supplies which the light railway to Jakalswater had allowed him to accumulate. He concentrated four mounted brigades at Riet, and directed two under Brits northwards to Karibib and the other two under M. W. Myburgh eastwards up the Swakop to Okohandja, so cutting off Franke to the north and forcing Kleist to the east as he retreated on Waterberg. On 3 May the Germans abandoned Karibib and its wells. Two days later the South Africans, their horses desperate for water, and confronting disaster if they did not get it, entered the town. Despite the broken terrain, they had encountered no German resistance.

Karibib was the railway junction which linked the north of the colony with the centre and the south. Its possession consolidated Botha's hold on all the objectives set by London. On 13 May he was able formally to take possession of Windhoek. At the start of the war Windhoek's wireless station had been out of commission, as it was undergoing repairs. But after Kamina's fall it had become the new pivot of communication between Africa and Nauen. Its signals were liable to daily interruption because of atmospheric conditions, and were entirely suspended in November. But full links were restored by January. Without Windhoek, the Germans depended on the wireless at Tsumeb in the north. Constructed from materials taken from the station at Swakopmund, it had begun operation on 24 November 1914. It provided good links throughout the colony and into Angola, but it could not communicate with Mwanza and Bukoba in German East Africa, as had been hoped, nor could it signal Nauen.[29] Thus the campaign's principal strategic objectives, the wireless stations and the ports, had been secured. Smuts's southern force was dispersed, most of it returning to South Africa and only part reinforcing Botha.

Botha calculated that a field force of 8,000 mounted men, giving a total of four brigades would be enough for the final stage of the campaign. What dictated the size of his command was his wish to have sufficient supplies and transport to be able to sustain continuous marches for three to four weeks. Getting the ratio between men and wagons right imposed a halt of six weeks. Karibib was virtually without food when it was occupied. On 15 May the railway from Karibib to Usakos and Swakopmund was reopened, thus allowing Botha to shift his line of communications from the Swakop and to begin the accumulation of stocks. The process was slow: on one day seven out of twelve engines broke down. The railways gave priority to the needs of humans rather than of horses. There was little grazing around Windhoek, and in desperation animals were reduced to eating their own dung. When Botha resumed his advance, 10,000 horses and mules had to be left behind. But their fitness, given their privations, was more striking than their sickness. At the outbreak of the war the Union Defence Force had one veterinary officer, who was on the sick list, one veterinary NCO, and one civilian storeman. Its complement of veterinary officers and NCOs swelled to forty-seven and 450 respectively. Annual equine mortality on the campaign was only 9.09 per cent. Such disease as occurred was principally a product of starvation rather than other causes.[30] By 11 June Botha had collected sufficient wagons to carry two to three weeks' supplies, giving him a total of 100 for each mounted brigade. The fact that the north was more fertile than the territory he had so far traversed also enabled him to reckon on feeding off the land.

German strategy remained unaltered: its objective was to retain sufficient territory to uphold Germany's claim to South-West Africa at the

[29] Klein-Arendt, *Kamina ruft Nauen*, 276–89.
[30] Blenkinsop and Rainey, *Veterinary Services*, 385–402.

final peace negotiations. Seitz therefore proposed, on 21 May, that the two sides agree an armistice on the basis of the territorial status quo, to be valid for the duration of the war. He gave his efforts bite by threatening the involvement of the black population in the campaign. But the negotiations failed. Botha's aims were now patently South African rather than imperial—to complete the conquest of German South-West Africa with Union troops, so reinforcing Pretoria's claim to the colony. Seitz and Franke therefore reworked their strategy in the light of an imminent renewal of Botha's offensive. A German presence would be sustained by forces in being rather than by territorial possession: the *Schütztruppen* should give ground and should avoid battle, because in their size and cohesion rested the symbols of German authority.

Both Botha and Smuts were worried that Franke would go over to guerrilla warfare, as they themselves had done in comparable circumstances. But the *Schutztruppe*'s commander discounted the possibility. Small bush patrols would represent no real threat to the South African forces, and would be easily outnumbered and crushed; the victims would be the German settlers, caught up in the plundering and looting which guerrilla operations would license. Instead, Franke proposed to fall back up the railway line from Omaruru to Kalkfeld, regrouping with Kleist's forces retreating northwards on a more easterly line to Waterberg. The munitions dump, originally at Keetmanshoop, 1,200 kilometres distant, had been shifted to the railhead at Tsumeb, and a stiff defensive battle could be staged at Otavi. Beyond Tsumeb the battle could be continued no further than Namutoni. The Germans lacked the wagons to operate far from the railway. The famine in Ovambo territory ruled out a retreat into Angola. Botha considered that the Germans might even try to break through to East Africa, but Franke does not appear to have given the idea serious consideration.

On 18 June Botha began his advance, with a total of 13,000 men and 20,000 animals. His command was divided into four columns, two hugging the railway and two far out on either flank, the left under Coen Brits and the right under Myburgh. He now had a far better picture of the enemy's intentions; he knew from wireless intercepts that Namutoni was the terminus for the Germans' withdrawal, and since the end of May six Henri Farman reconnaissance aircraft had given him the ability to track Franke's movements over vast distances. Nonetheless, the key remained supply. The mounted brigades operated without a pause, using the open flanks to envelop the Germans and advancing with a speed that caught them unprepared. By the end of the campaign Brits's brigade had advanced 735 kilometres from its base, and had covered the last 545 kilometres in twenty days. Myburgh's moved 767 kilometres from its base. Even the infantry brigade following the railway sustained a marching rate of 22.5 kilometres a day for sixteen days.

The Germans fell back to Otavi on 26/7 June, mistakenly imagining that they had created sufficient breathing space to organize their defences, and assuming that Botha would be slowed by his supply and water problems. Franke had a total of nine regular and eight reservist *Schütztruppen* companies, three infantry companies, and eight-and-a-half artillery batteries. He placed himself at Tsumeb, and entrusted the key position at Otavifontein to seven companies and ten machine-guns under Major Ritter. Ritter's task was to buy eight to fourteen days while the Germans prepared further defences. The flank to the east and Grootfontein were protected by a line of mountains, its passes guarded by Kleist's group.[31]

On 1 July Botha's two central mounted brigades, about 3,500 men, approached Otavi. The South Africans believed that they were about to encounter the main German body, and thought that, with their strength disposed to the flanks, they would be outnumbered. In fact Ritter had about 1,000 men, and had not had time to prepare his defences. He decided to deploy in depth, reflecting the fears that the South Africans' penchant for envelopment had now generated. Thus, the low hills screening Otavi and Otavifontein, and giving fields of fire over both the railway and the road, were only thinly held, and the troops there so posted on either flank as not to give each other mutual support. Botha moved forward on his left, threatening the western flank of the hills and, further back, of Otavi. Ritter drew back to Otavifontein and to Otavi mountain behind it. But he had no artillery positions prepared, and the bush which covered the area broke up the co-ordination of his units as they retreated. By 1 p.m. Ritter was pulling back to Gaub. His total losses were three dead, eight wounded, and twenty captured. A defence of only two days would have compelled Botha to retreat for lack of water.

[31] Hennig, *Deutsch-Südwest*, 272–90.

On 3 July Seitz and Franke met to review their position. Kleist had been ordered to fall back on Gaub the previous night, Myburgh's men having appeared before his front on the 2nd. Reports from Outjo suggested that Brits would be in Namutoni in a couple of days. An attack to retake Otavifontein was mooted, but the feebleness of its defence on the 1st suggested that the *Schutztruppe*'s morale had collapsed. Certainly there was little fight in Franke. Seitz the civilian was the most reluctant to surrender; Franke the soldier saw only needless casualties through continuing. Seitz was persuaded to ask for an armistice.

The South-West African campaign was characterized by a maximum of movement and a minimum of casualties. Its heroes were the horses and mules which had enabled the deep envelopments favoured by Botha. On occasion they had covered 64 kilometres a day. More than half of Botha's force was mounted, a ratio redolent of warfare in the sixteenth century and earlier. But it was a composition made possible by the internal combustion engine. Rapid advances across sandy wastes, the wells poisoned by the retreating Germans, relied on lorry-borne water; only in the final stages, north of Karibib, had the horses been able to draw to any great extent on local supplies.

The concomitant of mobility was a low casualty rate. The Union suffered greater losses in the rebellion than in the South-West African campaign proper: 113 had died through enemy action and 153 through disease or accident; 263 had been wounded. The determination of the Germans to keep their forces intact, and their readiness in pursuit of this policy to give ground rather than to fight, were only too evident at the final surrender: 4,740 men, with thirty-seven field guns, twenty-two machine-guns, and large stocks of ammunition (even after guns had been sunk in a deep-water lake, and 2 million rounds and 8,000 rifles at Tsumeb had been burnt[32]), had agreed terms without a climactic battle. Of the total of 1,188 German casualties, only 103 were killed and fully 890 were prisoners of war. The campaign's legacy, for all its failure to cement English–Afrikaner relations as Botha and Smuts had hoped, was a rapid reconciliation between German and South African.

On 9 July Botha agreed to terms which allowed the German reservists to return to their homes, German schools to continue to function, and

[32] Schoen, *Deutschen Feuerwerkswesens*, 1356–7.

the German civilian administration to remain in place. Botha's aim was white settlement. He recognized clearly the need for the ruling minorities to collaborate. The Germans could provide stability while Boer immigration got under way. On 25 June 1915 the Cape railway, extended from Prieska to Upington on 20 November, reached the German railhead at Kalkfontein. Into this local co-operation other, imperially derived considerations did not intrude. The glut of diamonds on the London market, and the freezing of diamond sales to prevent their export to Germany via Holland, put a major commercial pressure on South-West Africa into temporary abeyance. The vivid portrayal of German colonial atrocities, fed by the vicious suppression of the Herero rebellion, which had been ignored before 1914, took off after the war's outbreak. Nonetheless, the cause of humanitarianism did not prompt the South Africans to remove Germans from South-West Africa. In 1918 there were still about 12,000 Germans resident. Only after the deportation of half that number in the same year were the remainder outnumbered by immigrant Afrikaners.[33] By biding his time in 1915, Botha laid the foundations for South Africa's own brand of colonialism in 1918.

[33] M. W. Swanson, 'South West Africa in Trust 1915–1939', in Gifford and Louis (eds.), *Britain and Germany in Africa*, 635–7, 645–50; Louis, 'The origins of the "sacred trust"', 56–8; Newbury, *Journal of Imperial and Commonwealth History*, XVI (1988), 92–4, 100–3.

5

EAST AFRICA
1914–1915

On 2 March 1919 the Germans who had returned from East Africa marched through the Brandenburg Gate to be received by representatives of the Weimar government. At their head rode Paul von Lettow-Vorbeck, wearing the slouch-hat of the *Schütztruppen*, his neck adorned with the *pour le mérite*. It was a victory parade. The following year, in his book *Heia Safari!*, Lettow-Vorbeck would tell German youth of his exploits, of how with inferior forces he had sustained the war in Africa until surrender in Europe had forced him to lay down his arms. The *Schütztruppen* of East Africa embodied the German army's notion of its own invincibility; leadership and determination had enabled the few to prevail against the many; morale had triumphed over matériel.

Lettow-Vorbeck was indubitably a fine commander, who led by example and drove himself as hard as he drove his men. The loyalty he inspired in his troops became a key element in the agitation of German colonialists for the return of their territories after 1919. But his reputation has rested not simply on the needs of German militarism or German imperialism, nor on its supporting role in the argument that Germany was stabbed in the back. Beyond his own country, the *Schütztruppen* commander came to be venerated as a master of guerrilla war. The origins of such an interpretation lay with the South Africans who had fought him in 1916. The Boers among them, mindful of their own war against the British, and perhaps sensitive about their performance when the roles were reversed, responded happily to the idea that they had influenced Lettow's strategic outlook.[1] Lettow lived on until 1964. By then the practice of communist insurgency gave the techniques of guerrilla warfare fresh fascination, providing the lens through which Lettow's achievements were reassessed, and augmenting his band of Anglophone admirers.

Thus, the campaign in East Africa has not met with the neglect meted out to the other sub-Saharan theatres of the First World War.[2] But its analysis has been skewed by two mistaken premisses.

First, while it is true that Lettow himself remained active in the field throughout the war, his sustained defence of German East Africa extended to only twenty months (March 1916 to November 1917). Zimmerman's battle in the Cameroons was comparable in length. Indeed, without the Cameroons and without South-West Africa British forces would have been able to concentrate against Lettow much earlier in the war and at a stage when he was much less ready. If Lettow had taken the command in the Cameroons and not in East Africa (as was originally intended in 1913), or if the Entente had elected to deal with East Africa before the Cameroons and not vice versa, Zimmerman, not Lettow, might have ridden through the Brandenburg Gate in 1919.

Secondly, Lettow was never consistently a practitioner of guerrilla warfare. The *Schütztruppen* were trained to bush fighting, and in this both they and their commander excelled. But Lettow's own operational priorities remained those of the German military doctrine in which he was trained. His memoirs contain no theory relevant to the guerrilla; instead, they again and again bear testimony to his desire for envelopment, encirclement, and the decisive battle. Wintgens's great raid into the north of British-occupied territory in 1917, a model of guerrilla practice,

---

[1] Deppe, *Mit Lettow-Vorbeck*, 459.

[2] The recent English-language accounts of the campaign, all of them 'popular' histories, include Farwell, *Great War in Africa*; Miller, *Battle for the Bundu*; Mosley, *Duel for Kilimanjaro*; Miller is the most stimulating. They have all now been overtaken by Anderson, *Forgotten Front*, which is based on primary sources. The fullest operational narrative is Boell, *Operationen in Ostafrika*: Boell served on Lettow's staff. The British official history, Hordern, *Military Operations: East Africa*, is good, but only Volume I appeared (up to September 1916). Lucas, *Empire at War*, Volume IV, covers the whole campaign. Two of the more illuminating memoirs are British. Fendall, *East African Force*, covers the campaign to 1918 and is provocative on supply and administration. Meinertzhagen, *Army Diary*, is opinionated, runs only to 1916, but is full of insights. Of the Germans, Schnee, *Deutsch-Ostafrika im Weltkriege*, both discusses civil administration and, surprisingly, gives a clearer account of operations than does Lettow-Vorbeck, *Reminiscences*. Deppe, *Mit Lettow-Vorbeck*, is particularly full for 1917–18.

was criticized by Lettow as undermining the principle of concentration.[3] Most telling of all, contemporary theories of guerrilla war are grounded in ideas of national liberation; nothing could have been further from Lettow's mind.

The primary strength of the guerrilla rests not on force of arms but on his knowledge of the country and on the material support vouchsafed him by its population. Lettow's protracted resistance was sustained by both factors. And yet Lettow himself never fully recognized the political and economic foundations on which his campaign rested. His views were shaped by the circumstances of his appointment. Both Heydebreck in South-West Africa and Zimmerman in the Cameroons were creatures of the military department of the Colonial Office; hence, their priority was to protect their respective colonies. Lettow was the product of a bureaucratic takeover, an appointee of the general staff.[4] On 15 May 1914, four months after arriving in East Africa, he reported to Berlin that war in the colony should not 'be treated as a self-sufficient episode. It and the great war can react off each other.'[5] By taking the offensive, the *Schütztruppen* would draw British troops away from the main theatre and employ British warships in oceanic escort duties distant from home waters. German East Africa was therefore a means to an end. African interests were subordinate to German, local political stability and economic progress secondary to European military necessity. On 15 September 1918, as the war drew to its conclusion, Ludwig Deppe, a doctor with Lettow's force, wrote in his diary: 'Behind us we leave destroyed fields, ransacked magazines and, for the immediate future, starvation. We are no longer the agents of culture; our track is marked by death, plundering and evacuated villages, just like the progress of our own and enemy armies in the Thirty Years War.'[6] 'Lettow-Vorbeck's brilliant campaign', Tanganyika's historian has concluded, 'was the climax of Africa's exploitation: its use as a mere battlefield.'[7]

[3] Lettow-Vorbeck, *Reminiscences*, 4, 198, 205–6, 209–10, 213, on offensive-mindedness; 189 on Wintgens.

[4] Wolfgang Petter, 'Der Kampf um die deutschen Kolonien', in Michalka (ed.), *Der Erste Weltkrieg*, 399–400.

[5] Boell, *Operationen*, 23.

[6] Deppe, *Mit Lettow-Vorbeck*, 393.

[7] Iliffe, *Tanganyika*, 241.

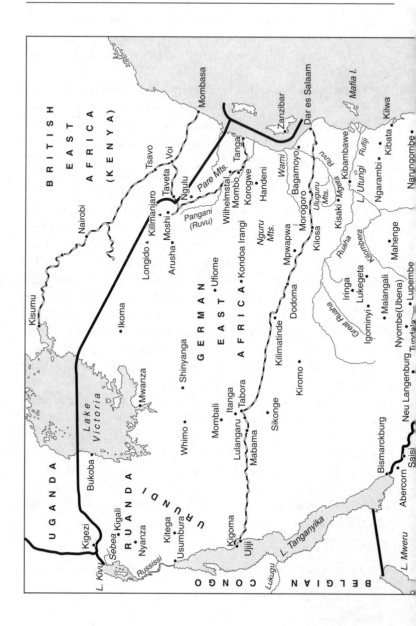

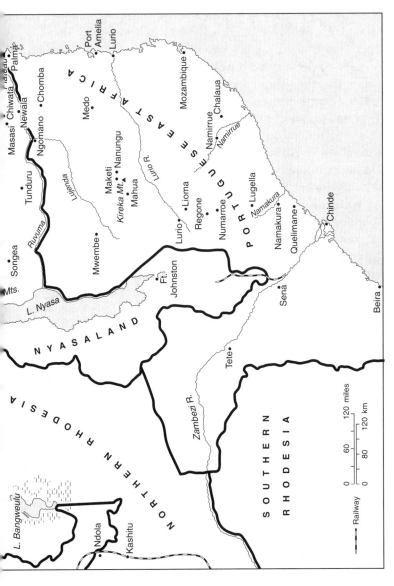

MAP 4. EAST AFRICA

Lettow's pre-war proposals never found formal sanction. The old East African hands, military as well as civilian, anticipated disaster. The concentration of the *Schütztruppen*'s field companies for the attack would remove the main peace-keeping force at the local level. Between 1889 and 1904 Germany had conducted over seventy-five punitive expeditions in the area, some of breathtaking brutality. As recently as 1905–6 the Maji-Maji rebellion had rocked Germany's hold on the south of the colony, and in 1914 two districts, Iringa and Mahenge, were still under military administration. For every German in East Africa there were 1,000 natives. To take away the soldiers, to enlist porters, to requisition food-stocks, to suspend overseas trade—all these were direct routes to the incitement of rebellion.

In Wilhelmstal a great redoubt was built, behind which the white civil population could seek refuge. But its wooden palisades became a joke. The great unspoken assumption on which Lettow's campaign in East Africa rested was the absence of rebellion. Broadly speaking, where German administration remained in place, there order and loyalty persisted. The exceptions were minor. In the north the Masai on the frontier used the power vacuum to revert to their cattle-stealing and lawless ways; during the course of 1915 some of them were won over to the British. In the south, fears of fresh rebellion—while persistent—proved greater than their actuality. The scorched-earth policies of the Germans after the Maji-Maji rising had caused famine and depopulation around Mahenge. The rains then failed in 1913. The Germans' war-driven demands for grain and manpower therefore struck a region ill able to provide either. The Wahehe, as well as the Watusi (or Tutsi) to the east, resisted, and punitive expeditions were mounted against both. When the actual fighting reached the Wahehe and the Makonde in late 1916 and 1917, their peoples helped the British and impeded the Germans. Nonetheless, early British hopes that Germany's position would be eroded from within proved groundless.[8]

Effective civil administration was thus the foundation-stone of Lettow's strategy. But precisely because Lettow's preoccupations were narrowly professional, the *Schütztruppen*'s commander was blinded to the achievements of German colonialism. The *Schütztruppen* had been

---

[8] Ibid. 251–5; Deppe, *Mit Lettow-Vorbeck*, 100–1, 191; Schnee, *Deutsch-Ostafrika*, vi. 77, 118–25, 218–24, 270–3. I am grateful to Ross Anderson for the point about the Makonde.

subordinated to civilian control in the wake of the military's brutal suppression of the Herero rebellion. Lettow, himself a veteran of that campaign, was determined to subvert this aspect of its legacy. Hostility characterized civil–military relations throughout the war. Efforts to maintain domestic order were interpreted, then and subsequently, as obstructive of military needs. Yet without them Lettow would have had no recruits, no porters, and no food.

East Africa's governor was the antithesis of the soldierly types required for the job in the early days of conquest. Heinrich Schnee was a lawyer and professional colonialist—'full of cunning, by no means a fool, but not a gentleman', in the view of one British general who met him in 1918.[9] In 1912 Schnee took over a German territory that was moving from conquest and suppression to prosperity and liberalization. In 1906 the colony's trade was worth 36 million marks; in 1913, with imports doubling and exports tripling, trade was valued at 89 million marks. The European population, which totalled 2,000 in 1901, reached 5,336 in January 1913, most of them planters drawn to the production of sisal, rubber, wool, copra, coffee, and groundnuts. Two railways thrust inland from the coast. The first, the northern or Usambara line, connected the port of Tanga with Moshi, situated at the foot of Mount Kilimanjaro. The fertility of the region and the healthiness of the uplands made this the major concentration of population and productivity. Further south, the colony's capital and major harbour, Dar es Salaam, stood at the head of the central railway, running through Tabora to Kigoma on Lake Tanganyika. In July 1914 preparations were afoot to celebrate the completion of this second railway, and in Dar es Salaam pavilions were being erected for an exhibition scheduled to open on 15 August.

Neither Schnee nor the rest of the German population of East Africa could muster much enthusiasm about the outbreak of war in Europe. The achievements of the previous decade were to be thrown into the balance. But while neutrality would serve Schnee's purposes, his hopes for its fulfilment were never unrealistic. On 2 August 1914 the colonial office in Berlin, uncertain about the likelihood of British involvement, instructed Schnee to quieten fears of war among the settler population. This, and not a naive faith in the Congo act, buoyed Schnee's hopes. On 5 August Schnee

---

[9] Fendall, *East African Force*, 129.

knew that Britain and Germany were at war, and told the German population to expect an attack from British East Africa. If the Congo act had really affected Schnee's calculations it would have been evident in his dealings with his western neighbours, the Belgians, who in August did pursue a policy of neutrality in Africa. But on 9 August Schnee (wrongly) concluded that Belgian belligerence embraced Africa as well as Europe, and it was an attack by a German gunboat against a Belgian on Lake Tanganyika on 22 August that precipitated Belgium's abandonment of neutrality.

Nonetheless, the neutrality question generated the first major clash between Lettow and his nominal superior, Schnee. Lettow argued in terms consonant with his European military priorities: neutrality would be to Britain's advantage, not Germany's, since Britain would be able to redeploy its assets in other theatres, whereas Germany, by dint of its naval inferiority, would not. Schnee's concern, however, was not with the grand strategy of European war but with the immediate issue of coastal defence. None of German East Africa's ports had been fortified. The only major naval unit in the region was the light cruiser *Königsberg*, based at Dar es Salaam. Dar es Salaam was a better harbour than any of those possessed by Germany on Africa's west coast. But a British colony, Zanzibar, lay athwart its entrance. The German navy, therefore, had no intention of using it in wartime. In accordance with her orders, *Königsberg* put to sea on 31 July rather than risk being blockaded in harbour. Her captain, Max Looff, was clear that he would be unable to return to Dar es Salaam. Schnee's position was most unsatisfactory: he possessed a port which he knew the British would regard as a base for cruiser warfare but which the cruiser in question had no intention of using. The Royal Navy's Cape Squadron already had *Königsberg* under surveillance; that it would bombard Dar es Salaam, killing women and children and destroying civilian installations, was highly probable; the Germans' inability to reply would dent their prestige with the native population. On 5 August Schnee declared Dar es Salaam an open town, and ordered the troops within it to positions outside. His solution to his defencelessness was therefore partial neutrality—to abandon the protection of the coast and so counter the only imminent external threat.[10]

[10] Marine-Archiv, *Krieg zur See. Kreuzerkrieg*, ii. 122–8; see also Ganz, *Militärgeschichtliche Mitteilungen*, 21 (1977), 40, 47.

Schnee's decision was in accord with the plan concerted with the German general staff before the war and essentially adopted by Lettow at its outset: to abandon the coast and withdraw inland to where the British could not easily follow.[11] But Lettow was furious. Schnee's plan appeared to deny the use of Dar es Salaam to the *Königsberg* but permit it to her British opponents. In reality the German navy, not Schnee, had deemed Dar es Salaam superfluous. To underline the point, the commander of the survey ship *Möwe* ordered that a floating dock be sunk across the harbour entrance, and then scuttled his own command in the harbour itself. On 8 August two British cruisers bombarded the harbour, their objective being to destroy the wireless station. Under the protection of a white flag, Schnee's representatives explained their policy, blew up the wireless station, and withdrew into the interior. On 17 August the Royal Navy's Cape Squadron accepted the neutralization not only of Dar es Salaam but also of Tanga. Thus was British naval weakness in the region writ large: inferior to the *Königsberg* in speed and no more than its equal in armament, the Cape Squadron was much more concerned about threats to the Indian Ocean's trading routes than it was about the East African coastline.[12]

Lettow's bellicosity in these early days of the war seemed faintly ridiculous: among the German population he acquired the nickname the 'Mad Mullah'.[13] Schnee's policy in relation to the coast infuriated him because of its connotations of cowardice; strategically, it served Lettow's purposes extraordinarily well.

In 1912 Schnee's and Lettow's predecessors had agreed a plan that anticipated an all-round defence of the colony combined with limited offensive thrusts. By leaving the *Schütztruppen* scattered, the purposes of domestic order as well as of colonial defence would be simultaneously satisfied. The plan presumed that the defence of the coast would be abandoned at an early stage. However, on his arrival in East Africa Lettow had proposed to recast the 1912 plan in the light of his European priorities. He argued that the Germans should not scatter their forces but should unite in the north for an attack into British East Africa, thus forcing the

---

[11] Deppe, *Mit Lettoew-Vorbeck*, 22.

[12] Corbett, *Naval operations*, Volume I, draws a veil over these Anglo-German negotiations, and their implications.

[13] Boell, *Operationen*, 43.

enemy over to the defence and so relieving the Germans of their own defensive obligations. Lettow's proposal had received an ambivalent response in Berlin. In East Africa itself the fear of rebellion cautioned against concentration. When war broke out, therefore, Schnee favoured a more limited grouping at Pugu, outside Dar es Salaam. But on 15 August the Germans captured Taveta, south-east of Kiliminjaro, just across the frontier into British territory and a vital staging post for any British advance. With his northern defences more secure, Lettow's case for thrusts against the Uganda railway, running from Mombasa to Kisumu on Lake Victoria, gained in credibility. On the German side of the northern frontier were the resources—both men and food—which would permit troop concentrations to be sustained and supplied; on the British side was a waterless expanse which would inhibit any enemy counter. British agreement to Dar es Salaam's neutrality, by relieving the Germans of any residual obligations to protect the coast, confirmed Schnee in his acceptance of Lettow's proposals. Between 20 and 24 August seven field companies began their move from the central railway to the northern.[14]

The strength of the *Schütztruppen* on the outbreak of war stood at 218 Europeans and 2,542 askaris, divided into fourteen field companies. Each company numbered between 150 and 200 askaris, and had sixteen to twenty German officers and NCOs. With its complement of porters and auxiliaries, its total ration strength could rise to 400. Four further companies were raised on mobilization, although the number of fit and young reservists was—owing to the long service of the regular askaris—small. The European civilian population had formed rifle associations in the years preceding the war, primarily for self-defence in the event of rebellion, and these contributed three more companies: by the end of 1914 1,670 German reservists had been called up. Finally, the police numbered fifty-five Europeans and 2,160 blacks. Lettow was scathing about their military qualities and resented their ability to draw recruits from the *Schütztruppen*. Moreover, not until 1917 was the last of them incorporated into the military forces. But it may not be fanciful to see in their numbers and in their subordination to civil control a reason for the unexpectedly good order of the colony during the war.[15]

[14] Boell, *Operationen*, 22–4, 39–41; Reichsarchiv, *Weltkrieg*, ix. 480–2.

[15] The minor variations given in 1914 strengths deny any attempt to be definitive. On the whole, Boell, *Operationen*, 28, has been followed in preference to Lettow-Vorbeck,

The *Schütztruppen* were a professional military elite, proud of their vocation and often the sons of soldiers. Originally their recruiting area had embraced the Sudan, Abyssinia, and Somalia, but by 1914 well over two-thirds came from within German East Africa itself, from Urundi, Tabora, Iringa, and Songea. Their initial period of enlistment was five years, and the combination of generous pay and enhanced status ensured frequent re-enlistment. Their officers served in the colony for a minimum of two-and-a-half years. In reality many served much longer, and six had been in East Africa since before 1908. Lettow himself, although only recently arrived, boasted experience far more relevant than most German officers could claim: he had visited the Boer republics, served in the Boxer rebellion, and had been wounded in the Herero uprising. The Germans' discipline was harsh, but clear and uncapricious: fifteen lashes with a horsewhip was the penalty for not obeying orders, and twenty-five for lying. The askaris' loyalty is a moot point. Of the 13,430 casualties which they suffered throughout the war, 4,510 were reported as missing, 4,275 as captured, and 2,847 as deserters. Sufficient indications of poor morale are present in these figures to give the lie to German claims of an extraordinary faithfulness to the Kaiser. Those who soldiered on frequently did so because their wives accompanied them: their homes and property rested in the *Schutztruppe*. But equally, the casualty figures were disproportionately swollen in 1917–18, when the askaris were far from their native territories with inadequate supplies and with pay considerably in arrears. No question-mark stands over askari loyalty until late 1916; and equally Lettow still had—for all its diminution—an effective fighting force in November 1918.[16]

In January 1914 all bar three of the field companies were armed with the 1871-model, black-powder carbine. Its retention had been justified on the grounds that bush warfare involved fighting at close quarters, success resting on surprise rather than on musketry. Lettow was anxious to increase the firepower of his troops, and by the outbreak of the war the number of companies equipped with the 1898 smokeless magazine rifle

---

Reminiscences, 19; Reichsarchiv, *Weltkrieg*, ix. 480, 483; Matuschka, 'Organisationsgeschichte des Heeres', 204–5.

[16] Boell, *Operationen*, 427, for casualties; on morale, see Ranger, *Dance and Society*, 53–4, 58, 66; Iliffe, *Tanganyika*, 248, is more critical; for punishments, review of Burkhard Vieweg, *Macho Porini*, in *Militärgeschichtliche Mitteilungen*, 56 (1997), 572; for problems in 1917–18, Deppe, *Mit Lettow-Vorbeck*, 385, 390, 392.

had risen to six. In addition, each company had two to four machine-guns. The thirty-one field guns were all obsolete, of small calibres and provided with insufficient ammunition.[17]

The askaris never achieved the level of markmanship to which Lettow aspired. The key weapon proved to be the machine-gun, more mobile than the field gun and manned by Europeans.[18] But their small-unit tactics were brilliantly adapted to the terrain in which they fought. Rather than embrace the 1906 German infantry regulations, the *Schütztruppen* of East Africa had their own manual based on their experiences against local insurgents. They recognized that retreat with minimum losses could be counted success, that pursuit of an apparently vanquished foe could be the prelude to ambush. The Germans had learnt the techniques of bush warfare, how to use ground but avoid fixed positions. Herein is the source of Lettow's claim to be a guerrilla leader. In reality, these tactics were the bread and butter of the *Schütztruppen* before his arrival. His achievement was to recognize their potential application in the event of conflict with the adjacent colonial powers.[19]

The British made no such imaginative leap. For them bush warfare and operations against European powers belonged in separate and largely self-contained compartments, at least until January 1917. They had, in the King's African Rifles, a unit comparable with the *Schütztruppen*. But in August 1914 it boasted only three battalions, one each in Nyasaland, Uganda, and Kenya. A fourth, also based in Nyasaland, had just been disbanded. Many of its members had crossed the frontier to Neu Langenburg to enlist in the better-paid *Schütztruppen*, with the result that the company there used British bugle-calls and English words of command. Both the Uganda and the Kenya battalions were engaged in operations on their northern frontiers, in Turkana, Jubaland, and Somalia. Thus, of the King's African Rifles' total strength of 2,319 askaris, only about 150 were available in Nairobi to protect the Uganda railway. Moreover, the battalion organization, apparently so much better adapted for war against a European opponent than the field-company structure of the *Schütztruppen*, was misleading. Each battalion consisted of eight small and therefore weak companies, not four large ones as had just been adopted in the

[17]　Again figures vary; those given here are maximums.
[18]　Reitz, *Trekking On*, 84; Young, *Marching on Tanga*, 215.
[19]　Miller, *Battle for the Bundu*, 15–19.

British army proper. The ratio of Europeans to blacks was much less favourable than in the German units: the numbers of officers were comparable (sixty-two British to sixty-three German), but there were only two British NCOs to sixty-seven German. Like the *Schütztruppen*, the King's African Rifles had no supporting units, no transport and supply services; unlike them, its administration was based not in East Africa but in London.[20]

Therefore, when the CID subcommittee met on 5 August 1914 it had to reckon with the problem that British East Africa had insufficient local forces for defence, let alone attack. The most recent operational plan for the area, that of 1912, recognized this: its thrust was entirely defensive, relying on the Royal Navy and developments in Europe. But the subcommittee's decision to target the port and wireless station of Dar es Salaam demanded an offensive capability. Its solution, first adumbrated in an ill-worked-out plan of 1898, was to call on the Indian army. Present at the meeting was Brigadier-General A. R. Hoskins, the inspector-general of the King's African Rifles, who was home on leave. Hoskins warned the committee of the problems of campaigning in East Africa, reminding them that the low-lying coastal strip was hot, humid, and malarial. The favoured point of invasion in the 1898 plan had been from Voi towards Moshi, via Taveta, in the much healthier uplands of the foothills of Kilimanjaro. Seaborne attacks along the coast were to prevent the Germans concentrating to the north. Thus, the immediate naval priorities in 1914 were at odds with the likely area of land operations. Moreover, the limited objectives of the former contrasted with the ambition of the latter: the 1898 plan reckoned on the conquest of all German East Africa.[21] The subcommittee's conclusion was to ask for not one but two Indian Expeditionary Forces (IEFs), B to go to Dar es Salaam and C to reinforce the King's African Rifles in British East Africa. Hoskins apart, the committee was deprived of intelligence or serious studies to support what it now proposed. The campaign and the King's African Rifles were the responsibility of the Colonial Office; the Colonial Office had asked the India Office for

[20] Moyse-Bartlett, *King's African Rifles*, 259–60, 265, 335; Hordern, *East Africa*, i. 9, 11, 15, 561–4, 575, 579; Lucas, *Empire at War*, iv. 209, 225, 229.

[21] Hodges, *Carrier Corps*, 18–19; Geoffrey Hodges, 'Military labour in East Africa', in Page (ed.), *Africa and the First World War*, 137.

troops; those troops were to fulfil objectives set by the Admiralty. The War Office was not directly involved and yet was the only ministry that possessed a general staff with which to work through the implications of the undertaking.[22]

By September East Africa came low in the priorities of the India Office. Its first need was for India's own security and good order, particularly on the north-west frontier; secondly, it had agreed to send two divisions to Europe; thirdly, Indian Expeditionary Force D was being readied for operations in the Persian Gulf in the event of war with Turkey. On 28 August IEF B's raid on Dar es Salaam was postponed. But, for the Admiralty, the cruiser threat, and German East Africa's position along-side the main shipping lanes through the Indian Ocean to the Red Sea and the Suez Canal, made the dispatch of IEF B increasingly urgent. *Königsberg* had, by virtue of her speed and the prevailing bad weather, eluded the Cape Squadron, and had captured a British merchantman off Aden on 6 August. Deprived of Dar es Salaam, *Königsberg* profited from the coastal survey completed in early 1914 by the *Möwe*. It revealed eight useable channels in the delta of the Rufiji river, more than the Royal Navy could blockade even if it had known about them, which it did not. It was here that *Königsberg* established her lair. On 20 September she sallied forth once more, raided Zanzibar, and sank a British light cruiser. The material damage done by *Königsberg* was sustainable. But the inability to track her, the suddenness of her incursions, and—from September—the combined effect of *Emden*'s entry on the eastern end of the scene were creating havoc with the maritime traffic of the Indian Ocean.

IEF B was resuscitated. But its objectives were now expanded to meet Admiralty needs, and far exceeded the resources allocated to them. Major-General A. E. Aitken, IEF B's commander, was instructed to take possession of all the bases on the German East African coastline, begin-ning not with Dar es Salaam but with Tanga. If IEF B took the more northerly port first, its operations could—so Aitken was advised—be combined with a thrust by IEF C from Tsavo towards Moshi. Having got control of both ends of the northern railway, Aitken would be in a position to advance on the central railway. The Germans would probably

<hr>

[22] Hordern, *East Africa*, i. 12–13, 16–18, 29–31; Callwell, *Experiences of a Dug-out*, 175–7; Maxon, *Struggle for Kenya*, 79–80.

then seek terms. On 5 August the CID subcommittee envisaged a limited raid; on 1 October it was aiming 'to bring the whole of German East Africa under British authority'.[23]

The version of his instructions telegraphed to Aitken seemed to leave him no discretion with regard to a landing at Tanga. That at least was the view in India. The supporting document, sent by post and only received by Aitken on his arrival in Mombasa on 31 October, did leave him with a choice. But by that stage Aitken had fallen victim to the optimism prevailing in the British camp. The British ex-consul in Dar es Salaam, Norman King, was its principal author, encouraging the view that rebellion would ensue the moment the British attacked, that the German civilian population had little fight, and that Tanga itself would be virtually undefended. At the conference held in Mombasa on 31 October IEF B's intelligence officer, Richard Meinertzhagen, a man of considerable Kenyan experience, did not disagree with the last point. But he observed that the Germans were concentrated in the Moshi area, and that they could therefore move troops by train to Tanga within thirty hours; at the very least they could operate on interior lines against IEF B and C, commands too far apart to have reciprocal effect, and thus liable to defeat in detail. Meinertzhagen's views should have weighed more heavily with Aitken in view of the—for him—major revelation of the Mombasa conference, that the British would not enjoy the advantage of surprise. The navy's agreement to respect the neutrality of Dar es Salaam and Tanga had been rejected by the Admiralty on 26 August. Rear-Admiral King-Hall, commander-in-chief at the Cape, was duly informed, but decided that the two towns would not be told until 'shortly before any further offensive action', in order to avoid the Germans preparing their defences. The abrogation of the neutrality agreements was confirmed in Mombasa on 22 October. By now the East Africa station had been transferred to the East Indies command, and administrative confusion may explain the determination of Captain F. W. Caulfeild, commanding the light cruiser *Fox*, that a separate notice of intention to resume hostilities was required at Tanga. If King's appreciation of German morale was right, a peaceful approach might pay dividends. Aitken agreed, albeit reluctantly, that one hour's notice be given.

[23] Hordern, *East Africa*, 65.

The planning of the Tanga landing was deficient in many respects, but the real stumbling-block was the shambolic state of IEF B. Originally built round a brigade subsequently purloined for the Gulf, it was composed of units that encountered each other and their commanders for the first time a week before embarkation. One brigade came from Bangalore, not one of the 'martial' areas of India, and the other was formed of the troops of the Indian princely states. Meinertzhagen thought them 'the worst in India'. Aitken, however, remained confident that 'the Indian army will make short work of a lot of niggers'.[24] With a command 8,000 strong against an anticipated 4,500, most of whom he expected either to be at Moshi or to desert, Aitken felt that he could refuse the offer of the 3rd King's African Rifles. Thus, none of his force was versed in bush warfare. Two battalions had not seen field service for a generation, and their equipment was accordingly antiquated: short-magazine Lee-Enfield rifles and machine-guns were only issued just prior to departure. Once aboard, the force remained at anchor for a week awaiting escorts before sailing. The troops were not allowed to disembark and refit at Mombasa for fear of losing surprise. Therefore, when IEF B's convoy stood off Tanga on 2 November its members had been afloat for the best part of a month, many of them seasick throughout that time, and all of them losing what little battle-fitness they had.

At 7.05 a.m. on 2 November Caulfeild took HMS *Fox* into Tanga and called on the German district officer, Dr Auracher, to surrender the town or be exposed to bombardment. Auracher procrastinated, saying he must refer to higher authority. At 10.40 a.m. Aitken received a signal from *Fox* to say that Tanga had not surrendered. The convoy carrying IEF B was 15 miles off shore in order to be over the horizon while these negotiations were conducted. Not until the afternoon did the British ships approach land. Caulfeild meanwhile was obsessed with the fear of mines across the harbour entrance, and refused to bring *Fox*'s guns to bear to cover Aitken's landing. HMS *Goliath*, a battleship with 12-inch armament, had broken down off Mombasa, and thus its firepower too was lost. Aitken therefore decided to disembark not at Tanga itself but at a beach sufficiently distant from the town to be undefended. The light was already

[24] Meinertzhagen, *Army Diary*, 82, 84, 105; Hordern, *East Africa*, i. 60–78, is full on the planning, if too generous to Aitken. See also Anderson, *War in History*, VIII (2001) 294–322, and *The Battle of Tanga*.

going when the first battalions began to come ashore; the unfamiliar process of disembarkation, carried out in the dark, left the Indian states forces exhausted and bewildered on a crowded beachhead as dawn broke on 3 November. The lead units, part of M. J. Tighe's brigade, set off towards Tanga at 4.30 a.m., but they were pinned down on the eastern edge of the town by 5.30. Dense bush impeded Tighe's communications and observation, and he was outflanked on his left. By 10 a.m. his demoralized brigade was back at its start point.

When the action began Tanga was held by a single company, consisting of former policemen and charged principally with the maintenance of order. Although Lettow had received abundant intelligence from spies and wireless intercepts of IEF B's coming, his attention had remained fixed on the north. He believed that any British attack on the coast was likely to be co-ordinated with an advance on Moshi. This made an attack on Tanga more likely than one on Dar es Salaam to the south, but to meet it head on conflicted with the pre-war plan to abandon the coast. Therefore, Lettow's initial response to the threat was to want to blow up 40 kilometres of railway track inland from Tanga, so as to isolate any beachhead the British might establish.[25] Such a course of action could have made sense if the British had indeed simultaneously attacked from the north, but they did not: they did not even consider the idea until the Mombasa conference on 31 October, far too late for there to be a realistic chance of its being effected.

Schnee stopped Lettow blowing the line. Lettow's sole response was to pre-position two further companies some kilometres to Tanga's west. Admittedly, his plans were complicated by Schnee's continuing to argue that Tanga was an open town. But by late October its population was no longer under such illusions, and on the 29th Lettow reminded Auracher that his duty as a reserve officer was to obey the military commander, not the governor. On 2 November Auracher, the moment he had finished his parley with Caulfeild, donned his uniform and placed himself under military command. Three further companies had already begun the move from Moshi to Tanga. Each company required an independent train. Between 2 and 6 November the northern railway's locomotives covered 6,443 kilometres compared with the 2,785 normal in peace for the

[25] Deppe, *Mit Lettow-Vorbeck*, 22.

same period, and on 3 November (the crucial day) they tripled the peacetime performance.[26]

Lettow himself arrived at Tanga on the night of 3/4 November to find that the three pre-positioned companies had been withdrawn. Mounting a bicycle, the *Schütztruppen* commander went through the deserted town on a personal and unimpeded reconnaissance of the British beachhead. He now had the equivalent of seven companies immediately available, with two more due to arrive during the course of 4 November. He decided to hold Tanga to its east, and to position his reserves behind his right wing with a view to counter-attacking the British from that quarter.

IEF B's advance began at noon on 4 November. It was very hot; units lost touch with each other in the thick bush; the fighting was mostly at ranges of 50 yards or less; the Indians were already wilting before they reached the eastern environs of Tanga. Because of the congestion on the beach, Aitken had decided not to disembark his artillery but to work the guns from the ships' decks. Caulfeild, however, remained reluctant to bring *Fox* in close, and there were no observation officers forward on land to direct the guns' fire. Thus the infantry was deprived of effective artillery support. Aitken's right, formed of the best Indian battalion and a British regular battalion, made satisfactory progress nonetheless, and got into Tanga. But the heaviness of the fighting at the town's eastern end pulled them towards the right and away from the left, which by the afternoon had disintegrated. One battalion broke and ran, causing what remained of the others on the left to bunch even further to the right. At 4.30 p.m. Lettow, his position apparently desperate, but now optimistic of accomplishing the cherished envelopment despite his inferior numbers, committed his reserve company against the British left. A further German company arrived from Moshi, but, to Lettow's chagrin, in the confusion followed and supported the first, rather than extended the German right. To regain control of their units some company commanders ordered their buglers to sound the recall. The call was taken up and an effort to regroup became a signal to fall back.

Thus, as darkness began to descend Aitken's position was far from irredeemable. Meinertzhagen recognized the German bugle call, but others on Aitken's staff insisted it was the charge. Aitken himself had

---

[26] Boell, *Operationen*, 74–6, 83.

lost confidence. He had kept no reserve in hand to exploit such an opportunity as now presented itself. At 8 p.m., rather than occupy the untenanted German positions, he ordered re-embarkation.

By 5 November Lettow had collected 1,500 troops. He awaited a fresh British onslaught, his defences far from secure, and conscious that only three companies remained to hold the area around Kilimanjaro. Tanga itself was at last under naval gunfire. At 5 p.m. Lettow concluded that the town was untenable, and prepared to fall back out of range. But IEF B was already on its way. By 3.20 p.m. the British evacuation was complete. All the heavy stores, whose rapid reshipment had not been envisaged, were abandoned on the beachhead. In the north IEF C had fallen back, its attack on 3 November too late to hold the Germans around Moshi and too lackadaisical to reach the water at Longido. Aitken had handed his adversary a major victory.

Aitken was relieved of his command. His successor, Major-General R. Wapshare, was 'a kindly old gentleman, nervous, physically unfit and devoid of military knowledge'.[27] Four months later he too had gone, replaced by Tighe, a much more pugnacious character, but given to drink. Overall responsibility for the East African theatre was shifted from India to the War Office. IEFs B and C were amalgamated, and distributed along the northern German frontier. Wapshare reckoned two further brigades were required to enable him to go over to the offensive, Tighe said one-and-a-half. Kitchener allowed them one British battalion. In addition he sent his brother to look into the expansion of the King's African Rifles. Wapshare thought two new battalions could be raised; the Colonial Office approved an increase of only 600 men, to be absorbed within the existing battalion structure; and the secretary of war's brother reported that it would require European units to do the job. Kitchener's policy was adamantly defensive.

Colonial Office concerns not only postponed the real growth of the King's African Rifles, they also blocked the exploitation of other sources of manpower. In August 1914 Gaston Doumergue, first as France's foreign minister and then as colonial minister, had suggested joint French and British operations in East Africa, hoping thereby to boost France's claims in that quarter of the continent. The Colonial Office had no wish to excite

[27] Meinertzhagen, *Army Diary*, 109.

French ambitions in an area where hitherto they had been non-existent. Thus, French troops in Madagascar remained unemployed.[28]

More serious was the question of Belgian co-operation. At the very least, Belgian gains at the expense of German East Africa might be used as bargaining counters to ensure the restoration of Belgian territory in Europe. But Belgium too had its advocates of colonial expansion; 'the country', the colonial minister, Jules Renkin, was to tell a sceptical King Albert, 'will never pardon its leaders for a peace without advantages and aggrandisements'.[29] The poor reputation of Belgian rule and Anglo-German desires for détente in Africa after 1911 had both fuelled Belgium's fears for its continued sovereignty in the Congo. The possibility that in any peace negotiations Britain and France would foster a German central African colony at Belgium's expense persisted into 1916. Therefore the seizure of Ruanda and Urundi from Germany might be traded for a more secure recognition of Belgium's status as an African power. More specifically, a slice of German East Africa might be given to the Portuguese in exchange for Portugal's allocation of northern Angola to the Belgian Congo, so lengthening the colony's exiguous 40-kilometre coastline.[30]

On 24 September 1914 the Germans confirmed their control of Lake Kivu by taking Kwijwi Island. The Belgian garrison, somewhat implausibly by this stage, said that they had not realized there was a war on. Their uncaptured compatriots behaved rather as though they subscribed to the same belief. They claimed that they were confronted by 2,000 Germans, when by October Lettow's concentration of his forces to the north had reduced the strength in the west to twenty-four Europeans and 152 askaris. The energy of the Germans' commander, Wintgens, did much to mask their numerical weakness, and the line of the Russissi river to the south of Lake Kivu impeded the offensive efforts of both sides.[31]

During 1915 the Belgians' ambitions grew with their increasing awareness of the true balance of forces. In February Charles Tombeur was appointed commander-in-chief in the Congo. His role was in part to moderate the more exaggerated notions of the colonialists. However,

[28] Andrew and Kanya-Forstner, *France Overseas*, 60, 62; Digre, *Imperialism's New Clothes*, 79–80.

[29] Overstraeten, *War Diaries of Albert I*, 79; also 88–91.

[30] Digre, *Imperialism's New Clothes*, 105–16; Thielemans, *Albert Ier*, 252.

[31] Louis, *Ruanda-Urundi*, 209–15.

Tombeur inherited a plan whose military ambitions now far exceeded any political illusions. In a sketch drawn up in January 1915 and intended for execution in April, the Belgians proposed an offensive in two converging thrusts, one Belgian from the area between lakes Kivu and Tanganyika into Ruanda and Urundi, and the other Anglo-Belgian from northern Rhodesia. The Germans still dominated the waters of Lake Tanganyika itself; the Belgian columns were widely separated and out of direct communication; the supply arrangements for such a large-scale advance were nowhere in place.[32]

In London, Lewis Harcourt, the colonial secretary, was as unenthusiastic about Belgian co-operation as he was about French, and for similar reasons. British control of German East Africa would open the link from the Cape to Cairo, and would provide a focus for Indian emigration.[33] In Nairobi, on the other hand, Wapshare was anxious to secure all the support he could get. Ignorant of the Belgian plan, he sent Brigadier-General W. Malleson to discuss with the local Belgian commander, Henry, the possibility of joint Anglo-Belgian operations between Lake Kivu and Lake Victoria. Malleson proposed an idea of his own making, an Anglo-Belgian concentration in Uganda, which would proceed to capture Mwanza and move south on Tabora. Such a scheme rested on a major British effort on the eastern side of Lake Victoria, and yet this was exactly what the War Office would not counsel, at least for the moment.

Tombeur's first response to this mixture of messages and confusion of intentions was to want to take the offensive everywhere at the same time. He argued that invasions from Uganda, British East Africa, the Indian Ocean, Portuguese East Africa, Nyasaland, Rhodesia, and the Congo would present the Germans with seven or eight attacks and leave them unable to decide which was the most important. But in due course Tombeur realized that, despite the contrary impression created by Malleson, the British did not propose an offensive for 1915. Most importantly, Northern Rhodesia, whose front was still under Colonial Office, not War Office, control, announced itself unwilling to co-operate in the Anglo-Belgian thrust adumbrated in the January 1915 Belgian plan. This, together with the situation on Lake Tanganyika itself, persuaded

[32] Belgique, Ministère de la Défense Nationale, *Campagnes coloniales belges*, i. 173–220; Hordern, *East Africa*, i. 198–209.
[33] Digre, *Imperialism's New Clothes*, 85–6.

the Belgians to restrict their preparations to independent but limited operations against Ruanda and Urundi, renouncing all thought of converging on the axis of the central railway. Tombeur accordingly ordered the Belgian troops south of Lake Tanganyika to move to its northern end.

It would not be totally just to say that planning confusion kept 7,000–8,000 Belgian troops idle. In reality logistic constraints made the Belgian plans unrealizable in 1915. Moreover, the Congo would not be free of its commitment to the Cameroon campaign until early 1916. Belgian inactivity nonetheless conformed to the sense of increasing weakness in the British camp. Tanga caused Aitken to inflate German strengths (he claimed that the Germans had had 4,000 troops deployed against him), and to write down his own effectives. Even Meinertzhagen fell prey to the prevailing depression, reckoning in March 1915 that of the British strength of 15,000 rifles 4,000 only were reliable.[34] The Indian troops were the main source of concern, their officers proving as inefficient as their men were demoralized. Friction flourished between the Indian army and the King's African Rifles. The former saw the latter as irregulars; the latter were accustomed to look down on Indians as the traders and artisans of East Africa. Tanga supported that judgement, and the vulnerability of the Indians to malaria confirmed it. Although the War Office had assumed direction of the campaign, the administrative responsibilities for the units fighting it remained divided over their parent ministries. Thus, the complications of supply, already profound with so many racial and religious dietary preferences, compounded to dampen morale yet further.

Not only was the army divided within itself, it was also at odds with the civil administration of British East Africa. The Colonial Office's role in the region had been marginalized when it forfeited its control of operations. Harcourt, its minister until May 1915, was weakened by a heart attack in early November; he was succeeded by Bonar Law, who as leader of the Conservative party had other priorities. The balance of power therefore swung to the periphery. Sir Charles Belfield, Kenya's governor, disowned the war and its conduct, which he saw as an unwelcome intrusion on civilian priorities. He had a point: 64.6 per cent of his officials served in the army during the war, thus severely weakening his administration. He responded to the demands of headquarters with

---

[34] Meinertzhagen, *Army Diary*, 120; see also Mosley, *Duel for Kilimanjaro*, 105–6.

indifference or even passive resistance. To escape Tighe (and his own wife), Belfield preferred to reside in Mombasa rather than Nairobi. The deadlock was not broken until 11 August 1915, when the fear of a German thrust into Kenya prompted a joint meeting of the War and Colonial Offices in London. On 14 August Belfield was instructed to support the army and to improve civil–military relations.

The beneficiaries of the power vacuum in Kenya in 1914–15 had been the settlers. The Crown Lands ordinance of 1915 gave them effective control of all land hitherto occupied by Africans, even if that land had been reserved for native use. The value of Kenyan exports, which fell from 5.8 million rupees in 1913 to 3.35 million in 1914, recovered to 4.24 million rupees in 1915 and 5.9 million in 1916. These figures obscured the boom in exports of coffee and—above all—sisal: the value of the latter soared 2,400 per cent between 1912 and 1916. But neither was a crop produced by Africans. They grew cotton, whose price fell 25 per cent in early 1915, and a further 56 per cent in 1915–16. In 1913 settlers provided 14 per cent of Kenya's exports, in 1915 42 per cent, and by 1919 it would be 70 per cent. In part they were reaping the benefits of pre-war plantings and investment; but they were also maximizing the opportunities which the war vouchsafed them.

Belfield's response to the Colonial Office's instruction was to create a war council made up of four civil officials, two military representatives, and three Europeans who were not officials. He then accepted a demand that three 'practical farmers' be added. The balance of power in the committee swung from the government to the settlers. In September the settlers, prompted by the machinations of British military intelligence, staged a mass meeting suggestive of greater enthusiasm for the war than they had expressed hitherto. But underpinning their love for the army was the realization that it constituted a new and large domestic market. Furthermore, compulsion was applied to native labour more readily than to the settler population, which was protected by virtue of the War Office's demand for sisal. Settler dominance of the war council was evident in the passage of the Native Followers Recruitment ordinance, which created powers to mobilize labour and to control wages. Porters' pay was reduced from the prevailing 10-to-15 rupees per month to 5 rupees for the first three months of service and 6 rupees thereafter. The settlers thus brought carrier pay into line with the rates general in agriculture. In December the war council ruled that those who left employment without passes from their employers would be liable to conscription as carriers. But these powers were not utilized until 1917. Their immediate effect was the reverse—to exempt from portering those Africans working on alienated land. The war council's action represented the desire of white settlers to maximize the available labour pool for farming more than it constituted a recognition of wartime exigencies.[35]

The only apparent operational glimmer was a raid on the German town and wireless station of Bukoba on 21–3 June 1915. Launched from Kisumu across Lake Victoria (over which the British established control in March 1915), its main purpose was to counter apathy and deterioration by offensive action. Looting and rape were sanctioned—perhaps for this reason, perhaps themselves indications of the problems that the attack was designed to arrest. One German eyewitness said that not a house was untouched by the British troops' barbarity. Although successful, the attack's outcome was nonetheless disadvantageous. The destruction of the wireless deprived Tighe's intelligence services of a valuable source of intercepts. Bukoba was abandoned.[36]

British gloom, however, was in itself a good indication of how distracted and divided British strategy had become. In reality 1915 represented not setback, but the achievement of the CID subcommittee's initial objectives. The threat of cruiser war in the Indian Ocean, the prime reason for grappling with German East Africa at all, was finally removed in July 1915.

After her raid on Zanzibar *Königsberg* returned to the Rufiji delta, her operational capacities hamstrung by lack of coal and by engine problems. While her boilers were being lugged overland for repair in Dar es Salaam three British cruisers searched the East African coast. On 30 October 1914 they found her. But her berth was inaccessible except at high water, the delta being barred by mudbanks, and her position unidentifiable from the sea owing to a screen of mangrove swamps. Although blockaded, *Königsberg*'s value to the German naval effort was not exhausted. While she yet floated she consumed the attentions of twenty-five vessels, a significant drain when, first, von Spee remained at large, and then in the

[35] Maxon, *Struggle for Kenya*, 79–82, 98–102, 103–5; Overton, *Journal of African History*, XXVII (1986), 79–103; Savage and Munro, in ibid., VII (1966), 319–22; Meinertzhagen, *Army Diary*, 149–51, and also 103, 106, 118; Lucas, *Empire at War*, iv. 210–13.
[36] Occleshaw, *Armour against Fate*, 117; Klein-Arendt, *Kamina ruft Nauen*, 312.

new year naval operations began in the Dardanelles. Furthermore, keeping track of the *Königsberg* was no easy matter, as she drew further up the river, her form shaded by overhanging trees. Efforts to bomb her with aircraft of the Royal Naval Air Service failed. Finally two shallow-draught monitors, their indirect fire corrected by airborne observers, sank the *Königsberg* on 11 July 1915.

This was not the outcome that had been envisaged by the Admiralty Staff in Germany. Looff's mooring was the antithesis of pre-war cruiser doctrine; it was exactly what the abandonment of Dar es Salaam had been designed to avoid.

Communications between German East Africa and its mother country remained effective—if sometimes intermittent—until at least September 1916. Despite the loss of first Kamina and then Windhoek, Nauen could be heard with reasonable regularity provided the atmospheric conditions were right. Transmission was more of a problem: all three of the existing stations in 1914, Dar es Salaam, Mwanza, and Bukoba, had only limited ranges, and the construction of a station of greater capacity at Tabora had been postponed in favour of those in West Africa. But the Dar es Salaam wireless was rebuilt after its destruction in August 1914, and this— together with *Königsberg*'s own wireless and the possibility (until autumn 1915) of communication through Portuguese East Africa—ensured sufficient two-way communication.[37] On this basis plans were laid to convey coal and ammunition from Germany so as to enable *Königsberg* to break out and make for home.

Rubens, disguised as a Danish merchantman bound for the River Plate, left Wilhelmshaven on 18 February 1915. On 3 March Looff received a signal via Windhoek telling him to communicate directly with *Rubens* on 1 April in order to arrange a rendezvous. Looff was well aware that these messages would not pass unnoticed by the British; he also came to realize that the Admiralty was reading German naval codes. To distract attention from *Rubens* he filled the air with wireless traffic designed to obscure the signals that were important and to create the impression that a second (but apocryphal) blockade-runner was imminent. Most importantly, he realized that *Königsberg* had no chances of breaking the blockade and

[37] Marine-Archiv, *Krieg zur See. Kämpfe der Kaiserlichen Marine*, ii. 214–20; Schnee, *Deutsch-Ostafrika*, 24–5, 64, 96, 158–9, 232–3; Klein-Arendt, *Kamina ruft Nauen*, 292, 295, 299.

effecting a junction with *Rubens*. By endeavouring to confirm the impression that *Königsberg* would be coming out, he drew British attention onto the *Königsberg* and away from *Rubens*. Looff therefore put the needs of the East African campaign ahead of those of cruiser warfare, his efforts being bent on saving *Rubens*'s cargo for the benefit of Lettow's troops. *Rubens* was instructed not to make for the Rufiji but for Mansa Bay, north of Tanga and adjacent to the front for land operations. Hotly pursued by the British light cruiser *Hyacinth*, *Rubens* went aground in Mansa Bay. *Hyacinth* drew off, her captain made fearful of mines by further false signals from Looff, and a boarding party having been persuaded that *Rubens* was sinking. In reality the *Rubens* had executed a further deception on the British by setting fire to the wood battened across her hatches. The bulk of her cargo, preserved from total loss by being below the water-line, was brought ashore over the next five weeks. The principal losses were the coal for the *Königsberg* and the medical supplies and wireless equipment for the *Schütztruppen*.[38]

The voyage of the *Rubens* was of enormous significance for the course of the campaign in East Africa, first because of Looff's acceptance of Germany's decision that his priority was now to support Lettow's operations. The *Königsberg*'s guns, wireless, and crew proved major additions to Lettow's fighting power. Secondly, the Royal Navy's shame at its inability to impose a blockade formally declared on 1 March led it to hide from the army what had happened. Not until the Germans were found using ammunition marked '1915' were the implications of this lack of co-operation borne in on British military intelligence.[39] The failure to develop amphibious operations as a British offensive option in 1916 may stem as much from the subsequent lack of trust as from the Tanga debacle. Thirdly, the permeability of the British blockade suggested to the Germans that, provided they retained possession of the coastline, fresh munitions supplies from Germany could be forthcoming.

Nonetheless, owing to the German colonial office's exaggeration of the outcome of *Rubens*'s voyage, almost a year elapsed before a second blockade runner, *Marie*, reached East Africa. On Schnee's instructions *Marie* observed strict wireless silence, and in March 1916 arrived unob-

---

[38] Marine-Archiv, *Krieg zur See. Kreuzerkrieg*, ii. 181–6.
[39] Meinertzhagen, *Army Diary*, 140–5.

served in Sudi Bay, in the remote south of the colony. *Marie's* cargo had been packed into 50,000 porter-loads, and in a sequence of carefully orchestrated marches was brought to the central railway within three weeks with only 1 per cent loss. Plans for two more ships to make the journey were postponed in September as Germany heard of the British advance. In 1917 the demand for U-boats in home waters blocked a proposal that they be used to supply the colony. The final attempt to resupply Lettow's troops was made on 21 November 1917 by an airship from Jamboli in Bulgaria. This time, however, British use of wireless intelligence was more successful. Alerted by intercepts to the Zeppelin's flight and intentions, the British sent a false signal, reporting Lettow's surrender and recalling the airship when it had already passed over Khartoum.[40]

Rubens's cargo included two 6 cm ships' guns, four machine-guns, 1,800 1898-model rifles, and quantities of medical equipment and other stores. Potentially most important to Lettow was its ammunition: 5,500 shells out of 7,500 (including 1,000 rounds for the 10.5 cm guns of the *Königsberg*), and 2 million out of 4.5 million small-arms rounds were salvaged. Bullets were carefully unloaded, the powder dried, and then reloaded, the entire process being performed without the proper tools.[41] But in the process some rounds were double-loaded, and in any case up to 80 per cent of the rifle ammunition had been so long under water that 60 per cent misfired and was therefore fit only for training purposes. Small-arms ammunition consequently remained the outstanding need. *Marie* brought 4 million rounds for the 1898-model rifle and 1 million for the 1871-model. In addition, she delivered four 10.5 cm field howitzers, two 7.5 cm mountain guns, four machine-guns, 2,000 rifles, 3,500 grenades, and equipment and clothing for 12,000 soldiers.[42] The shells which she delivered were spoilt by humidity and moisture; like the small-arms ammunition from the *Rubens*, they were unloaded and black powder used instead. This work was carried out by the naval artificers from the

[40] Occleshaw, *Armour against Fate*, 115–16; Klein-Arendt, *Kamina ruft Nauen*, 319–25; on efforts to supply East Africa in general, see Marine-Archiv, *Krieg zur See: Kampfe der Kaiserlichen Marine*, ii. 149–51, 197–214, 234–5.

[41] Schoen, *Deutschen Feuerwerkswesens*, 1407.

[42] Boell, *Operationen*, 103, 179; Marine-Archiv, *Krieg zur See*, gives contradicting figures, *Kreuzerkrieg*, ii. 182, and *Kämpfe der Kaiserlichen Marine*, ii. 149–50, 199, as does Deppe, *Mit Lettow-Vorbeck*, 165.

Königsberg, who also salvaged shells from their own ship, washing them with water and cleaning them with sand.[43] Never, therefore, did German East Africa have to resort to producing its own munitions.[44] Furthermore, the capture of enemy munition stocks, which at Tanga netted eight machine-guns, 455 rifles, and half-a-million rounds,[45] did not thereafter play a major part in German calculations until 1917.

Thanks to the voyages of *Rubens* and *Marie*, the direct military consequences of the blockade, on which the British were tempted to pin their hopes in 1915, were by and large negated. But naval efforts were not without their economic consequences for the colony. The two railway lines ran from east to west; north–south links followed the line of the lakes in the west and of the coast in the east. Britain added to its offshore control by overrunning Mafia Island, opposite the Rufiji delta, in January 1915. Internal communications in the eastern half of the colony were restricted to the land routes, and became proportionately slower and more laborious. Most importantly, the loss of coastal navigation effectively excluded the exploitation of Portuguese neutrality for the import of supplies.

German East Africa's domestic and civilian economy therefore became largely self-sufficient. Its most spectacular achievements were the production of ersatz goods to replace the loss of European imports, of clothing and shoes, even of petrol and cigarettes. More fundamental was the shift in the cultivation and consumption of food.

Schnee reckoned that the colony, provided it remained intact, could produce sufficient sustenance to feed itself. What was at issue was the marketing and distribution of surpluses. Low rainfall in the south in 1913/14 and 1914/15 resulted in famine around Lindi; the European population was accustomed to a diet heavy in meat, fats, and white bread, much of it imported; the expansion of the *Schütztruppen* created a new demand for food in their area of concentration in the north. Regional imbalances had therefore to be corrected, and fresh sources of supply brought on stream. In the north European planters were given guarantees to encourage them to switch from the cultivation of export goods to that of maize. Thus, full employment was maintained in the area, political

[43] Schoen, *Deutschen Feuerwerkswesens*, 1452–5.
[44] Crowe, *Smuts' Campaign*, 32, says the opposite, but there is no German evidence to corroborate Crowe.
[45] Boell, *Operationen*, 82; Lettow's figures, *Reminiscences*, 45, seem inflated.

stability buttressed, and the troops fed. German diets were sustained virtually unchanged until 1916, in large part owing to the growing of wheat, concentrated in the remote south-west around Neu Langenburg. A retired Saxon major-general, Kurt Wahle, who was visiting his son on the war's outbreak, was given responsibility for *Schütztruppen* supply. Wahle established a network of purchasing points, designed to draw surplus native food production onto the market. Ninety per cent of the food brought for sale to points along the central railway was produced by Africans and only 10 per cent by Europeans. These measures tapped new sources of production but allowed patterns of consumption to remain unchanged. Not until late 1916, and the German evacuation of the major food-producing areas of the colony, did European diets follow African.[46]

Schnee was able to spurn the tools of state intervention, of rationing and requisitioning, and instead to foster the invigoration of free enterprise. It was a position that squared well with liberal colonialism. Price controls for domestic products, fixed in June 1915 at 25 per cent above the peacetime level, were a belated and largely ineffectual response to what was being done in Germany. The big European commercial houses had been driven out of business by the loss of export markets and by Wahle's direct dealing with the producers. Local trade was in the hands of small dealers and shopkeepers, and neither the market nor its prices could be adequately policed.

The fundamental difficulty confronting Schnee's faith in a demand economy was therefore financial. The economic mobilization required by the war accelerated the penetration and establishment of the cash economy as a whole. But the loss of overseas imports negated the increased purchasing power of the native producer and trader; with nothing to buy and with prices rising, his inclination was to hoard. Cash disappeared. Furthermore, it could not be readily replaced. Both the silver rupees and the notes of German East Africa were imported from Germany itself. The Deutsch-Ostafrikanischen Bank increased its rate of interest from 4 to 5 per cent in a bid to draw in cash, and outflow was sustained by paying salaries monthly rather than quarterly. The effectiveness of civilian administration meant that the tax yield of 1915 exceeded that of 1913.

[46] Schnee, *Deutsch-Ostafrika*, 141–8, 165–7; see also Deppe, *Mit Lettow-Vorbeck*, 136, 169; Monson, *Journal of African History*, XXXIX (1998), 116.

Nonetheless, by the second half of 1915 real shortages of cash became evident. Without it, food could not be bought nor porters paid: the German war effort would grind to a halt. The obvious solution, for the colony to print its own notes, encountered a number of practical difficulties: the paper was of poor quality, the notes became damaged in the heavy rains, and the currency did not command the confidence of its African users. Furthermore, British military intelligence forged several million 20-rupee notes and thus contributed to the discrediting of German paper currency. Schnee's riposte was to mint coins, using copper and brass for the lower denominations and gold for the 15-rupee piece. His efforts were sufficiently successful to ensure that where German rule pertained there German currency ensured exchange. Even in Portuguese East Africa in 1918 the local population was prepared to accept payment in German notes.[47]

These, then, were the economic foundations which during the course of 1915 underpinned the expansion and training of von Lettow-Vorbeck's command. Without the cargoes delivered by the *Rubens* and the *Marie* there would have been no weapons with which to equip or train an increased number of men; without a shift in food production and supply, and without the capacity to pay farmers and porters, an underdeveloped economy could not have sustained the formation and concentration of such a large force. By December 1915 the fighting power available to Lettow had grown to 2,712 Europeans, 11,367 black soldiers, and about 2,000 auxiliaries. In March 1916 the *Schütztruppen*'s strength embraced 3,007 Europeans and 12,100 askaris. The number of field companies rose to thirty, and the total number of all units to sixty.[48] The European rifle associations were integrated with the African companies, so perpetuating the *Schütztruppen*'s relatively high ratio of whites to blacks. Furthermore, during the course of 1915 two preconditions were fulfilled which allowed Lettow to maximize his strength even when in 1916 and 1917 he no longer enjoyed numerical equivalence.

[47] Schnee, *Deutsch-Ostafrika*, 124, 163–5, 280–90, 317; Deppe, *Mit Lettow-Vorbeck*, 284–8; both Franz Kempner 'Verwaltung und Verteidigung von Deutsch-Ostafrika', 63–6, in Draeger (ed.), *Gouverneur Schnee*, and Henderson, *German Colonial History*, ch. 7, repeat Schnee's own points. See also Meinertzhagen, *Army Diary*, 164.

[48] Reichsarchiv, *Weltkrieg*, x. 484; Belgique, *Campagnes Coloniales Belges*, i. 138–9; Boell, *Operationen*, 28–9, 158; Lettow-Vorbeck, *Reminiscences*, 71–2.

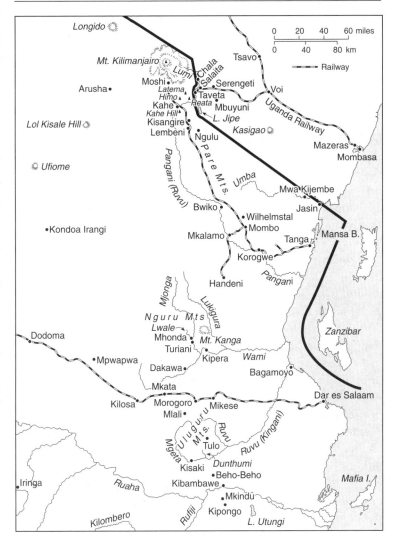

MAP 5. EAST AFRICA: NORTH EASTERN REGION

Most significant, relative to their opponents, was the fitness of the *Schütztruppen*. The sickness rates of the askaris never escalated as did those of the British forces. The explanation for this that points to the German use of native troops and to the British of European and Indian is only partial. As significant was the scale and quality of German medical care. When war broke out, a research programme on sleeping-sickness meant that the colony possessed a relatively large medical establishment. The *Schütztruppen's* complement of thirty-two medical officers immediately increased to sixty-three, without taking into account mission doctors, ships' surgeons, and others. Each company, therefore, had its own doctor, and the most prevalent illness, malaria, was treated in the field rather than in hospital. Vital to the management of malaria was the supply of quinine. The Germans used 1,000 kilograms of the drug during the war, and only half that supply represented pre-war stocks or wartime deliveries. Cultivation of the Peruvian bark from which quinine is derived had been begun in the north of the colony before the war, and from January 1915 the research stations at Amani and Mpwapwa were able to manufacture their own quinine. When the Germans were driven south of their laboratories on the central railway they could no longer take the medicine in pills, but had to boil the bark. The foul-tasting liquid which resulted became known as 'Lettow-schnapps'. The German practice, of giving quinine at lower doses but over a longer period, proved more efficacious than the British of administering it in larger doses but only during hospitalization.[49]

If a German officer died he could not be replaced. Therefore a bigger threat than malaria, whose effects were temporary rather than fatal, was dysentery. Much to their surprise, the Germans found that they were freer of dysentery than they had expected. Three things happened as they fell south of the central railway in late 1916. First, the shibboleths of European life in the tropics—with which in any case Lettow had little truck—were unsustainable. The idea of limited exertion in the midday heat was ditched along with pith helmets and mosquito nets. Long marches and sustained exercise made the Germans fitter. Secondly, their diet changed. It became set by local availability and local habit. Alcohol, fats, and salt became luxuries; vegetables and fruit, especially millet and mangoes, dominated; meat came in the form of game. Thirdly, even the doctors themselves—deprived of medicines and forced to create dressings from plants—came to see prevention rather than

[49] Taute, *Tanganyika Notes and Records*, VIII (Dec. 1939), 1–20; on quinine production, Schnee, *Deutsch-Ostafrika*, 149–50; Lettow-Vorbeck, *Reminiscences*, 70, 195.

intervention as the best cure. Ludwig Deppe, a doctor who stayed in the field until the very end of the campaign, argued that a new system of tropical hygiene had emerged. But bravado played a part in his thinking. The overall sickness rates for Germans in East Africa proved very similar to those of the British. The key point was that Deppe and his colleagues did enough to sustain the high ratio of European officers and NCOs deemed so important to the fighting effectiveness of the *Schütztruppen*.[50]

Again, Lettow used the lull in major operations to establish a more effective network of internal communications. To compensate for the loss of the south–north coastal route, the road from Kibambawe on the Rufiji river to Mombo on the northern railway was divided into stages, so that porters could be locally recruited, accommodated, and provisioned. From Mombo itself a light railway, using equipment from the plantations of the north, snaked its way south at a rate of 2 kilometres a day: by March 1916 it had reached Handeni. The telegraph line was extended to Mahenge and to Neu Langenburg, which before 1914 could only communicate with the rest of the colony via South Africa. The *Möwe* brought 500 kilometres of cable. Line was captured from the Belgians or improvised from barbed wire, and insulators formed from beer bottles with the bottoms broken out. By the beginning of 1916 the colony was linked by a telegraph network of 3,000 kilometres, and Lettow reckoned to have news from even the most distant of his fronts within one or two days. Although the Germans took the line with them as they fell back, and created a fresh system between the rivers Rufiji and Ruvuma, the combination of wear and tropical weather degraded its performance. Nonetheless, even in the last stages of the campaign, in Mozambique, the Germans plundered Portuguese cable and improvised insulators from bones and bamboo.[51]

The victory at Tanga made Lettow a hero. It gave him the authority to deal with Schnee, and it inclined Schnee to accept Lettow's point of view. Moreover, the faith of the *Schütztruppen*, both in themselves and in their commander, was confirmed. But it also encouraged Lettow in his pursuit of the decisive battle. On 25 December 1914 the British occupied the coastal town of Jasin in order to stabilize the frontier tribes in the Umba valley. The area was unhealthy, and any further threat to Tanga,

[50] Deppe, *Mit Lettow-Vorbeck*, 149–52, 169–76, 384–5. For a corrective to Deppe, see Anderson, *Forgotten Front*
[51] Deppe, *Mit Lettow-Vorbeck*, 281; Klein-Arendt, *Kamina ruft Nauen*, 314, 317

64 kilometres to the south, remote. But Lettow could not resist the temptation to concentrate nine field companies for an attack on Jasin. On 19 January 1915 the four Indian companies holding Jasin surrendered before relief could arrive; British morale—and prestige—took a further blow. But in reality the defences were much stronger than Lettow had anticipated, and his losses—15 per cent of his total strength, thirteen out of twenty-two regular officers wounded, twenty-three out of 265 Europeans killed—unacceptably high. In addition, 200,000 rounds of ammunition had been expended. Jasin was a gross error of strategic judgement, and a clear indication that guerrilla warfare was not Lettow's first option.

Recognizing, albeit reluctantly, the unwisdom of major actions in the north, Lettow adopted an operational style more appropriate to his means. In April 1915 the Germans inaugurated a series of raids against the Uganda railway and against the line under construction from Voi towards Taveta. By May 1916, the date of the last raid, they had executed forty-eight attacks, and claimed to have destroyed sixteen trucks and twenty-five locomotives.[52] However, their initial successes, the product in part of inadequate British precautions, were not sustained. The waterless buffer between the frontier and the railway limited the German parties to a maximum of ten men. The British, operating close to their own bases, responded by organizing large fighting patrols of 100 men, able to defeat the Germans, or much smaller reconnaissance groups of three to four men, able to track and report the Germans' movements. By placing vans loaded with sand in front of the engine, and by travelling at slower speeds, the locomotives of the Uganda railway increasingly escaped serious damage.

Both more promising and more urgent as a theatre of operations in 1915 was the west of the colony. Lettow had three vital strategic interests vested in the defence of the west—the wheat production of the Neu Langenburg area, the head of the central railway at Kigoma, and the navigation of Lake Tanganyika. Reports reached him of the preparation of a Belgian flotilla at Lukugu, opposite Kigoma, and of Tombeur's plan to invade Ruanda and Urundi. Both posed a long-term threat to the flank and rear of the *Schütztruppen* in the north. In May Lettow began the build-up of a German concentration around Bismarckburg, at the south-

---

[52] Boell, *Operationen*, 107–10, 112–15; Mosley, *Duel for Kilimanjaro*, 97, has different figures.

ern end of Lake Tanganyika, its mission either to forestall the Belgian gunboats at Lukugu or to push south-east against the flank of any invasion of the Neu Langenburg area. On 29 May Wahle was given the command, his task—in Lettow's words—'not border protection or the pushing back of the enemy, but a decisive success'.[53]

In reality Wahle had neither the men nor the guns for such an objective. On 28 June he attacked the British post of Saisi (Jericho to the Germans), situated east-south-east of Abercorn and across the frontier in northern Rhodesia. The attack was repelled but then renewed on 25 July. Again Wahle was held, and on 2/3 August fell back on Bismarckburg. The slowness of Belgian preparations at Lukugu suggested that a switch to that quarter would be premature. Instead, a new German concentration was formed to the north, its task to thrust across the Russissi river, linking lakes Tanganyika and Kivu, with a view to capturing Belgian equipment stockpiled for the invasion of Ruanda. On 26 October Wahle was given command of the entire western area of operations, and by late November had ten companies grouped around Tabora, his headquarters. Nonetheless, on 12 December the Russissi project was abandoned, a recognition of increasing Belgian strength in the area as well as of more pressing realities in other sectors. Wahle had not achieved Lettow's more grandiloquent objectives. Instead, both he and Tombeur had successfully negated each other's offensive intentions. The attack on Saisi had been sufficient to upset the Belgians' plan to concentrate their forces north of Lake Tanganyika for the invasion of Ruanda and Urundi. Equally, by leaving two battalions on the north Rhodesian frontier until late October, Tombeur successfully distracted the Germans from concentrating all their efforts on the Russissi sector.[54]

Lettow's strategy for 1914 and 1915 lacked coherence. In the pursuit of a major victory, the operations in the west augured well: the Germans had better communications to the rear, the British and Belgian forces were weaker, more isolated, and less well trained. But to have shifted its headquarters and even more of the *Schütztruppen* to Tabora or Bismarckburg would have left the north and east exposed. As it was, the fear of another amphibious attack caused Wahle and three companies to be

[53] Boell, *Operationen*, 117.
[54] Ibid. 115–27; Hordern, *East Africa*, i. 183–91; Belgique, *Campagnes coloniales belges*, i. 121, 200, 211–12.

shifted from the west to Dar es Salaam from late August 1915 until October. The *Kleinkrieg* in the north can only be seen as the centrepiece of Lettow's strategy in the retrospective context of guerrilla warfare. In practice, the attacks on the Uganda railway were a holding operation, engaging only small bodies of German troops while freeing others either for the west or for training in the more salubrious climate of Wilhelmstal. Formally, Lettow may have rebutted the premises of the 1912 plan; in reality, its prescription, all-round defence with limited offensive thrusts, was exactly what he ended up doing.[55]

However, in October 1915 Lettow began to plan a major offensive. The British adoption of the defensive, their concentration on Europe, and their beleaguered state at Gallipoli—all of these factors suggested that no major threat was imminent. The projected thrust across the Russissi, which drew in troops from Dar es Salaam on the coast and Mwanza on Lake Victoria, reflected that confidence. On 2 November Lettow received a message dispatched from Berlin in May reporting revolution in Sudan; simultaneously, the prospect of a Turkish victory at Gallipoli opened the door to an attack by the Central Powers on Egypt. With the British assailed in north-east Africa, and tied to their defence of the Suez Canal, Lettow could unleash his *Schütztruppen*—their strength now waxing, comparable in quantity and probably superior in quality to the British forces in East Africa. His immediate objective was Mazeras, a railway station on the Uganda line 25 kilometres from Mombasa itself. A road pushing north from Karogwe had been begun in late September, and in mid-December had reached Mwakijembe, with munitions dumps established on its route. On Christmas Eve Lettow ordered three companies forward to support the Germans holding the mountain at Kasi-gao, hitherto a forward base in the raids on the Uganda railway and now about to be the flank guard for the thrust on Mombasa.[56] Lettow's conception was Napoleonic—to place himself athwart his enemy's main line of communications. The British would have no alternative but to turn and face him. Lettow was bent on achieving the decisive battle which had so far eluded him.

---

[55] The only really effective criticism of Lettow, albeit slightly misconceived, is Buhrer, *L'Afrique orientale allemande*, 336–9.

[56] Boell, *Operationen*, 124–5, 134–5.

The possibility that the forces of South Africa would be dispatched to East Africa once South-West Africa had been overrun had been considered by Lettow and Schnee in June and July. A descent on Dar es Salaam or Bagamoyo, a landward thrust following the railway under construction from Voi, or a combination of the two—all contributed to Lettow's concerns for protection to the north and east. But by October he had convinced himself that the South Africans would go to the western front or to Gallipoli. His illusions were shattered on the very day he ordered the support for Kasigao. The district commissioner of Lindi reported that the press of Portuguese East Africa and of South Africa had announced that Smuts and up to 25,000 men were bound for the East African theatre in order to launch an attack early in the new year. Moreover, Portugal, German East Africa's southern neighbour, seemed bound to enter the war. A week later a letter captured at Tsavo, originating from London, confirmed the intelligence.

Lettow abandoned his offensive. He was still uncertain whether the attack would come from the sea or from Voi. But the coastal climate, and its unsuitability for white mounted troops, suggested the Kilimanjaro area as more likely. British reconnaissance activity corroborated Lettow's analysis. From mid-January the thrust of British strategy was manifest. Longido, a hill north-west of Kilimanjaro, was occupied on 15 January, Mbuyuni to the south-west was taken on the 22nd, and Serengeti on the 24th. The Germans abandoned Kasigao. On 12 February a major British attack on Salaita Hill (known to the Germans as Oldorobo), which barred the way to Taveta, was repulsed. Lettow concentrated almost half his total forces, 800 Europeans and 5,200 askaris, together with forty-seven machine-guns and ten field guns, in the Kilimanjaro area.[57] His indirect bulwark, South-West Africa, had collapsed; the fight for German East Africa was about to begin.

[57] Ibid. 142.

6

EAST AFRICA
1916–1918

The conquest, rather than the neutralization, of German East Africa, had already entered the minds of the CID subcommittee when it issued its orders to Aitken in October 1914. In February 1915 Wapshare recommended the construction of the railway line from Voi to Taveta, an essential preliminary to an offensive action from British East Africa. Thus Kitchener's insistence on defence, sustained throughout 1915, smacked of procrastination. Not even his own director of military operations, Sir Charles Callwell, had much enthusiasm for the policy.[1]

Nonetheless, British soldiers in East Africa concluded—rightly—that their needs and preoccupations did not attract much attention in the War Office. The London department much more concerned by the fights at Jasin and Saisi was the Colonial Office. The German raids across the frontier into Northern Rhodesia had created a lawless strip, whence colonialism had retreated and where a scorched-earth policy to create a neutral buffer appeared to be the only viable option. In British East Africa, the tribes around Jasin had fallen back northwards to escape German rule, and inland British prestige was being eroded by the attacks on the Uganda railway.

On 23 January 1915 John Chilembwe, an American-educated black missionary, had led an attack directed against the employment practices of white-owned estates in Nyasaland. Chilembwe's rebellion was limited

---

[1] Callwell, *Experiences of a Dug-out*, 178–9.

and easily contained. But a number of elements gave cause for concern. Millenarianism, anticipating that the war would eliminate the colonial powers and would enable the black elect to enter the New Jerusalem, found an audience among the African educated elite. Traditional, tribal divisions had been overcome, even if only in a limited and specific way. Secondly, economic pressures, already evident before the war, had been compounded by the loss of labour through the recruitment of porters, and threatened to give a mass appeal to a minority movement. Thirdly, Chilembwe challenged the basis on which the war was being fought. In a mixture of Christian pacifism and natural law, he repudiated the notion that Africans should fight for white men's rivalries, not least when their lack of property and of civic rights should have relieved them of military obligations. Chilembwe's death did not prevent his spectre haunting colonial minds thereafter. The withdrawal of white administrators for military service, the preoccupation of those that remained with wartime needs, and the progressive Africanization of Christian missions all served to reinforce the bases of Chilembwe's original appeal.[2]

The Conservative leader Bonar Law, who succeeded Harcourt at the Colonial Office with the formation of the coalition government in May 1915, was soon convinced that the need to restore British prestige in East Africa demanded the conquest of German East Africa 'once and for all'.[3] What he needed was a sufficiently large body of troops with which to do it. Tombeur's preparation of the Belgians' *Force publique*, far from solving that problem, added urgency to Colonial Office considerations: the brutality of the Belgian askaris had not contributed to good order in Northern Rhodesia, and a successful Belgian invasion around Lake Tanganyika, if independently conducted, would weaken Britain's relative status yet further.

As in the case of South-West Africa, London's short-term needs conveniently merged with Pretoria's long-term ambitions. The implicit agenda in South Africa's act of Union was its extension to the line of the Zambezi. The motivations were at once elevated, economic, and national. Smuts identified himself with Cecil Rhodes, and saw South

---

[2] Shepperson and Price, *Independent African*; S. E. Katzenellenbogen, 'Southern Africa and the war of 1914–18', in Foot (ed.), *War and Society*, 117–19; E. J. Yorke, 'A crisis of colonial control', 20–36, 127–8, 133–4, 150–8.

[3] Yorke, 'A crisis of colonial control', 131–2.

Africa's task as 'the progress of European civilization on the African continent'. Commercially, the adjacent ports for the Transvaal were not Capetown and Walvis Bay but Delagoa Bay and Beira, both in Portuguese hands. Thus, the development of Pretoria and of Afrikaner interests was stunted by the geographical configuration of the Union. The addition of South-West Africa would increase the weighting in favour of Capetown and the English population, not diminish it. The solution suggested in April and May 1915 by Harcourt and by South Africa's governor-general, Lord Buxton, was to persuade Portugal to swap Mozambique for South-West Africa. Smuts, however, recognized that the deal would be too poor to commend itself to the Portuguese. His idea was to conquer German East Africa, and then allocate its northern territory to Britain and its southern to Portugal. In exchange, Portugal would be asked to give the southern part of its existing colony, including Delagoa Bay and Beira, to South Africa. To achieve this the South Africans were prepared to provide troops for the East African campaign, initially at imperial expense, but—if the deal worked—eventually at South Africa's.[4]

The obstacle remained the War Office. The case for allocating South African troops, Europeans of proven military worth, not to East Africa but to the western front or at least to Gallipoli was supported by Kitchener's own determination that the main fronts were European. However, two political factors weighed against the strategic argument. First, the use of Boers in the conquest of South-West Africa, despite being an area of immediate South African interest, had aroused anti-imperial sentiment; thus, their deployment outwith the African continent was likely to be even more provocative. Secondly, imperial rates of remuneration were two-thirds less those paid to South African troops. To reward South Africans in Europe at South African rates promised ill-feeling between them and the British troops, and would create friction between London and Pretoria as to who should pay the difference. Sending the South Africans to East Africa, therefore, sidestepped the pay issue, albeit in part and only temporarily.[5] The War Office could console itself with

---

[4] Hyam, *Failure of South African Expansion*, 23–9, 36; Hancock and Poel, *Smuts Papers*, iii. 307–10; Warhurst, *South African Historical Journal*, XVI (1984), 82–8.

[5] Garson, *Journal of Imperial and Commonwealth History*, VIII (1979), 76–7; Hancock, *Smuts*, 408; Hancock and Pool, *Smuts Papers*, iii. 296–7.

the prevalent notion that East Africa was ideal country for the operations of Boer commandos. It was not; but then nor was the western front.

Even so, War Office agreement was not secured without subterfuge. Kitchener was absent from London, visiting Gallipoli, when the CID subcommittee reported to the War Council on 12 November 1915. The subcommittee recommended that 10,000 troops be sent to East Africa with a view to commencing operations before the April rains and to conquering the German colony with as little delay as possible. Kitchener was not at all happy when he returned. Both Sir Archibald Murray, the chief of the imperial general staff, and Callwell had colluded with Bonar Law to force his hand. Kitchener's riposte was to ensure that no British brigade was sent as part of the 10,000 and to withhold the proper complement of supporting arms, including artillery and engineers. During December the staff of the East African force planned their campaign in daily anticipation of its cancellation.[6]

Sir Horace Smith-Dorrien, the hero of Le Cateau but subsequently Sir John French's scapegoat, was appointed to the command. Smith-Dorrien's principle was 'more haste less speed'. Having built up a staff of East African and colonial experience, he was convinced that nothing should be attempted until training was complete, lines of communication secure, and the rains over. He anticipated doing no more by March than drive the Germans in on Taveta; the main offensive would not be launched until June, but would then be sudden, complete, and inexorable. Kitchener had never formally sanctioned the campaign. Now Smith-Dorrien forfeited South African and Colonial Office approval as well: both were anxious for an attack before the rains. They got it. Smith-Dorrien became ill en route for Mombasa and was replaced by Smuts.[7]

Bonar Law had wanted Smuts for the job all along, but the latter had initially pleaded the state of the Union's domestic politics as reason against his going. This was an argument weakened by Botha's victory at the polls in October 1915. In every other major British command of the war, professional experience with the regular army counted for more than the qualities of intellect and personality possessed by many amateurs. But Bonar Law was convinced by reports from France that 'we are

[6] Hordern, *East Africa*, i. 211–13; Callwell, *Experiences of a Dug-out*, 178–9; Fendall, *East African Force*, 39–49.

[7] Smith-Dorrien, *Memories*, 482–9

suffering from the want of brains in the higher command'. So anxious
was he not to appoint a soldier to the job that he (if nobody else) was
prepared to take seriously Churchill's request to go as governor-general
and commander-in-chief, equipped with a fleet of armoured cars.[8] The
fact that Law got his way is indicative both of the War Office's indifference
to East Africa and of the divided counsels emanating from the War Office
during Kitchener's absence. Callwell, the British army's leading authority
on colonial operations, supported Smuts. In reality, Smuts's military
experience was almost entirely irrelevant to the task that now faced
him. In the Boer War he had led a commando of 300–400 men with
minimal logistical needs in a defensive campaign in a moderate climate
over familiar terrain. In East Africa he was responsible for a ration
strength of 73,300 men, committed to the conquest of a tropical colony,
much of it barely mapped. His South African experience made him 'a
remarkable soldier', often to the front and admired by his men; but it also
rendered him 'a bad tactician and strategist' and 'an indifferent general'.[9]

The obvious foil to such a commander was his staff. But Smuts, albeit
gently, dismantled the body created by Smith-Dorrien. Thus, not one
officer in Smuts's field headquarters had 'ever previously filled an appointment on the General Staff with troops'.[10] Hoskins, whose local
knowledge was to have found sensible employment as chief of staff, was
shunted out to a division; J. J. Collyer, his replacement, was an ex-ranker
of entirely South African experience. British commanders—Tighe, Malleson, and Stewart—were, with good reason, removed, but their places
were taken by South Africans of experience comparable to Smuts's own—
Deventer, Brits, and Enslin. Divisions therefore fought their own battles,
failing to report back to a staff that lacked the authority to exercise
initiative. Smuts followed the procedure ordained in *Field Service Regulations*, but modified in practice in France, and divided his headquarters
in two, with himself and a small group at his advanced headquarters, and
the heads of the administrative services at base. Thus, field command
and logistics were separated in a theatre of operations where their mutual
dependence was paramount. Supply was initially in the hands of an

[8] Gilbert, *Churchill*, iii. 563–6; see also *Companion*, 1251–2.
[9] Meinertzhagen, *Army Diary*, 194; see also Fendall, *East African Force*, 57; Page, *International Journal of African Historical Studies*, XIV (1981), 467–9.
[10] Crowe, *General Smuts' Campaign*, 4.

Indian army colonel with a tendency to over-centralization and peace-time economies, and communications in those of a former chief of East African police, who knew the area but was highly strung and fearful of giving offence. At the end of January a veteran of the western front and a rare survivor from Smith-Dorrien's appointees, P. O. Hazelton, took charge of transport. But lack of existing records prevented him from determining what resources units already had, and lack of time forestalled his remedying any deficits. Smuts's continued, if paradoxical, reliance on the higher formations of European warfare, divisions and brigades, increased the logistical burden, and contrasted with the Germans' preference for the more flexible and self-contained field company. Never resolved but constantly disputed was the chain of command—between supply, transport, and communications; between the rear and the front; and between the operational and administrative branches of Smuts's headquarters.[11]

Smuts justified his practice of placing himself well forward by reference to the difficulties of communication in the bush. But although this impressed his troops, it militated against effective command. Close liaison with the heads of his administrative services was further jeopardized. Wireless was unreliable, visual signalling impossible. Cable was therefore vital. Laying it was another job for the porters; in places it had to be raised 8 metres to avoid damage by giraffes; telephones were superimposed on a single line also operating as a telegraph circuit. The entire service was described by Collyer as composed 'of men of different nationalities—of different training—speaking different languages, with equipment of varying patterns thrown together without any co-ordinated training to carry out an important operation in unknown country'.[12] None of the confusions generated by his polyglot force, logistic or linguistic, was resolved before Smuts advanced.

During the course of 1915 Meinertzhagen had taken the intelligence services in hand. By a variety of methods, including the recovery of German orders that had been used as lavatory paper, he built up a picture of Lettow's order of battle.[13] But there was still a tendency to exaggerate

---

[11] Ibid. 3–4; Fendall, *East African Force*, 144–8; also 53–6; Collyer, *South Africans with Smuts*, 60; Beadon, *Royal Army Service Corps*, ii. 297, 299–301; cf. Ian Brown, *British Logistics*, 44–51.

[12] Collyer, *South Africans with Smuts*, 280.

[13] Meinertzhagen, *Army Diary*, 127.

the Germans' strength: Smith-Dorrien put it at 2,200 whites and up to 25,000 blacks.[14] Moreover, the use of captured German maps created a false security. Plausible because they 'were presented in a form which [commanders] associated with accuracy', in reality they omitted much. Roads built since 1914 were frequently unmarked; duplications and difficulties with place-names were not resolved; marching distances proved much greater than cartographic distances. Thus, orders based on maps proved consistently over-optimistic.[15] Reconnaissance could rarely fill the gap. Thick bush obscured the ground from aerial observation and tsetse fly limited the value of mounted troops.

Smith-Dorrien's plan had been to attack around Kilimanjaro, while the Belgians thrust in from the north-west and a third attack from Northern Rhodesia entered in the south-west. When Lettow had been forced to commit his forces to the west, a brigade was to be landed at Dar es Salaam or Tanga, supported by four cruisers. The decisive thrust would thus have rested on secure and short lines of communications. Neither Smuts nor his staff was sea-minded. No landing at Dar es Salaam or Tanga was attempted. The main blow ran across rather than along the two main land lines, the northern and central railways. Smuts's invasion, therefore, played to the strengths already bestowed on the German defence by the nature of the terrain. The available axes of approach were limited by the mountain ranges, and the valleys were covered with bush. As he pushed on, his line of communications lengthened. The halts to allow his supply services to catch up gave the Germans the opportunity to regroup. Thus, his onset lacked the momentum that his dispatches suggested. Throughout 1916 Smuts's rate of advance failed to match his strategic conceptions.

Moreover, for all his talk of battle, Smuts's aim was to manoeuvre rather than to fight. Lettow's avoidance of a decisive engagement throughout 1916 can be attributed to Smuts's supply difficulties, the consequent loss of operational flexibility, and the German desire to avoid fighting in order to preserve lives and ammunition. But it can also be seen in the context of Smuts's political preoccupations. By the end of 1916 the conduct of the campaign would be the focus of public outcry

[14] Smith-Dorrien, *Memories*, 486.
[15] Hordern, *East Africa*, vol. i., pp. vi–vii; Young, *Marching on Tanga*, 195, 213.

in South Africa. Smuts was constantly reminded from Pretoria of the difficulties of raising men; he dreaded returning to the Union dubbed a butcher.[16] The fighting in South-West Africa suggested that indeed wars could be won by sweat rather than by blood, by mobility rather than by hard fighting. Neglecting or even abandoning lines of communication had been made possible by the speed of envelopments conducted by mounted troops. And so Smuts planned a sequence of envelopment battles, where success eluded him because of Lettow's refusal to fight. In reality, East Africa was—particularly thanks to the tsetse fly—not appropriate for mounted troops. His flank attacks, partly no doubt because of his supply problems, never extended sufficiently far to master German communications. Instead, he would probe towards the German wing without fixing the enemy frontally, so dispersing his troops and enabling the numerically inferior Germans to use the bush to break the battle up into a series of isolated fire-fights. Forced to deploy on ground of Lettow's choosing, Smuts would have to wait for the arrival of heavier weaponry; no attempt would be made to retain contact as night fell. Thus Lettow could escape because he had never been gripped.[17]

Plans for the initial attack east and west of Kilimanjaro had already been drawn up when Smuts arrived. The main German concentration was in the sector bounded by Salaita–Moshi–Kahe. Lettow had left only weak forces west of Kilimanjaro. His main concern was for his line of retreat down the northern railway, and he therefore watched with anxiety the Ngulu Gap through the Pare Mountains, opposite Lembeni. The original British intention was to launch their mounted troops not here but west of Kilimanjaro, past Longido, on to Moshi, in order to cut off the Germans protecting Taveta.

Smuts amended this plan. He recognized the strength of the German defences at Salaita, but calculated that Lettow had too few troops for his area of concentration. He therefore brought the major thrust east of Kilimanjaro, directed not at Salaita itself but in a flanking move to its north. On the night of 7/8 March the South African brigades under Deventer marched on Chala, north of Salaita, and on the morning of

---

[16] Hancock and Poel, *Smuts Papers*, iii. 356–7, 359; Hancock, *Smuts*, 412–13; Meinertzhagen, *Army Diary*, 166, 200.

[17] Meinertzhagen, *Army Diary*, 191; Buhrer, *L'Afrique orientale allemande*, 352–3, 355. I have also profited from Ross Anderson's tactical analysis.

the 8th the 2nd division moved into positions in front of Salaita. Despite the British patrols sent towards the Ngulu Gap, Lettow realized the true direction of the advance only on the 8th. When the 2nd division launched its attack on Salaita on 9 March it found the German trenches untenanted.

The Germans fell back west of Taveta to the hills of Reata and Latema. This position was well prepared but it was 19 kilometres long, too extensive for the troops available, and Lettow kept his main concentration to the rear at Himo. Smuts was determined to follow up as fast as possible, but owing to the need to consolidate his rear, had only three battalions available to attack. The main hills rose to 330 metres, and an attempt to seize the nek between the two during the course of 11 March was unsuccessful and costly. The bulk of the artillery was still being brought up, and the efforts of forward observation officers to direct its fire were hampered by the bush. Tighe, commanding the 2nd division, decided to use the cover of night to attack with the bayonet. Lettow, meanwhile, concluded that the major threat lay to his left, in the north, and at 5.30 p.m. sent two companies thither. But at 7.50 p.m. he received reports that Kraut's positions on the Latema side of the nek had been broken. At 9.30 p.m. he lost telephone contact with Kraut, and by 10.30 Kraut was reported as in full retreat. Lettow therefore ordered the whole position to be abandoned, and his forces to take up a new line backing onto the River Ruvu, facing north, with their left on Kahe.

In reality, although Kraut had ordered a retreat at 10 p.m., one company had not received the order and Latema could have been held. Moreover, there was comparable confusion in the British command. Smuts had never intended the frontal attack to precede Deventer's envelopment to the north. Nor did he appreciate that some of his troops had reached the summits of both Reata and Latema in the course of the night. On the morning of 12 March he ordered the 2nd division to fall back, while Deventer's outflanking move to the north—Lettow's original fear—took effect. Deventer pushed on towards Moshi to link up with the 1st division on 14 March.

Smuts had opened the door into the northern part of German East Africa. But he had not inflicted a major defeat on the *Schütztruppen*. The blame was laid on Stewart, commanding the 1st division. The advance west of Kilimanjaro, although no longer the major thrust, began from Longido on 3 March, so giving Stewart three days to get across the

German line of retreat before Deventer's and Tighe's attacks took effect. Stewart's progress was slow, manifesting an undue concern about problems of supply. But the real difficulty was that Smuts's plan did not make clear in which direction he thought the Germans most likely to withdraw. Stewart's advance would have its greatest and most immediate effect if Lettow planned to fall back to the west, from Moshi to Arusha. Moreover, Deventer's move to the north of the Taveta Hills rested on a similar assumption. As Lettow planned to fall back down the northern railway, an advance on Moshi by Stewart and Deventer could only shoulder the Germans in the direction which they already planned to follow. Stewart would have had to reach Kahe by 12 March to have fulfilled Smuts's hopes of true envelopment. It must, therefore, be presumed that Smuts, given his predisposition to see Lettow as a guerrilla, imagined that the German commander would seek the interior, would show the same disinclination to use railways and harbours as Smuts did himself, and would be confirmed in that tendency by the demonstrations around Ngulu. On this basis Lettow could only be expected to fight if not threatened with envelopment; wide turning movements by mounted troops would only keep the Germans moving, and were therefore a way of avoiding battle, not of seeking it.[18]

Lettow's new position was a strong one which sustained the threat to Taveta and to the railway line from Voi, but which also gave further opportunities for a British tactical success. His right flank rested on the River Lumi and Lake Jipe, his left on the Pangani, as the Ruvu became after Kahe. Any British frontal attack would be channelled by the crocodile-infested rivers flowing north–south into the Ruvu. But Lettow had both the Ruvu and the Pare Mountains to his back. His principal line of withdrawal, the railway, lay behind his left, while his own inclinations were to concentrate for a counter-attack on his right.

Smuts's plan was to attack frontally with the 1st division while sending Deventer's mounted brigade from Moshi, west of the railway, to Kahe in order to cut off the German retreat. The difficulties confronting the 1st division in its attack caused it to move against Kahe more than against the centre. On 21 March Deventer was unable to find crossings on the Pangani. Eventually part of his command swam the river and took Kahe

---

[18] Collyer, *South Africans with Smuts*, 68, 267–9.

Hill. Deventer then pushed back north on Kahe, while sending two dismounted squadrons south to cut the railway below Kahe. The Germans had already abandoned Kahe, and were in positions south of the Pangani strong enough to check Deventer's relatively weak command from working round their southern flank to the railway. Sheppard, Stewart's successor in command of 1st division, did not know that Deventer had control of Kahe, and at 4.45 p.m. ordered his men to dig in 3 or 4 kilometres to the north. Thus the South Africans failed to push in the attack at the vital moment. To the south, Deventer's two detached squadrons were blocked by impenetrable and seemingly endless bush. However, their efforts did not go unobserved. They were reported to Lettow as threatening Kisangire. A determined German counter-attack might have regained Kahe and Kahe Hill. But the danger to Kisangire decided Lettow that he should withdraw there himself, pulling his troops south of the Ruvu during the night of 21/2 March. Thus the British gained command of the Ruvu, and so secured their communications from Voi to Moshi. But once again they had failed to trap the German troops.

The March–May rainy season came late in 1916. Smuts was therefore lucky to have got as far as he had. But when the rains did arrive they were the heaviest for some years. All operations on the northern railway were suspended. Elsewhere the effects were less severe. In the west the Belgians advanced into Ruanda and Urundi; in the south-west a force under Brigadier-General Northey began its push from Northern Rhodesia; and to the south Portugal declared war on Germany in March. Tombeur's plan of a year previously, that of a number of converging but independent thrusts along the circumference of the German colony, thus found practical application. Co-ordination was admittedly non-existent. Smuts had no direct line of communications to Tombeur; Northey was answerable directly to the Colonial Office, not even to the War Office; no joint commander was appointed nor planning conference held. But the momentum of the allied onset was not lost.

Smuts's transport and supply services had banked on the rainy season for a moment's pause and consolidation. However, Smuts was unhappy at the prospect of inactivity on the northern front until June. He assumed that the Germans did not intend to fall south of the central railway. Thus neither Northey's column nor any Portuguese effort promised immediate effects. The pivot of Lettow's resistance seemed to be Tabora. Schnee had transferred his capital there, given the danger to Dar es Salaam; it was the *Schütztruppen's* major recruiting centre; and its inland position on the central railway played to German strengths and British weaknesses in matters of supply and communication. Intelligence gathered by Deventer, when he took Lol Kissale on 6 April, confirmed this analysis of German intentions; it pointed to plans for the defence of Ufiome and Kondoa Irangi, in order to bar the western route to the central railway.[19] Smuts was committed to accepting Belgian co-operation in the west, but on the assumption that Tombeur's operations would be secondary, not primary. However, if Smuts did nothing during the rains, the Belgians not the British would spearhead the advance on Tabora. Britain's credit in Africa would not be fully restored; South Africa's war aims might be forfeit to Belgium's.

Smuts briefly reconsidered the amphibious option favoured by Smith-Dorrien. Given his assumptions about the significance of Tabora, Tanga seemed remote and unimportant. Dar es Salaam, by virtue of its position at the head of the central railway, gave directly onto Tabora, but heavy seas and the unhealthy coastline helped confirm Smuts in his predisposition against such a scheme. Communication difficulties precluded the formation of a major British concentration at Mwanza for a direct drive on Tabora. Instead, Smuts opted to march on Kondoa Irangi. Although supported in his decision by Meinertzhagen, the conception and execution were essentially Boer. Afrikaner settlers in the north assured Smuts that the rains to the south and west would not be as severe as those around Kilimanjaro. His forces were reorganized into three divisions, two of them exclusively South African and each composed of an infantry brigade and a mounted brigade: mobility was emphasized over firepower. Smuts's aim was less the defeat of Lettow than the occupation of territory. The lessons of South-West Africa were being applied in circumstances that were totally different.

Success in their first campaign had made the South Africans heedless of the needs of horse management. The remounts they had employed had been shattered by the punishing marches imposed upon them. But the campaign had not collapsed; railways and motor-transport had kept some form of supply going, and disease in itself was not a major threat.

---

[19] Crowe, *General Smuts' Campaign*, 113; more generally Hordern, *East Africa*, i. 263–70.

In East Africa mechanical transport was not so readily available, and great areas, embracing a zone up to 400 kilometres inland or until the altitude reached 1,000 metres, were home to the tsetse fly. Ultimately all horses in East Africa would succumb to the fly. The task of the veterinary services was to keep it at bay for long enough to enable the advance to take effect. This could be achieved in two ways, prophylactically or operationally. The first was undermined by the inability of regimental veterinary officers to establish their authority over the decentralized commands of Boer units, whose squadron and troop leaders had powers of discretion. Arsenic powder could prolong the horse's life, but it was issued in pills and soldiers gave it to their mounts whole, with the result that it was left unconsumed at the bottom of the feed-bag. The second was the casualty of Smuts's staff arrangements. The veterinary staff was 'always miles away' from the commander-in-chief and his chief of staff. The British knew—as a result of maps obligingly provided by German veterinarians before the war—the locations of the worst tsetse areas, but this intelligence was not incorporated in the campaign plan. Equine wastage in 1916 ran at 100 per cent per month, when the veterinary services reckoned it could have been half that.[20]

The newly constituted 2nd division, commanded by Deventer, left Lol Kissale on 8 April. Its mounted brigade, in the van, reached Kondoa Irangi on 19 April, and the infantry brigade arrived by the end of the month. The weather contradicted the predictions: nearly 18 inches of rain fell at Moshi in the last fortnight of April. The supplies dumped at Longido and destined for Deventer's men became bogged on muddy roads. Tsetse fly annihilated the mounted brigade's mobility: of 3,894 horses issued to the brigade by 23 May, 1,639 had died since March and 718 were unfit for service.[21] Fortunately Kondoa Irangi itself was a fertile area.

However, the weather was not partial in its effects. The 'short' rains, those that fell in November, had proved light in 1915, and accordingly the harvest yields in the Kilimanjaro area had been low. Throughout February and March the German troops in the north were threatened with starvation. Food was brought from the depots on the central railway.

[20] Blenkinsop and Rainey, *Veterinary Services*, 407–18.
[21] Hordern, *East Africa*, i. 278, 284

To bridge the gap between Kilosa and the light railway at Handeni, an extra 20,000 porters were required. Then came the heavy rains of late March. Although the nine-day hike between the railways was organized in relays, both shelter and provisions proved inadequate. About 20,000 porters died, and many others fell prey to dysentery and respiratory illnesses.[22] As the intelligence captured at Lol Kissale revealed, Lettow was already planning to regroup around Kondoa Irangi in order to ease his supply problem before Deventer began his main advance.

Smuts's strategy thus conformed to Lettow's intentions. It allowed him to use his railway communications and the availability of interior lines to maximum advantage. Leaving Kraut and ten companies (2,400 men) in the Pare Mountains, Lettow brought the strength facing Deventer's 3,000 rifles to eighteen companies (4,000 rifles) and six guns (two of them heavy guns from the *Königsberg*). Deventer began to look dangerously vulnerable. For the first time in East Africa the Germans countered artillery with artillery.[23] But the ground before Kondoa Irangi was open and exposed. Furthermore, German reconnaissance was inadequate, and failed to spot British positions south of the town. Lettow's decision to attack on the night of 9/10 May, reflecting the lack of cover for a daylight advance, did not take account of his shortage of intelligence. The Germans were checked with 35 per-cent losses. Thereafter, Lettow remained unwontedly passive. Deventer's position was entrenched, and in early June was supplemented with heavy artillery.

In concentrating south of Kondoa Irangi, Lettow decided to abandon the northern railway. If Smuts wished to end the campaign quickly, he should have used the advent of dry weather to reinforce Deventer and then risked heavy casualties in a battle for the Dodoma–Kilimatinde section of the central railway. Such counsels were not lacking at his headquarters.[24] But Smuts now insisted that the northern railway was vital and that the Pare Mountains should be cleared. Given his previous assumptions about the importance of Tabora and the irrelevance of Tanga, this was perverse; it confirms the supposition that the avoidance of major battle was not Lettow's strategy but Smuts's. Deventer was to be

[22] Schnee, *Deutsch-Ostafrika*, 143–4.
[23] Benary, *Ehrenbuch der deutschen Feldartillerie*, 642–3.
[24] Meinertzhagen, *Army Diary*, 187–8.

supported indirectly, through an advance on Mombo and then Handeni: Lettow was to be outmanoeuvred, not outfought.

The rains in the north abated in the second week of May. Smuts decided to follow the line of the Pangani rather than of the railway. The east bank of the river was apparently undefended. The railway, on the other hand, marked a succession of German points of resistance, and its destruction by Kraut could delay Smuts's progress if he allowed its repair to dominate the tempo of his advance. Smuts therefore organized his forces in three columns, the river column, the centre column (to follow the railway), and the eastern column (to move from Mbuyuni to the Ngulu Gap and then through the Pare Mountains). The centre column would threaten the German front, while the river and eastern columns moved to its flanks. Smuts's aim was speed, not battle. Convinced that Lettow intended to reconcentrate on the northern railway, and reckoning that it would take him fifteen days to do so, Smuts wanted to get to Handeni and its railhead as soon as possible.

Kraut's inclination was to fight. But the nature of the British flanking moves ensured that combat rarely occurred. The river column found its momentum slowed by thick bush. Thus, it threatened the Germans without ever endangering them. Kraut's offensive spirit took second place to common sense, Schnee's admonitions to prudence, and the availability of the railway line for rapid retreat. Only if the centre column had fixed the Germans in frontal assaults could Smuts's succession of enveloping moves along the Pangani have had any effect.[25]

Kraut's force was, of course, never designed to give battle. Nor did Lettow plan to reconcentrate at Handeni. Smuts's advance was therefore as fast as he could have hoped. Beginning on 21 May, in ten days his troops covered 208 kilometres and reached Bwiko. Smuts then directed the river column on Mkalomo, assuming that Kraut would hold Mombo against the centre column.

Kraut intended to do so but was manoeuvred out anew, and so fought a brief action at Mkalomo on 9 June. The same happened at Handeni. Finally, the Germans took up defensive positions on the River Lukigura, north of the Nguru Mountains. Smuts hoped to take Kraut in the rear from the west, but the poverty of the maps and the difficulty of the terrain

[25] Boell, *Operationen*, 189–95; Schnee, *Deutsch-Ostafrika*, 185.

once again betrayed the ambition of the manoeuvre. Smuts had advanced 400 kilometres in under five weeks. The major constraint on his progress was not enemy action but his line of communications. The nearest railhead was Bwiko, 144 kilometres to his rear. His men were on half rations, restricted to a diet of hard-tack and mealie flour. A halt was called.

Smuts imagined that his advance to the Lukigura had eased the pressure on Deventer at Kondoa Irangi.[26] He now envisaged the two columns advancing in tandem towards the central railway, pinning the Germans between Morogoro and Dodoma.[27] In reality, Deventer's lack of movement throughout May and June was due not to Lettow's attentions but to health and supply problems. Moreover, Lettow had no intention of being tied to the central railway. At the end of April he and Schnee had agreed to abandon their original intention of withdrawing west to Tabora. Instead, they proposed to plunge south to Mahenge. Lettow used the veterinary surveys which Smuts had spurned, deliberately posting his men so as to draw mounted troops into fly-infested areas. Thus tsetse and extended communications would slow the British pursuit.[28] Lettow began to move his troops away from the Kondoa Irangi front on 20 June, over three weeks before Deventer was ready to advance.[29] He joined Kraut at Turiani in the Ngurus, his aim being to cover the evacuation of supplies from the central railway southwards.

On 14 July Deventer resumed his advance, directing his main column on Mpwapwa, and smaller columns on Dodoma and Kilimatinde. By the end of the month Deventer was astride the central railway and pushing eastwards on Kilosa to link up with Smuts.

Smuts spent July in the shadow of the Ngurus and the *Königsberg's* guns. The main German positions were on Mount Kanga, facing the Lukigura. Smuts was informed that the valleys of the Mjonga and the Lwale, running north–south behind the Kanga massif, were practicable for troops. He therefore planned that one column (Sheppard's) should engage the Germans on Kanga, while two more marched first west and then south following the valleys through the hills, converging on Turiani, thus cutting off the Germans' line of retreat. Sheppard set off on 7 August,

---

[26] Crowe, *General Smuts's Campaign*, 163–4.   [27] Hordern, *East Africa*, 294.
[28] Schnee, *Deutsch-Ostafrika*, 182–3; Lettow-Vorbeck, *Reminiscences*, 141–2; Rainey and Blenkinsop, *Veterinary Services*, 419.
[29] Boell, *Operationen*, 188.

but found his progress through the bush and along the mountain slopes too slow. He therefore had to retrace his steps and skirt the mountains to the east, following the line of the Lukigura. Meanwhile, the advance of the two western columns, begun on 5 and 6 August, proved equally laborious. The 2nd mounted brigade, heading the Mhonda valley column, reached the Mjonga on 8 August. But its position was unobservable from the air owing to the thickness of the cover, and it had no wireless. Sheppard's column was at this stage back at its start position, and the main bodies of the other two were only just beginning their southward ascent into the hills. Although the 2nd mounted brigade was in the right position, in isolation it lacked the strength to cut the German communications. Lettow made good his escape through Turiani to the Wami.

On 16 August the two western columns debouched from the Ngurus and at Dakawa ran into German fire from across the Wami. Sheppard's column had already crossed the Wami at Kipera, and moving up the right bank threatened to strike the German flank on the 17th. The Germans fought a delaying action and then fell back on the night of 17 August, Lettow and the main force retiring on Morogoro and Kraut moving south-westwards towards Mahenge.

On 16 August Smuts began to realize that Lettow did not propose to oblige him by fighting it out on the central railway.[30] He nonetheless hoped to be able to pin the Germans against the Uluguru Mountains, a range rising in places to 3,000 metres, and whose northern tip extended to Morogoro and the railway. Deventer reached Kilosa on 22 August. But his division was exhausted, and he reported that he could not continue unless the Germans facing him were threatened from the rear. Smuts therefore directed Enslin's 2nd mounted brigade to the south-west, to strike the central railway at Mkata. Deventer and Enslin, with Enslin leading, were then to push south and west of the Ulugurus to Mlali, while Smuts's main body moved to the east of the range. Smuts did not know whether Lettow planned to retire to Mahenge or to the Rufiji river: his hunch in favour of the latter explained the greater weight attached to his eastern hook. But once again he ducked a frontal assault. Arguing that

---

[30] Hancock and Poel, *Smuts Papers*, iii. 396; Collyer, *South Africans with Smuts*, 153–4, gives indications that this would be so in late June.

the hills which screened Morogoro to the north would make a direct advance from the Wami a costly and protracted operation, he put all his weight into the flanks. Enslin reached Mlali on 23 August; Mikese, 32 kilometres east of Morogoro, was gained on the 26th. Thus, when Morogoro itself was occupied on the same day, no German troops remained to contest Smuts's entry. Abandoned German supplies bore testimony to the speed of the British advance, but by now Smuts's operational style was too manifest for there to be any likelihood of Lettow waiting to fight. Lettow's orders of 26 August established the main German positions at the southern end of the Ulugurus, on the further bank of the River Mgeta. By deploying his troops in depth to the north, he hoped to render them proof against British turning movements, and also to enable them to strike blows against isolated components of Smuts's forces, scattered by design and divided by the terrain.

On 5 September Brits's 3rd division, which had taken up the western movement from Deventer's shattered 2nd division, was approaching Kisaki. Lettow had 600,000 kilos of supplies dumped here, and the poverty of the region south of the Mgeta encouraged him to fight for their protection.[31] On Brits's left, plunging through the Ulugurus themselves, was Nussey's 1st mounted brigade, detached from Deventer's division and now without its horses. Both commanders had wireless, and on 7 September, the day Brits attacked, each was within 8 kilometres of the other. But 'once off the road . . . even the sky overhead was invisible, and one could not see one's next-door neighbour three feet away'.[32] Not even the sound of Brits's rifle fire was audible to Nussey. His wireless was lost over a precipice. Lettow was able to deal with each in turn, smashing Brits on 7 September and checking Nussey on the 8th.

To the east the pattern was repeated. Delayed by the need to repair roads and bridges, Hoskins's 1st division did not reach Tulo until 9 September. The Germans, in entrenched positions on the Dunthumi river, could therefore be reinforced by the victors of Kisaki. The Germans fought a stubborn action from the 10th to the 12th, but in their wish to counter-attack were as hampered by the terrain as the British were in

[31] Lettow, *Reminiscences*, 152–3; Boell, *Operationen*, 226.
[32] Reitz, *Trekking On*, 101.

their advances. On 14 September Lettow abandoned Kisaki, withdrawing across the Mgeta and establishing a new base at Beho-Beho.

Smuts now paused. Most of his staff thought he should have done so at Morogoro. Deventer's 2nd division was 650 kilometres from its railhead, Brits's 3rd division 390 kilometres, and Hoskins's 1st division 360 kilometres. All three were on half rations; Hoskins's had no forward dumps and depended on a daily lift of 17,000 to 20,000 pounds.[33] Smuts used lorries as far as he could. But, although formally speaking the rains had not yet begun, rain was falling and within a day tracks across the black cotton soil were turned into a sea of 'sticky, black mud'.[34] Baggage animals could not make good the deficiency. Of 54,000 mules, donkeys, horses, and oxen put to work on the supply lines around and south of the central railway between June and September 1916, all but 600 fell prey to the tsetse fly.[35]

The health of the humans was little better. By May 1916, within three months of their arrival, most South African units had already lost half their strength to disease. The 9th South African Infantry mustered 1,135 all ranks on 14 February; on 25 October its parade state stood at 116. The 2nd Rhodesia Regiment deployed 1,038 all ranks between March 1915 and its departure from the theatre in January 1917. Thirty-six were killed in action, eighty-four wounded, and thirty-two died of disease. But there were 10,626 cases of sickness, including 3,127 of malaria, and 2,272 of these resulted in hospital admission.[36] Some at least were the product of the punishing rates of march, and of malnutrition caused by insufficient food or inadequate cooking. Although typhoid was controlled by vaccination, rates of dysentery were more than three times those suffered in the South African War. Proven methods in the control of malaria were neglected, in large part because of poor discipline, but also due to failures in the issue of quinine and mosquito nets. From the second half of 1916 new troops were disembarked at ports like Dar es Salaam, notorious for their high incidence of malaria. Medical problems therefore arose in part because the advice of doctors was not coordinated with the needs of military operations—a further reflection of the malfunctioning of Smuts's staff. Thus, as Meinertzhagen observed, 'what Smuts saves on

[33] Hordern, *East Africa*, i. 393–4.   [34] Fendall, *East African Force*, 194–5.
[35] Mosley, *Duel for Kilimanjaro*, 153.   [36] Hordern, *East Africa*, i. 521.

the battlefield he loses in hospital, for it is Africa and its climate we are really fighting not the Germans'.[37] An early battle, a frontal assault when lines of communication were short, might ultimately have proved less costly than long-range but combat-free manoeuvring.

The means by which to improve the supply position were available. At the beginning of September 1916 Smuts's base was still Mombasa. And yet Tanga was taken on 7 July. Smuts, convinced that complete victory was imminent, saw its restoration and use as of no value. The British entered Dar es Salaam on 3 September. Little energy was put into its reopening. Smuts's administrative staff remained at Tanga to the north, while his shipping was securing the ports of Kilwa, Lindi, Sudi, and Mikindani to the south. The damage to the central railway was not as severe as it might have been. The Germans had destroyed the bridges and removed much of the rolling stock to its western end, around Tabora. But the track was largely intact. By converting Ford cars to run on the rails, the British were able to use the permanent way almost immediately. During November locomotives once again linked Dar es Salaam and Morogoro. If Smuts had paused on the central railway, and re-established his communications through Dar es Salaam before pushing on into the Uluguru, he might have been able to terminate the campaign north of the Mgeta, or at least of the Rufiji.

However, the advance to the central railway had inflicted at least one major blow on the *Schütztruppen*. Lettow's theatre of operations was bisected. In the west Wahle and his men were out of contact, left to conduct their own operations. The campaign which he and Tombeur waged was comparable in range and significance with that in the east. It served neither British colonial interests, nor the post-war publicity accorded to Smuts and Lettow, to acknowledge the fact. But Tabora, Wahle's headquarters, was the largest town in German East Africa, centrally positioned in the colony. According to a British estimate of 1 April 1916 as many as 373 European troops and 7,650 askaris were deployed in the square Kivu–Mwanza–Tabora–Ujiji.[38] In themselves

[37] Meinertzhagen, *Army Diary*, 200; also 195. On these points, see Anderson, *East African Front*. Statistics can be found in Mitchell and Smith, *Medical Services*, and further detail in Macpherson and Mitchell, *Medical Services*, IV, 416–504.

[38] Belgique, *Campagnes coloniales belges*, ii. 177. This is the fullest source on the Tabora campaign.

these figures confirm how exaggerated were Meinertzhagen's estimates of Lettow's total strength. Wahle's disposable force actually numbered about 2,000. But the calculation reveals how dependent Smuts's thrusts in the east were on Tombeur's simultaneous commitment in the west. The troops concentrated under Lettow's direct command in the north only just exceeded half the *Schütztruppen*'s total force.

The campaign in the west also showed how unsympathetic to guerrilla operations and how wedded to colonial stability were many Germans. Both at Bukoba and at Mwanza the principles of German peacetime administration persisted for the first two years of the war. The local economy was nurtured, porters only served within their own regions, and productivity was sustained. Loyalty to Germany enabled auxiliaries to be raised, and even prompted rebellion across the Ugandan frontier at Kigezi. The basis existed for a sustained popular defence of Ruanda and Urundi. But instead the people were prepared for the arrival of the British and told to co-operate with them. The commander of the Bukoba area's final words were that the Germans 'wished to find the country in the same condition as they left it when they returned in three months time after the approaching German victory in Europe'. A preference for German colonialism, not the prosecution of the European war, led to the rejection of revolutionary methods.[39]

The first phase of the Entente's offensive in the west was bizarre, even in a theatre of operations dominated by larger-than-life personalities. Lieutenant-Commander G. B. Spicer-Simson was one of the Royal Navy's less distinguished officers. In command of a destroyer he had sunk a liberty boat, and he had been ashore entertaining some ladies when a gunboat anchored under his orders had been torpedoed. Nonetheless, Spicer-Simson was selected to command two gunboats that were hauled overland from Capetown via Elizabethville to Lake Tanganyika. Most of the journey was by rail, but the significant sections were not. The expedition sailed from England on 15 June 1915; on Boxing Day Spicer-Simson's two craft put out into the waters of Lake Tanganyika. By February two German gunboats were accounted for, but a third, the *Graf von Götzen*, a much bigger vessel, only recently completed and mounting one of the *Königsberg*'s 10.5 cm guns, remained at large. Spicer-Simson, who had

---

[39] Austen, *Northwest Tanzania*, 118, also 113–18; see also Louis, *Ruanda-Urundi*, 213.

now taken to wearing a skirt with his commander's jacket, refused Belgian pleas to engage the *Graf von Götzen*. Instead, he set off to the southern end of the lake to support the British forces on the Northern Rhodesian frontier. The Germans' control of the lake was sufficiently dented to allow the Belgians to transport goods along its western coast, but the navigation of the eastern bank remained in their hands. Thus, both sides were able to use the lake route to feed their forces in Ruanda and Urundi.[40]

For the Belgians, supply was a major headache. In August 1914 the *Force publique* concentrated 1,395 men along the Congo; in May 1916 Tombeur's strength was 719 Europeans and 11,698 blacks (a much lower ratio of Europeans to blacks than the other powers thought advisable). They were deployed in three groups: a brigade north of Lake Kivu close to the Ugandan frontier (Molitor's); a brigade on the Russissi (Olsen's); and a defensive group on the western shore of Lake Tanganyika. No food reserves had been formed before the offensive. The Belgians hoped to live off the land. But the 1916 harvest was not yet in, and the 1915 crop was either eaten or destroyed.[41] Dispersing to requisition, the Belgian askaris developed a fearsome reputation. Tombeur had stressed that the Belgians' war was with the troops of Germany, not with the inhabitants of Ruanda and Urundi;[42] in reality, the lack of sufficient European officers to ensure adequate supervision undermined the hopes of local collaboration. Each of the groups needed 7,000–8,000 porters for its own needs in addition to the porters for the lines of communication. The former were locally impressed. Tombeur tried to recruit the latter from the interior of the Congo, but eventually had to ask the British for 5,000 porters and 100 ox-wagons. The effect of this British contribution was temporarily to rob the troops in Uganda, Lakeforce (commanded by Sir Charles Crewe), of their offensive capacity.

Tombeur, like Smuts, was more interested in the conquest of territory than in the defeat of the *Schütztruppen*. Moreover, the examples of Tanga and Kahe convinced him that his opponents were masters of the defensive battle. Although sixteen 70 mm howitzers, originally ordered by the

[40] Farwell, *Great War in Africa*, 217–49, tells the colourful story; Boell, *Operationen*, 131–4, emphasizes its limited outcome.

[41] Belgique, *Campagnes coloniales belges*, ii. 51–90.

[42] Ibid., i. 184–7.

Mexican government, had been promised him by the French, they had yet to arrive. Therefore, the *Force publique* was instructed to shun attacks on trenches and strong-points. The Germans would thus be denied the opportunity of crushing one Belgian column before turning against the other, and so would be robbed of any advantage to be derived from operating on interior lines. Tombeur wanted to combine tactical conservatism—the holding of ground once gained, the avoidance of defeat, the keeping of casualties to a minimum—with a strategy of manoeuvre. And yet the porter problem, the lack of intelligence, and the absence of effective communications between the brigades all constrained such operations. The best that Tombeur could do was to set down his general principles and to agree a common date on which Molitor and Olsen were to advance.[43]

On 5 April Wintgens, the officer commanding the three *Schütztruppen* companies in Ruanda, received a letter from the Belgians offering an armistice. Tombeur said that the war in East Africa had been begun by Germany, not Belgium, and therefore asked Schnee for compensation. Lettow, his mind focused on the eastern theatre, was not unenthusiastic; Schnee saw it as a Belgian ruse to lower Wahle's guard, and said he would have to refer the whole matter to Berlin. In fact Tombeur was behaving with remarkable consistency. An armistice on such terms would have fulfilled Belgian objectives to the letter.[44]

On 12 April the Belgians, without replying to Schnee, opened fire on the Russissi front. Tombeur imagined that the Germans would fall back to a line flanked by Kigali in the north and Nyanza in the south. The northern brigade demonstrated against German positions on the River Sebea while directing its main body towards Kigali. Wintgens's communications with Wahle were cut on 22 April, and on 2 May he ordered the evacuation of Kigali. Further south, Olsen got across the Russissi and took Nyanza on 21 May. The Belgians had won Ruanda by manoeuvre alone.

So far Molitor's and Olsen's columns had pursued convergent lines of march. But now annexationism and operational necessity created divergent objectives. Olsen thrust south at the end of May towards Usumbura and Kitega (entered on 17 June), in order to secure Urundi. Molitor

---

[43] Ibid., ii. 186–9.
[44] Schnee, *Deutsch-Ostafrika*, 205; Boell, *Operationen*, 260; no Entente source refers to this episode.

moved east towards the south-western corner of Lake Victoria in order to collaborate with Crewe's Lakeforce. Thus the Belgians fanned out, their force-to-space ratio diminishing and their units increasingly pursuing independent objectives. The Belgian government's priority was the seizure of Ujiji and the domination of Lake Tanganyika; Olsen, therefore, had the principal role. But for the British Molitor was more important. They wanted him to combine with Crewe in the capture of Mwanza. By the end of June both objectives had been adopted. On Crewe's suggestion Mwanza, once secured, was to be the base for a thrust on Tabora. Olsen would support by moving eastwards from Ujiji along the central railway.

In practice, Olsen's progress proved more rapid than Molitor's: thus Belgian aims prevailed over British. Wintgens had reckoned that the rains would cause Tombeur to halt on the Kigali–Nyanza line. In reality, the lack of porters proved a greater impediment to pursuit. Those recruited in Ruanda were reluctant to follow Olsen into Urundi. The southern brigade overcame its immediate problems by shifting its base to Usumbura on Lake Tanganyika. It then occupied Ujiji without opposition, Wahle having decided to concentrate his forces north of Tabora. The British took Mwanza on 14 July. By 19 September 40,000 loads were accumulated at Mwanza. But its value as a base was minimized by lack of porters to carry them forward. The area south of Mwanza was waterless, its resources stripped, and its population shifted by the Germans. In the Belgian column seven out of every twelve loads were needed to feed the porters themselves. Crewe's force had 10,000 porters for 2,800 combatants.[45]

By the beginning of August Molitor reckoned Wahle's major positions were at Kahama, south of Whimo, with a supporting group opposite Crewe at Shinyanga. Crewe concluded that the Shinyanga positions were stronger. Each, therefore, saw himself as having the principal task and requested his ally to support him. For Tombeur, Molitor's job was to continue due south, so relieving the pressure on Olsen as soon as possible. If Crewe was right, then Molitor's troops would turn the Germans at Shinyanga without their having to lose time by marching to the east. Crewe, nonetheless, insisted on Molitor's direct support. He was proved wrong, but not until 17 August was Molitor able to resume the

[45] Buhrer, *L'Afrique orientale allemande*, 381–3.

original direction of his advance.[46] On 28 August Crewe took the Shinyanga position without fighting.

In Tombeur's mind he was commanding a massive concentric attack on Tabora, with Olsen's southern brigade leading while Molitor's northern brigade fixed the Germans around Whimo. In reality, Tombeur was a spectator. By early September his forces described a quarter-circle of nearly 200 kilometres, each brigade's base 400 kilometres distant from the other. On 2 September an intercepted German signal reported a German victory over Olsen's brigade the previous day at Mabama. This was Tombeur's first indication of Olsen's current position. The check to Olsen was minor, only one battalion having been engaged at Mabama, but Tombeur now decided that the northern brigade should take up the running while the southern held its ground. However, the supply problems of Molitor's brigade made his advance sporadic and slow. Each daily stage of his route could accommodate only two battalions, and his troops carried sufficient ammunition for a single day's fighting. On 9 September he took up defensive positions in order to reconcentrate. The southern brigade, not the northern, made the offensive efforts of the next four days. Even when direct contact between the two brigades was established on the 14th, the northern brigade remained on the defensive. Olsen's push on Lulanguru on 16 September was thus unsupported.

Wahle knew of Tombeur's intentions from radio intercepts and therefore established his main positions north of Tabora at Itanga. The proximity of Itanga and Lulanguru, particular given the railway line, enabled him to move troops from one to the other. But his force had now fallen to 1,100 rifles. He disbanded the naval unit under his command in order to redistribute its Europeans among the field companies. Nonetheless, desertions multiplied. Many of the askari came from the Tabora region and had no intention of leaving it. The Germans no longer had the men to defend the town's perimeter. On 16 September a captured letter, intended by Crewe for Molitor, revealed that the main blow from the north would be delivered on the 19th. Wahle divided his command into three components, two to go east along the central railway before turning south to Kiromo, and one to go due south from

[46] Belgique, *Campagnes coloniales belges*, ii. 419–25.

Tabora to Sikonge. The Germans abandoned their positions under cover of dark on the 18th.[47]

The pursuit of the *Schütztruppen* was half-hearted and limited. The occupation of Tabora on 19 September marked the limit of Belgian territorial ambitions. Logistic constraints as well as political directives tied Tombeur to the town. Now that the *Force publique* was reconcentrated its demands for food exceeded the capacity of the local supplies. The plight of Lakeforce, outside Tabora to the east, and 390 kilometres from its base, was even worse. On 3 October Crewe's command was dissolved. Had military priorities carried more weight than colonial rivalries in allied counsels, Olsen's advance from the west would have been held back. Crewe might then have hit the railway to the east before the attack from west had made itself felt. As it was, Olsen's outpacing of Molitor and Crewe meant that Wahle's path to the south and east lay open. His three columns made off towards Iringa, in a bid to reunite with Lettow and the main force.

The Germans' retreat south of the central railway gave the British advance from Northern Rhodesia more than local significance. In origin, however, the Colonial Office's decision to switch from defence to attack related not to the East African campaign as a whole but to the increasing instability in Nyasaland and Northern Rhodesia. The colonization of the northern parts of both territories was not complete in 1914. The district staff in Northern Rhodesia fell from 102 in 1914 to seventy-six by the end of 1915. And yet the strains on the colony multiplied. The German incursion across the frontier—and the demand for labour to support the troops needed to counter it—threw the value of British protection into question and caused economic crisis. Famine was evident by late 1915. Brigadier-General Edward Northey, the only British general in East Africa for whom the Germans confessed admiration, was appointed to the command, and his force boosted to 2,500 men. Having established four posts from Karonga to Abercorn, he took the offensive on 25 May 1916.[48]

---

[47] Ibid., app., pp. 173, 176, 181–6; Boell, *Operationen*, 283–5; Marine-Archiv, *Kämpfe der Kaiserlichen Marine*, ii. 269; Schnee, *Deutsch-Ostafrika*, 206–13.

[48] Crucial background to Northey's offensive is Yorke, 'Crisis of colonial control', 20–54, 118–65, 272–91; on Nyasaland, see Page, *Journal of African History*, XIX (1978), 87–100.

But Northey's attack exacerbated many of the colonial and economic problems it was designed to mitigate. The railhead for his force was at Ndola, 960 kilometres from Abercorn and 730 kilometres from his main base at Kasama. The road cut from Kashitu, south of Ndola, to Kisama and Abercorn in 1915 was not suitable for wheeled traffic, particularly in the rains; an experiment in the use of oxen in 1914 fell victim to tsetse fly. So porters were vital. The demands on the adult male population were enormous. In Nyasaland alone, perhaps 200,000 men, or 83 per cent of the total available, were employed as labourers in Northey's campaign. In north-east Rhodesia 92,337 carriers were engaged between April 1915 and March 1916, and 138,930 between April 1916 and March 1917. At a local level Abercorn, with a population of 8,500 taxable males, contributed 5,000 carriers and 800 road-builders by August 1916; Luwingu, with 7,000 taxable males, drew in sufficient labour from outside to account for 12,786 engagements between March 1915 and March 1916. The effect of such massive new employment was to jeopardize local cultivation. The British South Africa Company could not introduce measures to encourage African food production without threatening the preferential arrangements for white settlers, already alienated by rising labour costs generated through the army's demands and rates of pay. Food production, therefore, fell. Increasingly, the porters had to carry their own supplies as well as those of the troops. Sir C. A. Wallace, the administrator of Northern Rhodesia, reckoned that if the porters carried their own food only 1/27 of their load from Ndola would reach its destination at Kasama. To deliver 1 ton of food a day (enough for 1,000 men) from Ndola to Kasama needed 2,250 carriers if food was available en route and 23,300 if not. The exponential effects of the lack of local produce raised these numbers to 3,000 and 71,000 respectively, if delivery was to Abercorn. At the end of 1914 about one load in twenty was actually reaching its destination. The decision to move from defence to attack increased the numbers of troops to be supplied, extended the lines of communication yet further, and took the porters away from their own territories. The major threat to Northey's advance was less the Germans than administrative collapse, and even rebellion.[49]

[49] Yorke, 'Crisis of colonial control', 71–102; Lucas, *Empire at War*, iv. 270–2, 290–309; Hodges, *Journal of African History*, XIX (1978), 113.

Northey developed two palliatives to ease his supply problem. The first was to use boats to cross the swamps in Belgian territory, between Ndola and Kasama. More than half the total food delivered in the build-up to Northey's attack came by this route, and in 1916–17 12,000 paddlers using 2,000 canoes delivered 2,500 tons. Secondly, as Northey advanced so he established bases at the head of Lake Nyasa, and was able to use the route from Beira to Chinde, thence up the Zambezi, and finally to Fort Johnston.[50]

By 4 June Northey had cleared the frontiers of Northern Rhodesia and Nyasaland, and had established his headquarters at Neu Langenburg. A thrust north towards Tabora and Kilimatinde would have taken Northey's force across barren country and extended his line of communications. Therefore, as the main German forces were pushed in on the central railway, Northey inclined north-east towards Iringa. For Lettow, Northey's attack was both a threat and an opportunity. Its impact on his plan to withdraw to the south was immediate, robbing him of the cultivated areas around Neu Langenburg and endangering Mahenge. On the other hand, Northey's command, kept small by its supply problems, and divided into separate columns spread over a broad front, created the chance of local German successes. Lettow boosted the forces around Iringa to five companies, drawing troops from Dodoma and Dar es Salaam to do so. However, on 24 July Braunschweig, the local German commander, was defeated at Malangali, south-west of Iringa, by two British columns. The British were scarcely superior in numbers, but their converging movements and Braunschweig's undue concern about his single but useless howitzer unhinged the German conduct of the battle from the outset.

Northey remained subordinate to the Colonial Office, not the War Office, until 7 November 1916. Although technically still not under Smuts's command he was nonetheless careful to coordinate his movements with him. Smuts now asked Northey to shun Iringa, and instead to aim south for Lupembe. He was worried that Northey's column would drive the Germans off the central railway before the main attack could trap them there. But on 27 August, with the Germans south of the central railway and concentrated around Morogoro, Smuts changed tack, telling

---

[50] Yorke, 'Crisis of colonial control', 76–8, 195; Lucas, *Empire at War*, iv. 268, 293–5.

Northey to take Iringa in order to discourage Lettow from any attempt to move in that direction. The combination of Northey's move to Iringa and of Deventer's to Kilosa kept Kraut—after the German retreat from the line of the Wami—to the south-east and Mahenge.

Northey was increasingly worried. His small command was spread over a 160-kilometre front, between Lupembe and Iringa, and his line of communications stretched back to Mwaya. Lettow's main forces were moving south and would be anxious to secure the harvest around Mahenge. Northey wanted Deventer to relieve his northern flank at Iringa, but the 2nd division was exhausted and in any case was required further east. Instead, Smuts urged Northey on, sensing the need to deny the Germans the use of the Mahenge area before the rains. By the end of September Northey's Lupembe column was 96 kilometres from its base on the Ruhuje, and a further force had been detached south to Songea. Although his total strength was raised to 3,800 men, his front was now 320 kilometres long, and his supply dependent on the 17,000 reluctant carriers north of the frontier.[51]

Facing him, Kraut had concentrated 2,450 rifles in the Mahenge area. Kraut's efforts to turn defence into local counter-attacks were hampered in part by the mountainous terrain and the extent of his front. The Germans had simultaneously to face west to the Ruhuje, between Lupembe and Mahenge, and north on the Ruaha. But Kraut's problems were not eased by the offensive instincts of his superior. Lettow's interventions, including direct communications with Kraut's subordinates, added to the difficulties of co-ordination.[52]

Onto this fragile and delicately balanced scene broke Wahle's force from Tabora. After setting a frantic pace for the first ten days in order to escape any Belgian pursuit, Wahle had found himself deep in unexplored and uninhabited terrain. Neither water nor food was readily available. A supply dump had been prepared at Malongwe, on the central railway east of Tabora. But the porters had run off, and with only 600 Indian prisoners of war as carriers Wahle had to leave most of the food, to concentrate on carrying munitions and medical supplies. After six days such food as he had was exhausted, and his men had to forage, and even harvest and thresh, as well as march. The Wahehe, whose territory he

[51] Hordern, *East Africa*, i. 468–508.   [52] Boell, *Operationen*, 250–8.

entered in November, secreted their food stocks and supported the British. An initial strength of 5,000 men was whittled away: 786 askaris were captured, 146 were reported as missing, 916 deserted, and 300 were left behind. Morale, even among the Europeans, slumped. But Wahle kept his command active. He knew from intercepts that Northey had captured Iringa and that Lettow was moving south from Morogoro. He therefore determined to attack Iringa, so threatening Northey's lines of communications and forcing the British to turn west away from Lettow. But his supply problems forced him to remain divided in three columns, and by 24 October, two days before the day appointed for the attack on Iringa, he had still not regrouped. The British, alerted by a German assault on Igominyi, were already turning back to cover Iringa. Wahle therefore abandoned the attack on Iringa, and instead pressed on towards Mahenge and Lupembe, believing he would effect a junction with Lettow. Northey's movements in response to Wahle's relieved Kraut, but also confused him, as he was unaware of Wahle's approach. On 9 November Wahle made contact with a patrol sent out by Kraut. On the 26th one of Wahle's columns was surrounded and surrendered, but the other two, a total of 750 men, four guns, and fifteen machine-guns, completed their junction with Kraut. At the end of November Wahle superseded Kraut in command of the Mahenge area. His force totalled 350 Europeans, 3,000 askaris, nine guns, and thirty-nine machine-guns, spread over a front of 450 kilometres. His task was to protect the area under cultivation and, if possible, extend it westwards to Ubena (or Nyombe).[53]

Thus, throughout November Northey's force was exposed to the dangers of defeat in detail, and was engaged in a series of small fights to its rear and to its front. In December Deventer took over responsibility for Iringa. Northey's sector now ran from Songea to Lupembe, his line of communications snaking across the Livingstone Mountains east of Lake Nyasa to Mwaya.

The Germans' withdrawal towards the south-east corner of their colony increased the potential significance of Portugal's entry to the war in March 1916. In practice, however, unlike Northey's advance, Portugal's impact remained local and limited. The prime reason was Portuguese

[53] Ibid. 286–98; Deppe, *Mit Lettow-Vorbeck*, 187–96.

incompetence; but, in addition, British interests no more than German would be served by Portugal extending its claims across the Ruvuma river.

In August 1914 reports that Portugal had declared war on Germany and that Portuguese agitators were at work among the native population north of the Ruvuma led to clashes and casualties. Schnee established the truth in September, and apologized to the Portuguese. But in German eyes Portuguese neutrality seemed increasingly fictional.[54] Lisbon allowed the passage of British troops through Mozambique and it authorized its Angolan administrations to co-operate with Pretoria in mopping up after the conquest of South-West Africa. In the autumn of 1915 the postal service via Portuguese territory was disrupted and then suppressed. More significantly, an expeditionary force of 1,527 men arrived in November 1914 from Lisbon to boost the existing garrison of twelve poorly equipped native companies. It was relieved by a second, comparably sized force the following year. The immediate task of this second force was to create a network of posts along the German frontier. But the real aim of the government was the recovery of the Kionga triangle at the mouth of the Ruvuma, seized from Portugal by Germany in 1894. Portugal continued to pursue its imperial ambitions against the background of European war, but until March 1916 contrived to do so without committing itself to the larger conflict: even after 1914 clashes in the colonies did not inevitably lead to belligerence in Europe. When at last it did formally enter the war against the Central Powers, its military actions remained confined to Africa for the time being. In April 1916 Portuguese forces occupied the Kionga triangle. The Germans retaliated by seizing sixteen Portuguese posts on the Ruvuma, largely without opposition.[55]

The apparent success of Smuts's campaign gave urgency to Portugal's ambitions. A British conquest of German East Africa without Portuguese participation would diminish its claims to territory. But, once south of the central railway, Smuts's own ambivalence on Portuguese co-operation became evident. If the Portuguese gained by their own efforts that which Smuts wished to give them, the case for getting them to hand

[54] Boell, *Operationen*, 68–70; Marine-Archiv, *Kämpfe der Kaiserlichen Marine*, 275–6.

[55] Pélissier, *Naissance du Mozambique*, ii. 687–90. Pélissier is the main work on Portuguese aspects of the East African campaign. On the diplomatic background, see Texiera, *L'Entrée du Portugal dans la Grande Guerre*, esp. 205–10, 239, 247–50, 308–11, 358.

over to South Africa Delagoa Bay and its adjacent territories would be considerably weakened. On the other hand, a Portuguese advance on Lindi would, militarily, be a considerable contribution. The successful voyage of the *Marie* clearly demonstrated how important to the Germans the continued possession of the coastline might be. Therefore, when a third Portuguese expeditionary force, mustering 4,642 men, arrived at Palma on 5 July, and its commander, General Jose Cesar Ferreira Gil, proposed to move up the coast, Smuts responded by saying that the British could do that. Instead, he asked Gil to move into the German food-producing areas inland around Masasi, and pointed to Liwale as an ultimate objective. No roads existed to aid such a march.[56] It was alleged that Gil himself had been appointed because of his political credentials (he was a good republican), rather than his professional aptitude. He lacked experience of Africa; his exercise of command was lackadaisical. He was reported to be far to the rear playing cards while his forward units pressed on without proper reconnaissance.[57] His men showed no interest in the rudiments of tropical hygiene; they would not take quinine; they were reluctant to drink boiled water; tuberculosis, syphilis, and malaria were rampant. By the beginning of September Gil's effective strength was 2,700 rifles. Smuts's proposed line of advance could only reduce such a force to total ineffectiveness.

Gil crossed the Ruvuma and on 26 October occupied Newala. The local population on the Makonde plateau welcomed the Portuguese. Lettow had been so anxious to concentrate all his forces in the north that in 1915 he had appealed to Berlin in a bid to override Schnee's wish to keep a company at Lindi.[58] Looff, whose *Königsberg* crew formed the kernel of the German garrison in the south-east in the autumn of 1916, agreed with Schnee. Despite having inferior numbers (a total of 840 men), Looff checked Gil's advance and encircled him in Newala. On 28 November, after six days' siege, Gil abandoned Newala and retired across the Ruvuma, leaving four mountain guns, six machine-guns, and 100,000 rounds. Portuguese credit among the tribes of the Makonde withered. Looff's resolute action secured the food-producing areas of the south and made possible Lettow's continued resistance a year later.

[56] Hordern, *East Africa*, i. 388–91.
[57] Ribeiro de Meneses, *Journal of Contemporary History*, XXXIII (1998), 90.
[58] Boell, *Operationen*, 122.

Smuts's support for Gil was indirect, delayed, and, ultimately, thwarted by Lettow. Forced to pause on the Mgeta in September, he at last began to exploit his naval supremacy to secure the coastline. Kilwa was seized in September, and during October and November the whole of Hoskins's division was transported thither. Smuts's intention was not so much amphibious envelopment—Kilwa was too far from the Mgeta positions for such a move to have reciprocal effects. Instead, Hoskins was to advance inland on Liwale, so converging with the Portuguese and laying waste the crops on which Lettow might rely in 1917. By using a division, where originally he had intended a brigade, Smuts prevented Hoskins being ready to move until 29 November. The tracks inland were barely passable, sand alternating with black cotton soil. The rains came early and the area was thick with fly. The whole scheme proved ridiculously ambitious, making more sense on the map than it did on the ground.[59]

Moreover, Lettow was not fixed to the Mgeta position by offensive action. The South African artillery plotted the German trenches and lines of communication, and kept them under well-directed harassing fire. But Lettow was still free to divide his force, switching his *Schwerpunkt* from the river to the coast. The first British troops to move inland from Kilwa had occupied Kibata to the north-west, as a guard for their right flank. Lettow saw the opportunity to inflict a defeat on a portion of the enemy forces. Increasing his strength to ten companies, he advanced on Kibata on 5 December. The battle that developed was one of the most desperate and sustained of the campaign, fought in incessant rain between positions often only 80 yards apart, and dominated by artillery and grenades. By 21 December each side had fought the other to a standstill. The British had progressively reinforced Kibata during the battle, so leading Lettow to claim the strategic victory as he had deflected the danger to Liwale. But Lettow had not overwhelmed the British post, and protracted, attritional combat made little tactical sense. By the end of the year he could muster only 1,100 Europeans and 7,300 askaris fit for service.[60]

Lettow's concentration at Kibata had left only 1,000 men on the Mgeta. Smuts therefore embraced the plan which earlier he had spurned. The

---

[59] Crowe, *General Smuts' Campaign*, is the best English source for this phase of the operations; see also Haywood and Clarke, *Royal West African Frontier Force*, 182, 187; Beadon, *Royal Army Service Corps*, ii. 317.

[60] Boell, *Operationen*, 241–2, 246–9, 300; Lettow-Vorbeck, *Reminiscences*, 168–70.

Kilwa force was to push north-west on Ngarambi, so pinning Lettow, while his main body crossed the Mgeta and then the Rufiji. On 1 January 1917 Smuts attacked the Mgeta positions, using his main force to envelop from the west. The British were on the Rufiji by the 3rd. But the Kilwa force had not been able to hold Lettow. He had already anticipated Smuts's men and placed himself in a central position between the two attacks, at Lake Utungi. The British crossed the Rufiji on 17 January, taking Mkindu and Kipongo. But German resistance was now hardening. Smuts discounted the rains, of whose effects he had received ample warning. They had never really stopped in December, and now began in earnest. The Rufiji turned into a torrent, hundreds of yards across, its current too strong for any of the available boats. As the Germans had already discovered, the area between the Mgeta and the Rufiji, afforested and uninhabited, was devoid of food. It was becoming a swamp. The nearest railhead was at Mikese, 255 kilometres distant. Although Dar es Salaam was open and the central railway functioning, the supply services had still not recovered from their punishing marches earlier in the year. 'The transport was used up; the mechanical transport broken down, and in need of thorough overhaul and reconditioning; the animal transport mostly dead, and the porters worn out and debilitated.'[61] The British advance again ground to a halt.

This time Smuts would not be able to renew it. On 27 December 1916 he heard that he was to go to London, to represent South Africa at the Imperial War Cabinet. He left on 20 January. He had continuously anticipated a short campaign; his cables had consistently reported great successes; he had avoided mentioning the effects of the weather; now he described the war in East Africa as all but finished. At one level he was right. South African war aims were territorial. Four-fifths of the colony and nine-tenths of its infrastructure had been overrun. This was conquest, even if it was not ultimate victory. Smuts had served the cause of imperialism rather than that of the Entente's war effort. In doing so he had behaved as a politician rather than a general, boosting his own reputation and aiming to hallow the integration of the Union with battlefield triumph.

Where propaganda turned to fiction was in the depiction of a great South African feat of arms. On their arrival both Smuts and his fellow

[61] Fendall, *East Africa Force*, 88–9; also 169–70.

countrymen had dubbed the German askaris 'damned Kaffirs'.[62] But they had learnt that blacks could outfight and outwit whites. Privately their respect had grown; publicly they could not admit it. The deadliness of the East African climate was exaggerated rather than acknowledge the effectiveness of the *Schütztruppen*. 'Hospitals', Meinertzhagen commented on 8 October, 'are full to overflowing with strong healthy men suffering from cold feet or an excess of patriotism.'[63] South African medical officers colluded. Invalids were sent to recuperate in South Africa, and then did not return. When convalescent camps were established in Kenya, wastage rates were cut by about half.[64] Carried to its logical conclusion, the South African arguments about health had to acknowledge that the British, like the Germans, should rely on black, not white, troops. In October 1916 Smuts himself eventually concluded as much. But, by saying that after January 1917 only policing duties remained, he simultaneously protected the *amour propre* of the white South Africans.[65]

The Africanization of the campaign began with the completion of the conquest of the Cameroons. In July 1916 the Gold Coast Regiment arrived, and it bore the brunt of the fighting at Kibata. But Lugard at first opposed the use of the major component of the West African Frontier Force, the four battalions of the Nigeria Regiment. Their losses in the Cameroons had been greater than those of the Gold Coast Regiment. About 1,000 men had been discharged when the campaign ended, and the remainder were anticipating a period with their families. Lugard asked the War Office for forty-two senior officers, but was told that, in view of the demands of the western front, he could have only fifteen subalterns. The advice that he enlist from the local European population, although eventually followed, filled him with apprehension for the internal security of the colony. Over a third of his pre-war administrators were absent on army duties. A rebellion among the Oujo in November 1916, prompted by the chiefs' methods of recruiting porters, lent credence to his fears. Nonetheless, the Nigerians sailed in the same month, their establishment of 5,000 filled by voluntary re-enlistment. Not until 1917 would an indirect form of conscription be necessary. They

---

[62] Meinertzhagen, *Army Diary*, 165.
[63] Ibid. 199; also 201.   [64] Fendall, *East African Force*, 153–5.
[65] See Smuts's remarks in Collyer, *South Africans under Smuts*, pp. vii–viii.

entered the line on the Mgeta, and occupied the Rufiji valley during the rains.[66]

In April 1916 Hoskins had prevailed on Smuts to sanction a moderate increase in the King's African Rifles. Four new battalions were raised, doubling the strength to 8,000 men. Smuts remained sceptical, bound by the idea that most tribes of the British East African possessions were not warlike, and that therefore the recruiting capacity of the colonies was restricted. Nonetheless, by January 1917 the King's African Rifles had thirteen battalions, and in February a target of twenty was set. By November 1918 the establishment was twenty-two battalions, and its total strength 35,424 all ranks.[67] One regiment, the 6th, raised its three battalions from former German askaris; elsewhere, recently pacified tribesmen enlisted in order to recover their traditional vocations. But generally the notion of 'martial races', imported from the Indian army, was abandoned, and the recruiting base accordingly broadened.[68]

The expanded King's African Rifles was designed ultimately for imperial, not simply East African, service. Smuts, after all, was predicting a rapid end to the campaign, and the conventional wisdom was that the formation and training of each new battalion would take a year. Sensing a fresh source of manpower for other theatres, and thinking particularly of Palestine, which took priority over East Africa from February 1917, the War Office took a more benevolent interest than might otherwise have been the case. In June 1916 the battalions adopted the four-company structure, thus aligning themselves with European norms. A year later the allocation of machine-guns for each battalion was increased to four. Smuts had argued that the efficiency of the *Schütztruppen* was due to their high proportion of European NCOs; the Germans agreed. From a ratio of one white for every 35.5 blacks in January, the King's African Rifles moved to one for 9.25 by the end of the war. However, not all the experienced campaigners shipped out from Britain proved valuable, some being selected because shell-shock had made them unfit for further service in France.[69] In the event, the King's African Rifles' only other service than in

[66] Osuntokun, *Nigeria in the First World War*, 119–24, 239–250; Haywood and Clarke, *Royal West African Frontier Force*, 188–9, 245–9.

[67] Hordern, *East Africa*, i. 265, 561–75; Moyse-Bartlett, *King's African Rifles*, 301, 413.

[68] Lewis J. Greenstein, 'The Nandi Experience in the First World War', in Page (ed.), *Africa*, 82–5; Savage and Munro, *Journal of African History*, VII (1966), 324.

[69] Fendall, *East African Force*, 198–9; Hordern, *East Africa*, i. 575; Moyse-Bartlett, *King's African Rifles*, 333–6.

German East Africa was on the northern frontiers of Kenya and Uganda, against Somalis, Swazis, and Abyssinians. Their contribution to the major theatres of war was therefore indirect. Henceforth, Lettow was not tying down white troops that could be deployed in France and Flanders. A major strategic rationale for his campaign had been eroded.

The Africanization of the British effort in East Africa did not resolve its logistical problems. On 28 November 1916 715 of 980 other ranks in the Gold Coast Regiment were on the sick list; ironically, the British officers, with nineteen out of thirty-six unfit, were rather more robust.[70] The supply arrangements reached their nadir on the Rufiji in February 1917. Half rations were ordered. The daily food allocation averaged 17 ounces, predominantly of maize. Carriers ate roots and berries, and consequently died of alkaloidal poisoning.[71] Labour was at a premium: 12,000 porters were needed for every 3,000 soldiers, and the British forces on the Rufiji required 135,000, and eventually 175,000.[72] A. R. Hoskins, Smuts's successor, had taken over an army robbed of offensive capacity. Only his West African units could be deemed reliable; it would be some months before the new battalions of the King's African Rifles were sufficiently trained to face the *Schütztruppen*.

Lettow's problems were worse. The area into which he had now retreated was the focus of the Maji-Maji rebellion: to the south the Makonde had welcomed the Portuguese, to the west some of the Wangeni in Songea had joined Northey. The rains had failed in 1913/14 and 1914/15, and famine ensued. Two armies had entered a region already made destitute. Lettow had reckoned on having 450,000 kilos of corn stored between the Rufiji and the Mbemkuru. On 26 January 1917 he learned he had only 350,000. There were a further 150,000 kilos in the Lindi area, but to bring them north would have required porters, and his ration strength was already a quarter above what he had anticipated. Lettow dispensed with all useless mouths, handing over to the British those not fit to fight. Each European was reduced to five porters, each company to 150, and those on the lines of communication were sent home: a total of 8,000 carriers were thus discharged. Rations, which might otherwise have been cut to a quarter, were set at a third.

---

[70] Haywood and Clarke, *Royal West African Frontier Force*, 183.
[71] Killingray and Matthews, *Canadian Journal of African Studies*, XIII (1979), 18.
[72] Miller, *Battle for the Bundu*, 256.

The askari (including his wife or boy) got between 600 and 700 grammes of meal a day, the Europeans about 6 kilos of food for twenty-eight days. Maize was eaten before it ripened. Sickness rates reached 80 per cent among the Europeans, and dysentery ravaged the blacks.[73]

Lettow's objective was to hold the ground south of the Rufiji until the harvest ripened in March and April. Even sowing the crops was complicated, given the loss of labour and the lack of pre-existing German administrative control in the area. But the rains were heavier and more prolonged than for some years. The harvest was good, although the water flooded the fields and impeded its distribution.[74]

On the Rufiji, Hoskins's paralysis saved Lettow. To the north-west, Deventer's line of communications from Iringa to Dodoma was sundered by the flooded Ruaha, which reached a width of 26 kilometres. His push on Lukegata was reduced to three battalions and a squadron, and then halted entirely. Only Northey remained active. His forces were healthier, not so much because half of them were blacks but because they were operating on the higher ground away from the coast. In January a captured German message revealed that the detachments under Kraut and Wintgens were dependent on supplies in the area north of Songea. Northey's columns began to converge on Iringa from Lupembe and Songea.

Wahle's main concentration was now to Northey's north, threatening Hoskins's right flank while converging on Lettow. The food available to him was not sufficient to support Kraut's and Wintgens's men, and on 29 January he ordered them to move south and north, to feed off the enemy lines of communication. Kraut entered the area between the Ruvuma and Lake Nyasa, marching first south-east and then north-west, before finally turning east along the Ruvuma to Tunduru.

Kraut told Wintgens to follow him. Wintgens refused and took his 524 men north-west towards Tundala, and thence along the Northern Rhodesian border towards Tabora. Wintgens fed off the land, causing mayhem on the supply routes stretched across German East Africa. The

[73] Boell, *Operationen*, 316–17; Lettow-Vorbeck, *Reminiscences*, 160–2, 175–80; Marine-Archiv, *Kämpfe der kaiserlichen Marine*, 253–5; Taute, *Tanganyika Notes and Records*, 8 (1939), 5–6, 14–15; Deppe, *Mit Lettow-Vorbeck*, 136–41.

[74] Schnee, *Deutsch-Ostafrika*, 141–2, 269–75.

pursuit, conducted initially by Northey's Lupembe column, traversed a land already laid bare.

As the Germans approached Bismarckburg early in March, the British asked the Belgians if they could use the western end of the central railway, within the Belgian area of occupation; they also requested permission to recruit. Two months previously, anxious to limit Belgium's gains, Britain had told it that its assistance was no longer required. Only 2,000 of the *Force publique* remained in German East Africa, others had been demobilized, many of the whites had returned to Europe, and the porters had dispersed or entered British service. By handing Tabora over to the British the Belgians had left the protection of Urundi and Ruanda against any fresh German offensive to their allies. Nonetheless, they preferred to offer the British troops rather than indirect support. At the beginning of April Hoskins and Huyghé, Tombeur's successor, agreed on a Belgian contribution of 6,600 askaris, 600 Europeans, and 18,000 porters. In reality, only 456 Europeans were available, and therefore junior officers occupied senior posts; 5,000 of the 18,000 porters were already in British service and could not be released. The Hoskins–Huyghé plan, to deploy 4,000 rifles in Wintgens's path, was unrealizable.[75] Without porters, the Belgians could not move with sufficient speed.

On 1 May the British element in the pursuit was changed. Northey's column fell back south, and a new force of 1,700 men, including a King's African Rifles battalion still under training, took up the running. The Germans were approaching Tabora. On 21 May Wintgens himself, sick with typhus, surrendered. Heinrich Naumann, his successor, planned to rejoin Wahle by marching south-east, but finding his path barred he moved north-east, across the central railway, towards Mwanza and Lake Victoria. Responsibility for this area had been passed over to the Colonial Office, and friction between the army and the civilian administration now added to the problems of British and Belgian co-ordination. The lack of a united command meant that the pursuit was devoid of consistency or purpose. Early in July Naumann, now operating in the north around Ikoma, flirted with the idea of a raid on Nairobi. But instead he decided to thrust south in an effort to reunite his troops with Lettow's. By August he realized that he could never get through, and divided his

---

[75] Belgique, *Campagnes coloniales belges*, iii. 11–17, 24, 33–52, 121.

command into three sections, each to go in divergent directions with the aim of drawing as many British troops from the main theatre as possible. The section sent to the south-east surrendered on 2 September. But the two northerly sections held out for a further month, Naumann himself raiding Kahe on 29 August. Naumann remained a reluctant guerrilla. At the end his intention, once again, was to link with Lettow, rather than maximize the effects of dispersion. Nonetheless, he had conducted a classic guerrilla operation.[76] His men had marched almost 3,200 kilometres since February; they had found a population that was passively, if not actively, supportive; they had drawn the attention of up to 6,000 men away from the main battle.

Wintgens's and Naumann's marches served to deepen London's frustration with Hoskins's failure to complete a campaign already pronounced victorious by Smuts. Hoskins, however, was the first, and last, British commander-in-chief in East Africa who appreciated the constraints under which he was operating. His knowledge of local conditions, his awareness of the training needs of the African troops, led him to avoid the hyperbole of Smutsian advances. From February to May the British forces in East Africa were rebuilt. Their demand for porters—they needed 160,000, and a further 15,000 a month to cover wastage—so exceeded supply (Hoskins had about 40,000 when he took over) that lorries became an increasingly vital component. Hoskins reckoned that one lorry was equivalent to thirty porters, and wanted 400 of them. But lorries were unusable in the rains, and therefore necessitated a pause in operations until May.[77]

Hoskins's demands embarrassed both Smuts and his new colleagues in the War Cabinet. Warnings against the presumption of speedy or easy victory chimed ill with the South African's claim that the campaign was effectively over. If the spoils of East Africa were to go to Pretoria, Smuts had to argue that his South Africans had done the job. If they had not, then the credibility of white South African citizen soldiers would be forfeit to the subsequent achievements of blacks. 'Military training of the native' in Central Africa would thereby be endorsed, and, he warned in May 1917, would eventually present 'a danger to civilization'.[78] Personal

---

[76] Boell, *Operationen*, 325–32.   [77] Hodges, *Carrier Corps*, 51–7.
[78] McLaughlin, *Small Wars and Insurgencies*, II (1991), 248.

pique coincided with the territorial needs and the racial policies of the Union.

Hoskins recognized that Lettow might well cross the Ruvuma into Portuguese East Africa. His plan, therefore, rested not on continued pushes southward to clear territory, but on a concerted effort to trap the Germans. The British agreement with the Belgians included provision for a column to join Deventer's forces south of Dodoma: their task, once they had dealt with Naumann, was to advance on Mahenge. The Nigerians on the Rufiji would also strike towards Mahenge. Liwale would be approached from the west by Northey and from the east by the 1st division at Kilwa. The brigade at Lindi, which had been occupied on 16 September 1916, was to break free of Looff's attentions and aim for Masasi, so cutting German communications to the south.

The chances of trapping Lettow seemed good. The main German forces were deployed along the coast rather than inland, presumably in the hope that a third supply ship might break the blockade. In April Lettow concentrated south of Kilwa. On 3 June Wahle, his junction with Lettow complete, was given overall authority around Lindi. But on 29 May, before the British offensive could get under way, Hoskins was relieved of his command. Smuts's lobbying had convinced Sir William Robertson, the chief of the imperial general staff, that Hoskins was losing his grip, and that his successor should be 'Jaap' van Deventer.[79] Once again a British regular had been replaced by an Afrikaner amateur. Deventer's instructions were to end the campaign as soon as possible; with merchant tonnage losses soaring in the Atlantic, the objective was to save shipping. He was given no territorial or operational objectives.

Lettow's strengths against the British converging movements remained interior lines and deployment in depth. For neither side was the apparent front line, the Rufiji, of major concern. The key battles of the second half of 1917 were fought around Kilwa and Lindi. The foundation of Lettow's strategy was the containment of the British attempt to break out from Lindi, thus keeping open the Germans' route to the south. In June Lettow reinforced Wahle at the expense of the Kilwa front.

Like Hoskins, and unlike Smuts, Deventer realised that his object should be the destruction of the *Schütztruppen* in battle, not the

[79] Hodges, *Carrier Corps*, 51.

occupation of territory through massive turning movements. Deventer was also aware, as Hoskins had been, that Lettow intended ultimately to move into Portuguese territory. He therefore remained loyal to Hoskins's plan, consolidating his position at Lindi so as to cut off the Germans' line of retreat. But Kilwa had the better harbour, and his main initial effort came from there. On 19 July the three converging British columns from Kilwa were fought to a standstill by a German force of 945 men, enrenched in strong positions at Narungombe. The Germans, reduced to five rounds of ammunition per man and unaware that Lettow was marching north to reinforce them the next day, fell back to Nahungu, on the Mbemkuru.[80] But Deventer's progress on the Kilwa front was halted until September. On the 19th of that month, his communications extended to enable the next advance, Deventer's Kilwa force moved on Nahungu. In the next eighteen days the Germans counted thirty-seven separate engagements, many of them battles for the control of water supplies. The thick bush impeded not only the British aerial reconnaissance but also the Germans' co-ordination on the ground. The British were again held on 27 September, but the Germans fell back once more. They were running low on smokeless ammunition, and by 1 October were having to rely on the 1871-model carbine, whose bullets used black powder, so providing targets for British guns.[81] Deventer now decided to put his weight on the Lindi sector. He ordered the Nigerian brigade to detach itself from the Kilwa force and march on Nyangoa, so converging with the Lindi force attacking from the east.

However, British intelligence had lost track of Lettow himself. The German commander moved between fronts, his attention during the August lull increasingly drawn south to Masasi and Tunduru, one of Northey's columns having begun operations along the Portuguese frontier. Whether the Nigerian brigade's task was to envelope Wahle as he faced the Lindi force, or to prevent a junction between Wahle and Lettow is therefore not entirely clear. Lettow himself saw the opportunity to strike a decisive blow, using his interior lines to effect a concentration in a way that had eluded him at Narungombe and Nahungu. The Nigerians' eight-day march, dogged by lack of water, halved their effective strength

[80] Schwarte, *Weltkampf*, iv. 406; Boell, *Operationen*, gives dates a day later than those given in British accounts.
[81] Deppe, *Mit Lettow-Vorbeck*, 296–305.

to 1,000 men. Rather than envelop the Germans, they themselves were encircled. Lettow had concentrated a total of eighteen out of twenty-five available companies. In a fierce four-day battle at Mahiwa, beginning on 15 October and fought at close quarters, ground was won and lost up to six times. The Lindi force found itself endeavouring to break through Wahle and so extricate the Nigerians from Lettow's clutches. British losses totalled 2,700 out of 4,900 engaged. But German casualties, though ostensibly light (about 600), were relatively more serious. By the second day the number of wounded exceeded the number of porters to carry them, and men with three or four injuries continued to fight. Wahle's command lost nearly 30 per cent of its combat strength, and two field companies were disbanded. Moreover, all their smokeless ammunition (500,000 rounds) was expended, machine-guns had to be destroyed, and only twenty-five rounds remained for each of the older-pattern rifles.[82] Command failures gave Lettow the opportunity to defeat the British in detail, but he could not take his chance. Mahiwa was the first sustained battle of the entire campaign. It confirmed that the avoidance of combat had been the strategy not of Lettow but of Smuts; it also demonstrated that such a strategy had served Germany's interests rather better than Britain's.[83]

The third major German group, in addition to those round Kilwa and Lindi, was the twelve companies in the Mahenge area, from 9 May under the command of Theodor Tafel. Deventer's plan was for the Belgians to advance on Mahenge from Kilosa. But the Mahenge region had been stripped bare by the Germans, and consequently the Belgians could not live off the land to the extent that they had done in the Tabora campaign. Too few porters were collected in time to allow them to take part in the first stages of the July offensive. Carriers recruited from the Belgian-occupied areas of East Africa proved useless in the pursuit of Naumann; the British therefore allowed the Belgians to requisition up to 6,000 porters in their zone of occupation to replace the 5,000 previously handed to the British by the Belgians; a further 10,000 were raised in the Congo between July and November 1917. The Belgians were finally

[82] Boell, *Operationen*, 377, gives total German losses of 580; Lettow, *Reminiscences*, says 800. See also Haywood and Clarke, *Royal West African Frontier Force*, 207–35; Schnee, *Deutsch-Ostafrika*, 255; Deppe, *Mit Lettow-Vorbeck*, 165, 260–1.
[83] Hodges, *Carrier Corps*, 51.

ready to move in September, and on 9 October occupied Mahenge. Tafel withdrew to the south-east. Further supply problems delayed the Belgian pursuit for eight days. Then the rains came and the road from Kilosa to Mahenge was rendered impracticable. Two Belgian battalions, the most that could be fed, were left at Mahenge, and the rest pulled back to the central railway for redeployment to Kilwa and Lindi.[84]

Tafel made good his escape to the south-east. Northey's columns, reorganized in July with bases at Lupembe, Songea, and Fort Johnston, entered Liwale on 29 October. But his force was now up to 480 kilometres from its Lake Nyasa bases and the striking powers of each component limited. Tafel broke through Northey's screen on 15 November and made for Newala, hoping to link with Lettow.

Lettow had gone. Between April and September 1917 a detachment of Kraut's force, 400 strong, had entered Portuguese territory, and reached as far south as Lurio and Fort Johnston. This preliminary reconnaissance suggested that the local population would be friendly and the country fertile. At a conference at Lukuledi on 24 October the German leaders debated their next step. Schnee, the defeat of his colony complete, advocated surrender. Lettow answered with an argument that drew its inspiration as much from Schnee's own creed, that of German colonialism, as it did from the needs of war in Europe. With German territory forfeit, Germany's claim to be an African power resided in the *Schütztruppen* themselves.[85] They must carry on the war across the Ruvuma, in Portuguese East Africa, so maintaining German presence in Africa until the peace. Schnee agreed.

Practical as well as political considerations shaped the German decision. The area between the Rufiji and the Ruvuma was on the brink of famine. The harvest was not due until March, and in the event the rains failed in November. Lettow had sufficient food for six weeks. His stocks of quinine would last a month. He could not fight in order to capture supplies because the ammunition situation made him reliant on the 1871-pattern carbines and two-thirds of his force were equipped with the 1898-models or captured British equivalents. The artillery ammunition, so painstakingly dried and reassembled in 1915–16, had got wet again: in 1917

---

[84] Belgique, *Campagnes coloniales belges*, iii. 121–219.
[85] Mosley, *Duel for Kilimanjaro*, 174–5.

the fuses in particular required refabrication. He now had only enough shells for two mountain guns, and the last of the *Königsberg*'s guns was destroyed. Lettow therefore shaped his force according to his resources. In July his rifle strength had been 800 Europeans and 5,500 askaris. On 25 November, when he crossed the Ruvuma, he took 300 Europeans and 1,700 askaris. One thousand fit askaris were left behind, as well as over 1,500 Europeans, mostly the sick and wounded, and women and children. At least 3,000 blacks—wives, porters, and boys—accompanied the *Schütztruppen*; their families' presence was a major factor in the continuing loyalty of the askari, and only a small number responded to British appeals to surrender.[86]

Mahiwa, for all its self-inflicted damage to the Germans, enabled them to break contact with the British. The Kilwa force, its line of communications now 200 kilometres long, could not open a shorter connection through Lindi until the Lindi force was ready to resume its movement. Deventer planned to round up Lettow's forces in the area of Chiwata. He asked the Portuguese to demonstrate north of the Ruvuma in the hope of blocking the Germans to the south, and so encouraging them to hold Newala. But the junction of the Kilwa and Lindi columns was not effected until 11 November. By then the major threat seemed not to be Lettow but Tafel. His command, a ration strength of 5,471, including 181 Europeans and 1,558 askaris, still had 262,000 smokeless rounds. On 20 November three out of four British columns were directed against Tafel. Uncertain of the whereabouts of the German western forces, Deventer also lost track of Lettow's lines of march, covered by the thick bush of the Makonde plateau from aerial observation. Deventer got Tafel. However, his success was the result, not of manoeuvre nor of battle, but of a loss of nerve on the part of the German commander. Tafel crossed the Ruvuma, failed to find either food or Lettow, and then returned into German East Africa, surrendering on 28 November.

Mindful of the experiences of a year previously, Deventer did not at first follow Lettow into Portuguese territory. Fear of the rains (which in practice proved far less heavy than on the Rufiji), and the need to regroup, brought the British to a halt. Deventer issued a somewhat optimistic summons to Schnee to surrender. It was ignored. He saw the move into

---

[86] Lettow-Vorbeck, *Reminiscences*, 216–25; Schoen, *Deutschen Feuerwerkswesens*, 1455–6.

Portuguese territory as short-lived, reckoning that the Germans would recross the Ruvuma once the harvest was ripe in the Songea region. His immediate operational objectives were consequently defensive—to stop the Germans breaking back into German East Africa and to guard Nyasaland. He reduced his forces, sending the Nigerians home and keeping only the Gold Coast Regiment and the King's African Rifles.

Nor was Lettow under any pressure from the Portuguese. A fourth expeditionary force, mustering 5,277 men, had arrived from Lisbon in 1917, and a further 4,509 reinforcements were dispatched to make good the losses to the 1916 expedition. But Portuguese strength in numbers and equipment was betrayed by the poverty of command and morale. Tomas de Sousa Rosa, a cavalryman in tsetse country, who had never been to Africa before, succeeded Gil in September 1917; his tenure 'went beneath the lowest levels of insignificance'.[87]

Portugal's preoccupations in 1917 were not with the Germans but with their own internal order. The Portuguese Makonde, south of the Ruvuma, had never been properly pacified. The tasks of the 1917 expeditionary force were the systematic reduction of tribal resistance in the area, and the construction of a road from the coast inland. By the time of the German invasion the first objective was almost fulfilled but the second was not; the road did not reach Chomba until 30 July 1918.

Concentration in the north weakened Portuguese presence in the south, while at the same time increasing labour demands. The Portuguese drafted their carriers, and neither paid nor fed them. In March 1917 the Makombe rebellion broke out in Portuguese Zambezia. The Portuguese themselves were defeated and besieged in Tete. The revolt derived its strength from traditional elites, who briefly overcame ethnic divisions in the rejection of Portuguese colonialism. The Portuguese held Sena, but their strategy for reconquering an area 800 kilometres broad, and embracing up to 20,000 rebels, was confused. The army and the Mozambique Company found themselves at loggerheads over how best to proceed. The British, aware that the Makombe saw their rule in Rhodesia in a favourable light, refused their allies troops, Nyasaland instead presenting 200 rifles and Southern Rhodesia somewhat belatedly contributing two obsolete machine-guns and 200 drill rifles. In the end African

---

[87] Pélissier, *Naissance du Mozambique*, ii. 704; see also 699–703.

divisions, not imperial co-operation, determined the fate of the rebellion. Between 10,000 and 15,000 Ngoni were called in as auxiliaries, and were promised all the booty they could carry away, including women and children. Thus, by condoning terrorism and slavery, the Portuguese broke the back of the rebellion by the end of 1917.[88]

Neither the Makonde nor the Makombe responded in any obvious way to the possibility of German support. The north-east of the Portuguese colony remained settled throughout the German invasion, an indirect tribute to the Portuguese army's work, and Lettow never penetrated Zambezia. But almost wherever they went the Germans were well received. The Yao in the north-west had accommodated those fugitives from the 1915 Chilembwe rebellion who had escaped into Portuguese East Africa, and had also welcomed the 1917 German expedition. The Lomue, south of the Lurio, and the Angoche, along the coast beneath Mozambique, proved equally hospitable. The Germans, for all that their paper money was worthless, did at least pay for their goods rather than seize them. German doctors attended to the sick. But Lettow did not take the opportunity to turn opposition to Portuguese rule into revolution. The Germans neutralized the African population rather than armed it. Thus, even in 1917–18, and even in Lettow's own hands, the anxiety to buttress collective European colonial rule outweighed immediate military advantage. Lettow still rejected a true strategy of revolutionary warfare.

Nonetheless, with his entry into Portuguese territory Lettow's actual style of operations for the first time conformed to that of a guerrilla leader. His supply position had forced him to reduce his fighting strength. Thus he had to quell his predilection for the offensive. He fought to feed, and to feed he had to keep moving to fresh sources of supply. Mobility, not striking power, was henceforth his major asset. When he crossed the Ruvuma his column was 30 kilometres long, the main body separated by one day's march from its advanced guard and two days' from its rear. Confined to jungle paths, frequently crossing precipitous terrain, the Germans trudged in single file. In such circumstances rapid concentration for battle was impossible. Lettow reorganized his forces into three columns, his own, Wahle's, and Kohl's, each with

---

[88] Ibid., ii. 650–79; Ranger, *St Antony's Papers*, XV (1963), 54–80.

its own supply train and field hospital. By following parallel routes the columns overcame the worst dangers of dispersion. The Germans marched for six hours a day, with a half-hour halt every two hours, and aimed to cover 24 to 32 kilometres a day. It was a considerable achievement. The porters frequently carried additional loads weighing up to 30 kilos; the askaris bore iron rations for fifteen days as well as their rifles and ammunition; their wives on occasion gave birth on the line of march and within hours had rejoined the column.[89]

The greatest potential impediment to mobility, the bush apart, was ill-health. In this respect Lettow's force began its trek with several advantages: only the fittest were selected, thirteen doctors were among them, and the small European complement was adjusted to the available supply of quinine. Plunder made good many deficits in medical supplies. But the Portuguese had done little to eradicate disease within their colony. Locally recruited porters and prolonged residence in native settlements introduced new sicknesses. Smallpox appeared in February and July 1918. In August 1918 pneumonia (not, the German doctors were sure, influenza) struck 250 of the force and killed at least twenty-two. By then only eighty sick could be carried. Periodically they would be collected into a hospital and left, together with a doctor, for the British. By the end of the war Lettow had only six doctors remaining.[90]

The area between the Ruvuma and the Lujenda did not prove as rich as Lettow had hoped. Game formed much of the diet, but the thick, tall vegetation made stalking and shooting difficult. However, now the Germans, effectively for the first time since Tanga, could plunder. The Portuguese frontier forts along the Ruvuma provided arms, ammunition, and European food. At Ngomano, on 25 November 1917, the Germans surprised 1,200 Portuguese troops and captured 600 rifles and 250,000 rounds. Three more forts were taken in December, and the *Schütztruppen* thus re-equipped themselves with Portuguese rifles and almost a million rounds.

Lettow commenced his march south before the rains ceased, so as to maintain his lead over Deventer. Two British battalions from Fort Johnston began to advance on Mwembe in January 1918, and Lettow concen-

[89] Schnee, *Deutsch-Ostafrika*, 353–5; Lettow-Vorbeck, *Reminiscences*, 233–4, 271, 280; Miller, *Battle for the Bundu*, 299–305.
[90] Taute, *Tanganyika Notes and Records*, VIII (1939), 3, 6, 10, 18–20.

trated around Nanungu at the end of February. As the rains eased the Germans were able to rig up a wireless. In late March they heard the news of the German victories in France, and of the imminent capture of Amiens. Their purpose in maintaining a German presence in Africa reaffirmed, Lettow briefly flirted once again with offensive options. His central position seemed to give him the chance to strike enemy forces in isolation, particularly those with longer lines of communication coming from the west. In late April and early May Lettow placed Kohl at Medo to guard him from the east, while he concentrated five companies for a blow to the west. The action at Kireka mountain on 5 May cost him 27 per cent of those engaged.

Deventer's concern was still to stop the Germans going north. He therefore planned to create a line of posts from Port Amelia to Fort Johnston, via Medo and Mahua. The conception was ridiculous: he never possessed the resources to create an impermeable barrier 560 kilometres long. His main base was still at Dar es Salaam. Therefore goods from Britain proceeded via the Cape and Dar, before being transshipped and routed south again to Port Amelia. The conviction that Lettow was about to be defeated had not, despite all the evidence to the contrary, dissipated. Thus, when Port Amelia and later Mozambique were established as intermediate bases, provision was made for 12,000 men to be fed up to 320 kilometres from the coast. Ultimately 33,000 men were dependent on the two ports.[91]

Deventer's other major obstacle was the Portuguese. The presence of Portuguese troops did little more than create supply dumps from which Lettow could replenish his food and ammunition needs. They also antagonized the local population, making it increasingly hard for the British to recruit porters. The British paid the hut tax of those Africans who enlisted as carriers. The effect, however, was to antagonize the local administrators, who were in the habit of appropriating a percentage of the tax for themselves. Ultimately the King's African Rifles lived largely off the land, an expedient which slowed their pursuit as they foraged over areas through which the Germans had already passed. The campaign was fought on Portuguese territory but increasingly without Portuguese participation. In July 1918 Sousa Rosa was recalled to Lisbon and arrested.

[91] The English-language sources on this phase of the campaign are few; see Fendall, *East African Force*, 114–42, and Moyse-Bartlett, *King's African Rifles*, 390–414.

On 22 May Lettow got his major battle. Kohl's column, now effectively his rearguard, was nearly trapped by the British forces from Port Amelia at Korewa, near Maketi. He managed to extricate himself, but at the price of losing all his supplies, including 70,000 rounds, 30,000 rupees, and all Schnee's official documents; Schnee himself was lucky to escape. The British completed their junction from east and west, and the Germans marched south.

On 16 June Lettow captured a Portuguese map showing the area as far as Lugella and Quelimane. Anxious to capitalize on what little intelligence he could garner, he pressed on, aware that the Lugella Company's base might provide rich pickings. He found them at Namakura on 1–3 July. The defences, 3,000 yards in extent, proved too great for the combined Portuguese-British garrison of 1,030 men to hold. Neither ally fought well; in their efforts to escape along the Namakura river many were drowned or eaten by crocodiles; the Germans lost nine men, the British and Portuguese 200 dead and 543 captured. Far more importantly, the booty included ten machine-guns, 350 rifles, 350 tonnes of food, and large quantities of ammunition. The Germans were almost entirely re-equipped with modern British and Portuguese rifles, and had a stock of 813,800 rounds. While the pursuing forces pressed on to Quelimane, anticipating that the next German move would be to strike the harbour there and then go up the Zambezi, the Germans rested at Namakura, drinking the abundant quantities of schnapps which they had looted, and then doubled back to the north-east.

Across the River Namirrue Lettow attacked an isolated British force on the night of 22/3 July, and then captured Namirrue itself. On 28 July he paused at Chalaua, recruiting and training 310 porters as askaris. A captured letter alerted Lettow to the next British move and on 8 August he quitted Chalaua. His direction at first was north-east, but then, having deceived his opponent, he switched to due west, reaching Numarroe on 24 August. The British hoped that Lettow would attack Regone, but their intention of enveloping him while he did so was known to Lettow. He marched north to Lioma. Here he was hard hit by three battalions of the King's African Rifles, losing 48,000 rounds and large quantities of stores. His total casualties between 27 August and 6 September included thirty-nine Europeans, 184 askaris, and 317 porters (242 were reported as missing). His intention now was to aim through the Livingstone

Mountains, around the northern end of Lake Nyasa, and then turn west. He calculated that Deventer would rein in his pursuit and reconcentrate on the central railway to cover Tabora. He was only partly right. Intelligence acquired on 22 September suggested that there were no troops on the Ruvuma, but that there were major concentrations in Nyasaland. Morale was slipping. Lettow's refrain, that their efforts were tying down 30,000 enemy troops, was less persuasive as the *Schütztruppen*'s strength dwindled, their supply and health problems multiplying. On 28 September the Germans recrossed the Ruvuma; they again speculated about a push to the north, aiming to get beyond the Ruaha before mid-December and the advent of the rains.

The projects discussed on 29 September bordered on the fantastical. Some favoured the northern thrust, even as far as Abyssinia, in the hope that it might be pro-German. Others suggested taking ship for Afghanistan (presumably via Persia). But opinion veered once again towards the west, and a march to Angola.[92] The morale of the askaris recovered as they regained their own territory. At Songea, the local population welcomed and resupplied them. At Ubena on 18 October Lettow found papers alerting him to the situation in Europe; thereafter, a number of reports confirmed that Germany was seeking an armistice. The British prepared their defences at Mahenge, Iringa, and Tabora, and, forewarned by the example of Wintgens's raid to the north, anticipated a dash across the central railway. But round Dodoma the requisitioning of grain and livestock in 1915–16 had driven those of the population not taken as porters into the forests and mountains. Cultivation had declined, and the lateness of the rains in 1918–19 meant that shortages turned into famine.[93] Lettow struck west towards Fife, not north. His intention was to raid the depots on the Kasama–Fife road, working along Northey's line of communications, and then push west between lakes Bangweulu and Mweru.

It was a brilliant move. Relations between the administrations of Rhodesia, the British South Africa Company, and the War Office, deteriorating from autumn 1916, had finally collapsed in September. The Company was alarmed by its increasing deficit, forced up by the costs

[92] Deppe, *Mit Lettow-Vorbeck*, 30, 368–9, 396–402.
[93] Maddox, *Journal of African History*, XXXI (1990), 183–5.

of the war, and above all by the requisitioning of carriers for Northey's columns. The Makombe rising, just across the border from Northern Rhodesia, had been a salutary reminder of the need to reward and compensate, not to terrorize and compel, the local population into war service. The strain of sustaining Northey's operations had rebounded. Colonial authority was itself being undermined by their side-effects: crime, illegal repression, and famine. The Colonial Office backed the company; the War Office and the Treasury did not. In September 1918 the Colonial Office acted unilaterally and banned compulsory war recruitment in Northern Rhodesia. When Lettow entered Northern Rhodesia, Northey's forces could not move for lack of porters. In two weeks the Germans advanced 160 kilometres.[94]

On 9 November 1918 Lettow's advance guard entered Kasama. The position of Major E. B. B. Hawkins and his 750 King's African Rifles was unenviable. Lettow was in unknown country but so, effectively, was Hawkins; his only map was a world atlas on a scale of 200 miles to the inch. Lettow's invasion had smashed British prestige, fomenting panic and looting. British askaris were deserting; the Northern Rhodesia Police was mutinous.[95] On 12 November the two sides clashed in the last engagement of the Great War.

The following day Lettow received the news of the armistice. The formal surrender at Abercorn on 25 November revealed a fighting force that, given the chaos in Northern Rhodesia, could easily have sustained itself well into 1919. Lettow's strength was 155 Europeans and 1,156 blacks, armed with thirty-seven machine-guns, 1,071 British and Portuguese rifles, and 208,000 rounds. They had captured sufficient quinine to last until June.

The real restraint on what Lettow might have achieved in November 1918 lay not in the possible efforts of his enemies—he had, after all, successfully struck at their weakest point—but in his own reluctance to embrace a revolutionary strategy. Lettow was an officer of resource and determination, ruthless in war and honourable in peace. He was not a guerrilla. He had proved reluctant to exploit the collapse of Portuguese authority for the purposes of the war. There is no reason to assume he would have behaved any differently in the case of Britain.

[94] Yorke, 'Crisis of colonial control', 272–370.
[95] Ibid. 362–70; Moyse-Bartlett, *King's African Rifles*.

Lettow justified his entire campaign in terms of the number of Entente soldiers committed to the East African theatre. About 160,000 British and Belgian troops, including naval forces, were engaged during the course of the war against the *Schütztruppen*; Smuts had 55,000 men in the field in 1916.[96] However, very few of these, if any, would have been available for the western front. The only point where the British consciously weighed Europe against Africa was over the deployment of the South Africans in 1916; but at that stage, given the political divisions within the Union, the existence of the East African theatre was a convenience rather than an embarrassment. Thereafter the Africans themselves took the burden. Total British losses in East Africa were 3,443 killed in action and 6,558 died of disease.[97] It is only with the inclusion of porters, a local resource not readily employable elsewhere, that casualty figures reach levels commensurate with the length and breadth of the campaign: British losses then rise to over 100,000 dead.[98] Africans, and to a lesser extent Indians, were Lettow's major foe, at least in numerical terms. Their only likely alternative area of operations was the Middle East, not Europe. In practice, Lettow's real diversionary achievement was to be measured in its maritime, not military, effects. In 1917–18, with U-boat warfare at its height, the length of the voyage around the Cape to Dar es Salaam engaged merchant vessels on long-haul voyages when they were badly needed elsewhere. The need for ships, not the need to defeat Lettow per se, underpinned the British war cabinet's impatience with Hoskins's lack of movement in February to May 1917.

During and after the war the Entente powers tried to appropriate the war in Africa as a war for liberalism, a crusade for civilization and enlightenment against repression and brutality. There is little evidence that those who did the fighting, and on behalf of whom these grand claims were advanced, thought in such terms. Many askaris had, by the end of the war, fought for the Germans and the British, and had done their duty to both. Their loyalty was that of the professional or the mercenary—the soldier who takes pride in doing his job well and who fights because that is his vocation. Similarly, the attractions of portering,

[96] The first figure is from Crowder, 'The First World War', 291; the second from Moyse-Bartlett, *King's African Rifles*, 413. Boell, *Operationen*, 32, gives 240,000.

[97] Iliffe, *Tanganyika*, 246.

[98] Hodges, *Journal of African History*, XIX (1978), 115.

if there were any, were pecuniary: the pay was better than in other comparable occupations. The causes so vehemently espoused in Europe relied on a well-developed sense of nationalism; in Africa no such nationalism yet existed, and if it had it would have undermined, not supported, the war efforts of both sides.

The Great War was the prelude to the final stage of the scramble for Africa, played out at Versailles. Despite all their misgivings at the outset, the European powers advanced rather than retarded the cause of colonialism between 1914 and 1918. The opposition which they encountered was tribal and traditional; glimmerings of modern resistance—the involvement of educated elites in the Chilembwe rebellion, inter-ethnic unity in the Makombe rising—remained short-lived. Instead, the marches of the armies, the wiles of the recruiting parties, the supply needs of their men, spread the colonial nexus through the agencies of the market, of cash, of cartography, and of communications. Because, by 1914, colonialism had begun to move from conquest to civilization, the armies' contribution to its advancement was not apparent: what the European powers saw was the withdrawal of white administrators and the Africanization of missions. But the war reinvigorated territorial ambitions dormant since the turn of the century. Annexation or retention remained the dominant European motivation in the war in Africa, even if not so clearly elsewhere. Ebermaier's and Schnee's primary concern was to sustain Germany in Africa, not Germany in Europe. Similarly, Smuts's emphasis on manoeuvre rather than on battle derived from his principal objective, the conquest of territory. Lettow-Vorbeck's principal achievement was, perhaps, the thwarting of the full extent of South Africa's annexationist ambitions.[99] He himself appeared a guerrilla because his interpretation of colonialism was contrasting, not congruent; for Lettow, as for Zimmerman, in the last analysis Germany's African claims resided not in the preservation of land but in the unity of the *Schütztruppen* themselves. In a war redolent with eighteenth-century parallels, it was perhaps appropriate that the heirs of Frederickian Prussia should still interpret the army as the embodiment of the state.

[99] Wolfgang Petter, 'Der Kampf um die deutschen Kolonien', in Michalka (ed.), *Der Erste Weltkrieg*, 406

FURTHER READING

The bibliography which follows this guide to further reading gives full details of author, title, place and date of publication. Therefore, unless strictly necessary for purposes of clarification, the discussion which follows refers to books by their author only.

In general the war in Africa has been neglected by scholars. However, the enthusiasm for war aims in the 1970s did not pass Africa by, not least because Fischer himself gave full attention to Germany's ambitions in central Africa. Since then France has been best served, by Andrew and Kanya-Forstner. Yearwood has done important work on west Africa, Louis looks at British aims in the German colonies as a whole, and Digre relates the wartime debate to the peace treaties.

Most historians of Africa have been more interested in the war's cultural, social and economic impacts. An excellent representative collection of their work is the volume edited by Melvin Page. This focuses particularly on the experience of the carriers, and further research in the same vein is to be found in the articles by Savage and Munro, Thomas, Hodges and Killingray. France's conscription of men in west Africa was the subject of an exhaustive work by Michel, but those without French will need to read Clayton or Echenberg, both of whom have remits broader than the First World War. The combination of labour demands and the withdrawal of colonial administrators created a crisis of imperial control which can best be understood through the studies of individual colonies. Iliffe is in a class of his own on Tanganyika, but Osuntukun is thorough on Nigeria, and Yorke revealing on Northern Rhodesia. For the lesser colonial powers, see Pélissier on Portugal in Angola and Mozambique, and Louis on Belgium in *Ruanda-Urundi*. The Belgian official history of its army's role in Africa is disproportionately massive.

Works like these expose the social and economic underpinnings of campaigns which more traditional historians have described in purely military terms. In all this military history is the poor relation. Killingray's essay in Strachan's *Oxford Illustrated History* is a brief survey which pulls

together most of the threads, but there is nothing which is simultaneously as scholarly while being more substantial. Lucas is dated, and he
provides succinct, readable accounts of all the African campaigns from a
British perspective. Farwell is more recent and more readily available, but
he does not go beyond the English-language memoirs and their assumptions. German first-hand accounts were collected by Foerster and Greiner, and by Heichen, but both were committed to a positive view of
Germans as colonisers. Lunn and Page, by the use of oral history, have
given Africans a voice that they were in danger of never finding.

A clutch of articles—by Garson, Katzenellenbogen, Nasson and Spies
—provide a synoptic and convergent view of South Africa's response to
the outbreak of the war. The rebellion is succinctly covered by Davenport
and Walker. Smuts—at least in respect to his wartime ambitions for
South Africa—remains an opaque figure in Hancock's hands. Hyam is
essential if the reader is to grasp the expansionist agenda of the Union.

There is no account of the campaign in South-West Africa written
from primary sources. L'Ange is the most recent from a South African
perspective, and supplements, if it does not replace, Collyer. Collyer was a
participant in the campaign, and so too was the more lively and intelli-
gent Reitz, a former Boer commando and a future High Commissioner in
London. Of the German narratives, Seitz is probably superior to Hennig
and Oelhafen, principally because as governor he had a broader perspective.

Grove is perfectly adequate on Togoland, and what he says can be
found at greater length in Moberley's official history. Sebald gives the
German story, and Klein-Arendt says more about its key strategic target,
its wireless station.

It is impossible to understand the Cameroons campaign simply from
the English-language sources, which remain hung up on Duala as the
pivotal objective. Moberley's detailed official history thus reflects the
inadequacies of British intelligence. Gorges is the other principal British
account, written by a participant. The French official history, volume IX
of *Les Armées françaises dans la Grande Guerre*, is vital for any sort of
balance, and Aymérich gives the perspective of the French columns in the
south of the colony. But he did not understand German strategy any
better than the British. If they had read Mentzel—the single best book on
the campaign—they would have been amazed.

Both Schwarte's multi-volume account of the war and the German official history of land operations, the Reichsarchiv's *Der Weltkrieg*, treated the campaigns in Africa superficially, although there is much useful information in the Marine-Archiv's volumes on the navy, especially for east Africa. Most historians have therefore fallen back on Lettow-Vorbeck's self-serving memoirs. The result has been that their understanding of the fighting in east Africa is almost as inadequate as of that in the west. Of the swathe of popular histories in English, Charles Miller's racy but cogent narrative does best. The others can be safely discarded. None of them used the full account by one of Lettow's staff officers, Boell, who was employed by the Reichsarchiv as the official historian of the campaign. His drafts were destroyed in the Second World War, but he painstakingly reconstructed them. Anderson's books use Boell, as well as primary sources in German and English. Moreover, he carries the story onto the war's end, unlike Hordern, the British official historian, whose death meant that he left off in 1916. Lettow apart, east Africa has produced some stimulating and suggestive memoirs. In English, both Meinertzhagen and Fendall are often scathing about Smuts's command. In German, Schnee puts Lettow in context, and goes much further in explaining how German East Africa held out for so long. Deppe is also a useful corrective to Lettow. English war literature tends to concentrate on the western front, but if there is a contribution to the genre from the war in Africa it is by Francis Brett Young.

BIBLIOGRAPHY

Afflerbach, Holger, *Falkenhayn. Politisches Denken und Handeln im Kaiserreich* (Munich, 1994).
—— 'Wilhelm II as supreme warlord in the First World War', *War in History*, V (1998), 427–49.
Afigbo, A. E., *The Warrant Chief: Indirect Rule in Southeastern Nigeria 1891–1929* (London, 1972).
Ageron, Charles-Robert, *Les Algériens musulmans et la France (1871–1919)*, 2 vols. (Paris, 1968).
Ahmad, Kamal Madhar, *Kurdistan during the First World War* (London, 1994).
Ajayi, J. F. A., and Michael Crowder (eds.), *History of West Africa*, vol. II, (London, 1974).
Albertini, Luigi, *The Origins of the War of 1914*, 3 vols. (London, 1957).
Ally, Russell, 'War and gold—the Bank of England, the London gold market and South Africa's gold, 1914–1919', *Journal of Southern African Studies*, XVII (1991), 221–38.
al-Rahim, Muddathir 'Abd, *Imperialism and Nationalism in the Sudan: A Study in Constitutional and Political Development* (Oxford, 1969).
Anderson, Ross, 'The Battle for Tanga', *War in History*, VIII (2001) 294–322.
——, *The Battle of Tanga 1914* (Stroud, 2002).
——, *The Forgotten Front: The East Africa Campaign 1914–1918* (Stroud, 2004)
Andrew, Christopher, *Secret Service: The Making of the British Intelligence Community* (London, 1985).
Andrew, Christopher M., and A. S. Kanya-Forstner, *France Overseas: The Great War and the Climax of French Imperial Expansion* (London, 1981).
—— and ——, 'France, Africa, and the First World War', *Journal of African History*, XIX (1978), 11–23.
—— and ——, 'The French colonial party and French colonial war aims 1914–1918', *Historical Journal*, XVII (1974), 79–106.
Andrews, E. M., *The Anzac Illusion: Anglo-Australian Relations during World War I* (Cambridge, 1993).
Anglesey, Marquess of, *A History of the British Cavalry*, 8 vols. (London, 1973–96).
Assmann, Kurt, *Deutsche Seestrategie in zwei Weltkriegen*, (Heidelberg, 1957).
Avery, Peter, *Modern Iran* (London, 1965).
—— Gavin Hambly, and Charles Melville, *From Nadir Shah to the Islamic Republic: The Cambridge History of Iran*, vol. VII (Cambridge, 1991).

Austen, Ralph A., *Northwest Tanzania under German and British Rule: Colonial Policy and Tribal Politics, 1889–1939* (New Haven, 1968).

Aymérich, J., *La conquête du Cameroun 1er août 1914–20 février 1916* (Paris, 1933).

Balfour, Michael, *The Kaiser and his Times* (London, 1964).

Barooah, Nirode Kumar, *India and the Official Germany 1886–1914* (Frankfurt, 1971).

Barrett, John, 'The rank and file of the colonial army in Nigeria', *Journal of Modern African Studies*, XV (1977), 105–15.

Beadon, R. H., *The Royal Army Service Corps*, vol. II (Cambridge, 1931).

Beckett, Ian F. W., 'The Singapore mutiny of February, 1915', *Journal of the Society for Army Historical Research*, LXII (1984), 132–53.

Beesly, Patrick, *Room 40: British Naval Intelligence 1914–18* (London, 1982).

Belgique, Royaume de: Ministère de la Défense Nationale—Etat-Major Général de l'Armée Section de l'Historique, *Les Campagnes coloniales belges 1914–1918*, 3 vols. (Brussels, 1927–32).

Bell, A. C., *A History of the Blockade of Germany and of the Countries Associated with her in the Great War, Austria-Hungary, Bulgaria, and Turkey* (London, 1937; actually published 1961).

Benary, Albert (ed.), *Das Ehrenbuch der deutschen Feldartillerie* (Berlin, [c. 1930]).

Bennett, Geoffrey, *Coronel and the Falklands* (London, 1962).

—— *Naval Battles of the First World War* (London, 1968).

Bernard, Philippe, and Henri Dubief, *The Decline of the Third Republic 1914–1938* (Cambridge, 1985; first published 1975–6).

Bernhardi, Friedrich von, *Germany and the Next War* (London, 1914).

Bidwell, Robin, *Morocco under Colonial Rule: French Administration of Tribal Areas 1912–1956* (London, 1973).

Bihl, Wolfdieter, 'Das im Herbst 1914 geplante-Schwarzmeer-Unternehmen der Mittelmächte', *Jahrbücher für Geschichte Osteuropas*, NS XIV (1966), 326–66.

—— *Die Kaukasus-Politik der Mittelmächte. Teil 1. Ihre Basis in der Orient-Politik und ihre Aktionen 1914–1917* (Vienna, 1975).

Bitsch, Marie-Thérèse, *La Belgique entre La France et l'Allemagne 1905–1914* (Paris, 1994).

Blake, Robert *The Unknown Prime Minister: The Life and Times of Andrew Bonar Law 1858–1923* (London, 1955).

Blenkinsop, L. J., and J. W. Rainey, *History of the Great War based on Official Documents: Veterinary Services* (London, 1925).

Boell, Ludwig, *Die Operationen in Ostafrika* (Hamburg, 1951).

Boemeke, Manfred F., Roger Chickering, and Stig Förster (eds.), *Anticipating Total War: The German and American Experiences 1871–1914* (Cambridge, 1999).

Borgert, Heinz-Ludger, 'Grundzüge der Landkriegführung von Schlieffen bis Guderian', in Militärgeschichtliche Forschungsamt, *Handbuch zur deutschen Militärgeschichte 1648–1939*, vol. IX (Munich, 1979).

Bosworth, Richard, *Italy and the Approach of the First World War* (London, 1983).

Bourne, J. M., *Britain and the Great War 1914–1918* (London, 1989).

Bourne, K., and D. C. Watt (eds.), *Studies in International History* (London, 1967).

—— and Roger Bullen, *The Great Powers and the European States System 1815–1914* (London, 1980).

Brock, Michael, and Eleanor Brock (eds.), *H. H. Asquith: Letters to Venetia Stanley,* (Oxford, 1985; first published 1982).

Brodie, Bernard, *Sea Power in the Machine Age,* 2nd edn. (Princeton, 1943).

Brown, Emily C., *Har Dayal: Hindu Revolutionary and Rationalist* (Tucson, 1975).

Brown, Judith, *Gandhi's Rise to Power: Indian Politics 1915–1922* (Cambridge, 1972).

—— *Modern India: The Origins of an Asian Democracy* (Delhi, 1985).

Buhrer, J., *L'Afrique orientale allemande et la guerre de 1914–1918* (Paris, 1922).

Bunselmeyer, Robert E., *The Cost of the War 1914–1919: British Economic War Aims and the Origins of Reparation* (Hamden, Conn., 1975).

Burdick, Charles B., *The Japanese Siege of Tsingtau: World War I in Asia* (Hamden, Conn., 1976).

Burke, Edmund, 'Moroccan resistance, pan-Islam and German war strategy, 1914–1918', *Francia,* III (1975), 434–64.

Busch, Briton Cooper, *Britain, India, and the Arabs, 1914–1921* (Berkeley, 1971).

Cain, P. J., and A. G. Hopkins, *British Imperialism: Crisis and Deconstruction 1914–90* (London, 1993).

Callwell, C. E., *Experiences of a Dug-out 1914–1918* (London, 1920).

Cassar, George H., *Kitchener: Architect of Victory* (London, 1977).

—— *Asquith as War Leader* (London, 1994).

Castex, Raoul, *Théories stratégiques,* 5 vols. (Paris, 1927–35).

Cecco, Marcello de, *The International Gold Standard: Money and Empire,* 2nd edn. (London, 1984).

Cecil, Hugh, and Peter Liddle (eds.), *Facing Armageddon: The First World War Experienced* (London, 1996).

—— and —— (eds.), *At the Eleventh Hour: Reflections, Hopes and Anxieties at the Closing of the Great War, 1918,* (Barnsley, 1998).

Charbonneau, Jean, 'La Grande Guerre sous l'équateur', *Revue militaire française,* 129, (1932), 397–420; 130 (1932), 80–99.

Clayton, Anthony, *France, Soldiers and Africa* (London, 1988).

Coetzee, Frans, and Marilyn Shevin-Coetzee (eds.), *Authority, Identity and the Social History of the Great War* (Providence, 1995).

Cohen, Stuart A., *British Policy in Mesopotamia 1903–1914* (London, 1976).

Cohen, Stuart A., 'The genesis of the British campaign in Mesopotamia, 1914', *Middle Eastern Studies*, XII (1976), 119–32.

Collyer, J. J., *The Campaign in German South West Africa 1914–1915* (Pretoria, 1937).

—— *The South Africans with General Smuts in German East Africa 1916* (Pretoria, 1939).

Corbett, Julian, *Some Principles of Maritime Strategy*, ed. Eric Grove (Annapolis, 1988; first published 1911).

—— and Henry Newbolt, *History of the Great War: Naval Operations*, 5 vols. (London, 1920–31).

Corrigan, H. S. W., 'German–Turkish relations and the outbreak of war in 1914: a reassessment', *Past and Present*, 36, (1967), 144–52.

Cron, Hermann, *Geschichte des deutschen Heeres im Weltkriege 1914–1918* (Osnabrück, 1990; first published 1937).

Crook, Paul, *Darwinism, War and History: The Debate over the Biology of War from the 'Origin of the Species' to the First World War* (Cambridge, 1994).

Crowder, Michael, *Revolt in Bussa: A Study of British Native Administration in Nigerian Borgu, 1902–1935* (London, 1973).

—— 'The First World War and its consequences', in A. Adu Boahen (ed.), *Africa under Colonial Domination 1880–1935*, vol. VII of *UNESCO General History of Africa* (London, 1985).

Crowe, J. H. V., *General Smuts' Campaign in East Africa* (London, 1918).

Cruttwell, C. R. M. F., *A History of the Great War 1914–1918*, 2nd edn. (Oxford, 1936).

—— *The Role of British Strategy in the Great War* (Cambridge, 1936).

Dahlhaus, Friedrich, *Möglichkeiten und Grenzen auswärtiger Kultur-und Pressepolitik dargestellt am Beispiel der deutschen–türkischen Beziehungen 1914–1918* (Frankfurt am Main, 1990).

Dallin, Alexander et al., *Russian Diplomacy and Eastern Europe 1914–1917* (New York, 1963).

Daly, M. W., *Empire on the Nile: The Anglo-Egyptian Sudan 1898–1934* (Cambridge, 1986).

Davenport, T. R. H., 'The South Afrcian rebellion 1914', *English Historical Review*, LXXVIII (1963), 73–94.

David, Edward (ed.), *Inside Asquith's Cabinet: From the Diaries of Charles Hobhouse* (London, 1977).

Davis, Lance E., and Robert A. Huttenback, *Mammon and the Pursuit of Empire: the Political Economy of British Imperialism 1860–1912* (Cambridge, 1986).

Davis, Shelby Cullom, *Reservoirs of Men: A History of the Black Troops of French West Africa* (Geneva, 1934).

Delbrück, Clemens von, *Die wirtschaftliche Mobilmachung in Deutschland 1914* (Munich, 1924).

Deppe, Ludwig, *Mit Lettow-Vorbeck durch Afrika* (Berlin, 1919).

Dignan, Don, *The Indian Revolutionary Problem in British Diplomacy 1914–1919* (New Delhi, 1983).

Digre, Brian, *Imperialism's New Clothes: The Repartition of Tropical Africa 1914–1919* (New York, 1990).

Dirks, Uwe, 'Julian S. Corbett und die Britische Seekriegführung 1914–1918', *Militärgeschichtliche Mitteilungen*, 37 (1985), 35–50.

d'Ombrain, Nicholas, *War Machinery and High Policy: Defence Administration in Peacetime Britain 1902–1914* (Oxford, 1973).

Draeger, Hans (ed.), *Gouverneur Schnee: ein Künder und mehrer deutscher Geltung* (Berlin, 1931).

Dua, R. P., *Anglo-Japanese Relations during the First World War* (New Delhi, 1972).

Dülffer, Jost, 'Limitations on naval warfare and Germany's future as a world power: a German debate 1904–1906', *War & Society*, III (1985), 23–43.

Duroselle, Jean-Baptiste, *La France et les français 1914–1920* (Paris, 1972).

—— *La Grande Guerre des français: l'incompréhensible* (Paris, 1994).

Duus, Peter (ed.), *The Cambridge History of Japan*, 6 vols. (Cambridge, 1988–99).

—— Ramon H. Myers, and Mark R. Peattie (eds.), *The Japanese Informal Empire in China, 1895–1937* (Princeton, 1980).

Echenberg, Myron, *Colonial Conscripts: The 'tirailleurs sénégalais' in French West Africa, 1857–1960* (Portsmouth, NH, 1991).

Ekoko, Elango, 'British war plans against Germany in West Africa, 1903–14', *Journal of Strategic Studies*, IV (1984), 440–56.

Elango, Lovett, 'The Anglo-French "condominium" in Cameroon, 1914–1916: the myth and the reality', *International Journal of African Historical Studies*, XVIII (1985), 657–73.

Elgood, Peter, *Egypt and the Army* (Oxford, 1924).

Ellinwood, DeWitt C., and S. D. Pradhan, *India and World War I* (New Delhi, 1978).

Evans-Pritchard, E. E., *The Sanusi of Cyrenaica* (Oxford, 1949).

Falkenhayn, Erich von, *General Headquarters 1914–1916 and its Critical Decisions* (London, [1919]).

Falls, Cyril, *The First World War* (London, 1960).

Farrar, L. L., jr, *The Short-War Illusion: German Policy, Strategy and Domestic Affairs, August–December 1914* (Santa Barbara, 1973).

—— *Divide and Conquer: German Efforts to Conclude a Separate Peace, 1914–1918* (Boulder, Col. 1978).

Farwell, Byron, *The Great War in Africa 1914–1918* (London, 1987).

Fendall, C. P., *The East African Force 1915–1919* (London, 1921).

Ferro, Marc, *The Great War 1914–1918* (London, 1973).

Fischer, Fritz, *Germany's Aims in the First World War* (London, 1967; first published 1961).

Fischer, Fritz, *World Power or Decline: The Controversy over Germany's Aims in the First World War* (London, 1974; first published 1965).

—— *War of Illusions: German Policies from 1911 to 1914* (London, 1975; first published 1969).

Foerster, Wolfgang and Helmuth Greiner (eds.), *Wir Kämpfer im Weltkrieg. Selbstzeugnisse deutscher Frontsoldaten in Feldpostbriefen, Kriegstagbüchern und Aufzeichnungen, vornehmlich aus dem Material des Heeresarchivs Potsdam* (Berlin, n.d.).

Forbes, A., *History of the Army Ordnance Services: The Great War*, 2nd edn. (London, 1931).

France—see Ministère de la Guerre

Fraser, T. G., 'Germany and Indian revolution', *Journal of Contemporary History*, XII (1977), 255–72.

—— 'India in Anglo-Japanese relations during the First World War', *History*, LXIII (1978), 366–82.

French, David, *British Economic and Strategic Planning 1905–1915* (London, 1982).

—— *British Strategy and War Aims 1914–1916* (London, 1986).

—— 'The meaning of attrition, 1914–1916', *English Historical Review*, CIII (1988), 385–405.

Friedman, Isaiah, *Germany, Turkey, and Zionism 1897–1918* (Oxford, 1977).

Frothingham, Thomas, *The Naval History of the World War*, 3 vols. (Cambridge, Mass., 1924–6).

Galbraith, John S., 'British war aims in World War I: a commentary on statesmanship', *Journal of Commonwealth and Imperial History*, XIII (1984), 25–45.

Ganz, A. Harding, 'Colonial policy and the imperial German navy', *Militärgeschichtliche Mitteilungen*, 21 (1977), 35–52

Garcia, Luc, 'Les Mouvements de résistance au Dahomey (1914–1917), *Cahiers d'études africaines*, X (1970), 144–78.

Garson, N. G., 'South Africa and World War I', *Journal of Imperial and Commonwealth History*, VIII (1979), 68–85

Gatzke, Hans W., *Germany's Drive to the West (Drang nach Westen): A Study of Germany's Western War Aims during the First World War* (Baltimore, 1950).

Gehrke, Ulrich, *Persien in der deutschen Orientpolitik während des Ersten Weltkrieges*, 2 vols. (Stuttgart, 1960).

Geiss, Imanuel *July 1914: The Outbreak of the First World War: Selected Documents* (London, 1967).

Gemzell, Carl-Axel, *Organization, Conflict, and Innovation: A Study of German Naval Strategic Planning 1888–1940* (Lund, 1973).

Gershoni, Israel, and James P. Jankowski, *Egypt, Islam, and the Arabs: The Search for Egyptian Nationhood, 1900–1930* (New York, 1986).

Gifford, Prosser, and Wm. Roger Louis (eds.), *Britain and Germany in Africa: Imperial Rivalry and Colonial Rule* (New Haven, 1967).

Gilbert, Martin, *Winston S. Churchill*, vol. III, *1914–1916*, and companion volume (London 1971–2).

Goldschmidt, Arthur, jr, 'The Egyptian nationalist party: 1892–1919', in P. M. Holt (ed.), *Political and Social Change in Modern Egypt* (London, 1968).

Goltz, Colmar von der, *Denkwürdigkeiten* (Berlin, 1932).

Gooch, John, *The Plans of War: The General Staff and British Military Strategy c1900–1916* (London, 1974).

—— *The Prospect of War: Studies in British Defence Policy 1847–1942* (London, 1981).

Gordon, Donald C., *The Dominion Partnership in Imperial Defense, 1870–1914* (Baltimore, 1965).

Gorges, E. Howard, *The Great War in West Africa* (London, 1930).

Görlitz, Walter (ed.), *The Kaiser and his Court: The Diaries, Note Books and Letters of Admiral Georg von Müller, Chief of the Naval Cabinet, 1914–1918* (London, 1961; first published 1959).

Gottlieb, W. W., *Studies in Secret Diplomacy during the First World War* (London, 1957).

Grigg, John, *Lloyd George: From Peace to War 1912–1916* (London, 1985).

Grove, Eric, 'The first shots of the Great War: the Anglo-French conquest of Togo, 1914', *Army Quarterly*, CVI (1976), 308–23.

Grundlingh, Albert, 'Black men in a white man's war: the impact of the First World War on South African blacks', *War & Society*, III (1985), 55–81

Guillen, P. (ed.), *La France et l'Italie pendant la première guerre mondiale* (Grenoble, 1976).

Guinn, Paul, *British Strategy and Politics 1914 to 1918* (Oxford, 1965).

Güth, Rolf, 'Die Organisation der deutschen Marine in Krieg und Frieden 1913–1933', in Militärgeschichtliches Forschungsamt, *Handbuch zur deutschen Militärgeschichte 1684–1939. VIII. Deutsche Marinegeschichte der Neuzeit* (Munich, 1977).

Hadley, Michael L., and Roger Sarty, *Tin-pots and Pirate Ships: Canadian Naval Forces and German Sea Raiders 1880–1918* (Montreal, 1991).

Hagen, Gottfried, *Die Türkei im Ersten Weltkrieg. Flugblätter und Flugschriften in arabischer, persischer und osmanisch-türkischer Sprache aus eines Sammlung der Universitätbibliothek Heidelberg eingeleitet, übersetzt und kommentiert* (Frankfurt am Main, 1990).

Haley, Charles D., 'The desperate Ottoman: Enver Pasha and the German empire', *Middle Eastern Studies*, XXX (1994), 1–51, 224–51.

Halpern, Paul, *The Naval War in the Mediterranean 1914–1918* (London, 1987).

—— *A Naval History of World War I* (London, 1994).

Hancock, W. K., *Smuts: The Sanguine Years 1870–1919* (Cambridge, 1962).

Hancock, W. K., and Jean van der Poel (eds.), *Selections from the Smuts Papers*, vol. III, *June 1910–November 1918* (Cambridge, 1966).

Hankey, Maurice, Lord, *Government Control in War* (Cambridge, 1945).

—— *The Supreme Command 1914–1918*, 2 vols. (London, 1961).

Hanssen, Hans Peter, *Diary of a Dying Empire*, ed. R. H. Lutz, M. Schofield, and O. O. Winther (Port Washington, NY, 1973; first published 1955).

Hardach, Gerd, *The First World War 1914–1918* (London, 1977; first published 1970).

Harper, R. W. E., and Harry Miller, *Singapore Mutiny* (Singapore, 1984).

Hatton, P. H. S., 'The Gambia, the Colonial Office, and the opening moves of the First World War', *Journal of African History*, VII (1966), 123–31.

Haycock, Ronald, and Keith Neilson, *Men, Machines, and War* (Waterloo, Ont., 1988).

Haywood, A., and F. A. S. Clarke, *The History of the Royal West African Frontier Force* (Aldershot, 1964).

Hazlehurst, Cameron, 'Asquith as prime minister, 1908–1916', *English Historical Review*, LXXXV (1970), 502–31.

—— *Politicians at War, July 1914 to May 1915: A Prologue to the Triumph of Lloyd George* (London, 1971).

Headlam, John, *The History of the Royal Artillery from the Indian Mutiny to the Great War*, vol. II 1899–1914 (Woolwich, 1937).

Heichen, Walter, *Helden der Kolonien. Der Weltkrieg in unseren Schutzgebieten* (Berlin, n. d.).

Heine, Peter, 'Sâlih ash-Sharîf at-Tûnisi, a North African nationalist in Berlin during the First World War', *Revue de l'Occident Musulman et de la Mediterra-née*, 33 (1982), 89–95.

Helfferich, Karl, *Der Weltkrieg* (Karlsruhe, 1925; first published 1919).

Heller, Joseph, *British Policy towards the Ottoman Empire 1908–1914* (London, 1983).

Henderson, W. O., *Studies in German Colonial History* (London, 1962).

Hennig, Richard, *Deutsch-Südwest im Weltkriege* (Berlin, 1920).

Herwig, Holger H., 'Admirals versus generals: the war aims of the imperial German navy, 1914–1918', *Central European History*, V (1972), 208–33.

Herwig, Holger H., *'Luxury' Fleet: The Imperial German Navy 1888–1918* (London, 1980).

—— 'The failure of German sea power, 1914–1945: Mahan, Tirpitz and Raeder reconsidered', *International History Review*, X (1988), 68–105.

—— *The First World War: Germany and Austria-Hungary 1914–1918* (London, 1997).

Herzfeld, Hans, *Der Erste Weltkrieg*, 7th edn. (Munich, 1985; first published 1968).

Hewins, W. A. S., *Apolgia of an Imperialist: Forty Years of Empire Policy*, 2 vols. (London, 1929).

Hiery, Hermann, 'West Samoans between Germany and New Zealand', *War & Society*, X (1992), 53–80.

—— *The Neglected War: The German South Pacific and the Influence of World War I* (Honolulu, 1995).

Hinsley, F. H., (ed.), *British Foreign Policy under Sir Edward Grey* (Cambridge, 1977).

L'Histoire, 14–18: mourir pour la patrie (Paris, 1992).

Hobson, J. M., 'The military-extraction gap and the wary Titan: the fiscal sociology of British defence policy 1870–1913', *Journal of European Economic History*, XXII (1993), 461–506.

Hodges, G. W. T., 'African manpower statistics for the British forces in East Africa, 1914–1918', *Journal of African History*, XIX (1978), 101–16.

Hodges, Geoffrey, *The Carrier Corps: Military Labor in the East African Campaign 1914–1918* (Westport, Conn., 1986).

Hoisington, William A., jr, *Lyautey and the French Conquest of Morocco* (Basingstoke, 1995).

Hopkirk, Peter, *On Secret Service East of Constantinople: The Plot to Bring Down the British Empire* (London, 1994).

Hordern, Charles, *Military Operations: East Africa*, vol. I, (London, 1941; no more published).

Horne, John, 'Immigrant workers in France during World War I', *French Historical Studies*, XIV (1985), 57–88.

Hough, Richard, *The Pursuit of Admiral von Spee* (London, 1969).

—— *The Great War at Sea 1914–1918* (Oxford, 1986).

Howard, Harry N., *The Partition of Turkey: A Diplomatic History 1913–1923* (New York, 1966; first published 1931).

Howard, Michael, *The Continental Commitment: The Dilemma of British Defence Policy in Two World Wars* (Harmondsworth, 1974; first published 1972).

Hull, Isobel V., *The Entourage of Kaiser Wilhelm II 1888–1918* (Cambridge, 1982).

Hunt, Barry D., and Adrian Preston (eds.), *War Aims and Strategic Policy in the Great War 1914–1918* (London, 1977).

Hyam, Ronald, *The Failure of South African Expansion 1908–1948* (London, 1972).

Iliffe, John, *A Modern History of Tanganyika* (Cambridge, 1979).

Ingram, Edward (ed.), *National and International Politics in the Middle East: Essays in Honour of Elie Kedourie* (London, 1986).

Jacobsen, Irmgard, 'German attempts to influence the intellectual life in the Ottoman empire during World War I', *Revue d'histoire Maghrebine*, 59–60 (Oct. 1990), 95–100.

Janssen, Karl-Heinz, *Der Kanzler und der General. Die Führungkrise um Bethmann Hollweg und Falkenhayn (1914–1916)* (Göttingen, 1967).

Jarausch, Konrad H., 'The illusion of limited war: Chancellor Bethmann Hollweg's calculated risk, July 1914', *Central European History*, II (1969), 48–76.

—— *The Enigmatic Chancellor: Bethmann Hollweg and the Hubris of Imperial Germany* (New Haven, 1973).

Jäschke, Gotthard, 'Der Turanismus der Jungtürken. Zur osmanischen Aussenpolitik im Weltkriege', *Die Welt des Islams*, XXIII (1941), 1–54.

Jeffery, Keith, *The British Army and the Crisis of Empire 1918–22* (Manchester, 1984).

Jenkins, Roy, *Asquith* (London, 1964).

Johnson, Franklyn Arthur, *Defence by Committee: The British Committee of Imperial Defence 1885–1959* (London, 1960).

Joll, James, *The Origins of the First World War* (London, 1984).

Jones, G. Gareth, 'The British government and the oil companies, 1912–1924: the search for an oil policy', *Historical Journal*, XX (1977), 647–72.

Jordan, Gerald (ed.), *Naval Warfare in the Twentieth Century 1900–1945: Essays in Honour of Arthur Marder* (London, 1977).

Jose, Arthur W., *The Royal Australian Navy 1914–1918* (Sydney, 1935).

Kakwenzaire, P. K, 'Sayyid Muhammad Abdille Hassan, Lij Yasu and the World War I politics: 1914–1916', *Transcaspian Journal of History*, XIV (1985), 36–45.

Kaspi, André, 'French war aims in Africa, 1914–1919', in Prosser Gifford and Wm. Roger Louis (eds.), *France and Britain in Africa: Imperial Rivalry and Colonial Rule* (New Haven, 1971).

Katzenellenbogen, S. E., 'Southern Africa and the war of 1914–18', in M. R. D. Foot (ed.), *War and society* (London, 1973).

Kautsky, Karl (ed.), *Die deutschen Dokumente zum Kriegsausbruch 1914*, 4 vols. (Berlin, 1922).

Kedourie, Elie, *England and the Middle East: The Destruction of the Ottoman Empire 1914–1921* (London, 1956).

Keiger, John F. V., *France and the Origins of the First World War* (London, 1983).

Kennedy, Greg, and Keith Neilson (eds.), *Far-flung Lines: Essays on Imperial Defence in Honour of Donald Mackenzie Schurman* (London, 1997).

Kennedy, Paul, *The Rise of the Anglo-German Antagonism 1860–1914* (London, 1980).

—— The Rise and Fall of the Great Powers: Economic Change and Military Conflict from 1500 to 2000 (London, 1988).

—— (ed.), The War Plans of the Great Powers 1880–1914 (London, 1979).

Kent, Marian (ed.), The Great Powers and the End of the Ottoman Empire (London, 1984).

Kielmansegg, Peter Graf, Deutschland und der Erste Weltkrieg, 2nd edn. (Stuttgart, 1980).

Killingray, David, 'Repercussions of World War I on the Gold Coast', Journal of African History, XIX (1978), 39–59.

—— 'Beasts of burden: British West African carriers in the First World War', Canadian Journal of African Studies, XII (1979), 5–23.

—— 'Labour exploitation for military campaigns in British colonial Africa 1870–1945', Journal of Contemporary History, XXIV (1989), 483–501.

Kimche, Jon, The Second Arab Awakening (London, 1970).

King, Jere Clemens, Generals and Politicians: Conflict between France's High Command, Parliament and Government, 1914–1918 (Berkeley, 1951).

Kiraly, Bela, Nandor F. Dreisziger, and Albert A. Nofi (eds.), East Central European Society in World War I (Boulder, Col., 1985).

Klein, Fritz, Deutschland im ersten Weltkrieg, 3 vols. (Berlin, 1968).

Klein-Arendt, Reinhard, 'Kamina ruft Nauen!' Die Funkstellen in den deutschen Kolonien 1904–1918 (Ostheim/Rhön, 1996).

Koch, H. W., (ed.), The Origins of the First World War: Great Power Rivalry and German War Aims (London, 1972); 2nd edn. (1984).

Koss, Stephen, Asquith (London, 1976).

—— 'The destruction of Britain's last Liberal government', Journal of Modern History, XL (1968), 257–77.

Kraft, Heinz, Staatsräson und Kriegführung im kaiserlichen Deutschland 1914–1916. Der Gegensatz zwischen dem Generalstabschef von Falkenhayn und dem Oberbefehlshaber Ost im Rahmen des Bundniskreiges der Mittelmächte (Göttingen, 1980).

Kress von Kressenstein, Friedrich, Mit dem Türken zum Suezkanal (Berlin, 1938).

Krieger, Leonard, and Fritz Stern (eds.), The responsibility of Power: Historical Essays in Honor of Hajo Holborn (London, 1968).

Kühlmann, Richard von, Erinnerungen (Heidelberg, 1948).

La Gorce, Paul-Marie de (ed.), La Première Guerre Mondiale, 2 vols. (Paris, 1991).

Lambert, Nicholas A., 'Admiral Sir John Fisher and the concept of flotilla defence, 1904–1909', Journal of Military History, LIX (1995), 639–60.

—— 'British naval policy, 1913–1914: financial limitation and strategic revolution', Journal of Modern History, LXVII (1995), 595–626.

Lambi, Ivo Nikolai, The Navy and German Power Politics, 1862–1914 (Boston, 1984).

Landau, Jacob M., *Pan-Turkism in Turkey: A Study of Irridentism* (London, 1981).

—— *The Politics of Pan-Islam: Ideology and Organization* (Oxford, 1990).

L'Ange, Gerald, *Urgent Imperial Service: South African Forces in German South West Africa 1914–1915* (Rivonia, 1991).

Larcher, M., *La Guerre turque dans la guerre mondiale* (Paris, 1926).

Lautenschlager, Karl, 'Technology and the evolution of naval warfare', *International security*, VII (1983), 3–51.

Le Révérend, André, *Lyautey* (Paris, 1983).

Lettow-Vorbeck, Paul von, *My Reminiscences of East Africa*, 2nd edn. (London, [1922]).

Lewis, Bernard, *The Emergence of Modern Turkey* (London, 1961).

Lewis, Geoffrey, 'The Ottoman proclamation of Jihad in 1914', in *Arabic and Islamic Garland: Historical, Educational and Literary Papers Presented to Abdul-Latif Tibawi* (London, 1977).

Liman von Sanders, Otto, *Five Years in Turkey* (Annapolis, 1927; first published 1920).

Louis, Wm. Roger, *Ruanda-Urundi 1884–1919* (Oxford, 1963).

—— *Great Britain and Germany's Lost Colonies 1914–1919* (Oxford, 1967).

—— 'The origins of the "sacred trust"', in Ronald Segal and Ruth First (eds.), *South West Africa: Travesty of Trust* (London, 1967).

Lowe, Peter, *Britain and Japan 1911–1915: A Study of British Far Eastern Policy* (London, 1969).

Lucas, Charles (ed.), *The Empire at War*, 5 vols. (Oxford, 1921–6).

Lumby, E. W. R. (ed.), *Policy and Operations in the Mediterranean 1912–14* (London, 1970).

Lunn, Joe, *Memoirs of the Maelstrom: A Senegalese Oral History of the First World War* (Portsmouth, NH, 1999).

Lutz, Ralph Haswell (ed.), *Documents of the German Revolution: Fall of the German Empire 1914–1918*, 2 vols. (Stanford, 1932).

Lyautey, Pierre, *Lyautey l'Africain: textes et lettres du maréchal Lyautey*, 4 vols. (Paris, 1953–7).

Macfie, A. L., *The End of the Ottoman Empire 1908–1923* (London, 1998).

McGibbon, Ian, *The Path to Gallipoli: Defending New Zealand 1840–1915* (Wellington, 1991).

McKale, Donald M., '"The Kaiser's spy": Max von Oppenheim and the Anglo-German rivalry before and during the First World War', *European History Quarterly*, XXVII (1997), 199–219.

—— *War by Revolution: Germany and Great Britain in the Middle East in the Era of World War I* (Kent, Ohio, 1998).

Mackenzie, S. S., *The Australians at Rabaul: The Capture and Administration of the German Possessions in the South Pacific* (Sydney, 1927).

McLaughlin, Peter, *Ragtime Soldiers: The Rhodesian Experience in the First World War* (Bulawayo, 1980).

—— 'Victims or defenders: African troops in the Rhodesian defence system, 1890–1980', *Small Wars and Insurgencies* II (1991), 240–75.

MacMunn, George, and Cyril Falls, *Military Operations: Egypt and Palestine*, 2 vols. (London, 1928–30).

Macpherson, W. G., and T. J. Mitchell, *Medical Services: General History*, 4 vols. (London, 1921–4).

Maddox, Gregory, ' "Mtunya": famine in central Tanzania, 1917–20', *Journal of African History*, XXXI (1990), 181–97.

Marder, Arthur J., (ed.), *Fear God and Dread Nought: The Correspondence of Admiral of the Fleet Lord Fisher of Kilverstone*, 3 vols. (London, 1952–9).

—— *From the Dreadnought to Scapa Flow: The Royal Navy in the Fisher Era, 1904–1919*, 5 vols. (London, 1961–70).

Marine-Archiv (ed.) *Der Krieg zur See 1914–1918. Der Kreuzerkrieg in den ausländischen Gewässern*, by E. Raeder and Eberhard von Mantey, 3 vols. (Berlin, 1922–37).

—— (ed.), *Der Krieg in den türkischen Gewässern*, 2 vols. (Berlin, 1928–38).

—— (ed.), *Der Krieg zur See 1914–1918. Die Kämpfe der kaiserlichen Marine in den deutschen Kolonien* (Berlin, 1935).

Martin, Gregory W., 'Revolutionary Projects and Racial prejudices: non-military perceptions of the colonial manpower effort', unpublished paper.

Matuschka, Edgar Graf von, 'Organisationsgeschichte des Heeres 1890–1918', in Militärgeschichtliche Forschungsamt, *Handbuch zur deutschen Militärgeschichte*, vol. V (Frankfurt am Main, 1968).

Maxon, Robert M., *Struggle for Kenya: The Loss and Reassertion of Imperial Initiative 1912–1923* (Cranbury, NJ, 1993).

Meaney, Neville, *The Search for Security in the Pacific, 1901–14* (Sydney, 1976).

Meinertzhagen, R., *Army Diary 1899–1926* (Edinburgh, 1960).

Meintjes, Johannes, *General Louis Botha: A Biography* (London, 1970).

Mentzel, Heinrich, *Die Kämpfe im Kamerun 1914–1916. Vorbereitung und Verlauf* (Berlin, 1936).

Mentzel, Heinz, *Die Kämpfe in Kamerun 1914–1916*, *Münchener historische Abhandlungen: zweite Reihe: Kriegs- und Heeresgeschichte*, 1. Heft (Munich, 1932).

Messimy, Adolphe, *Mes souvenirs* (Paris, 1937).

Meynier, Gilbert, *L'Algérie révélée: la guerre de 1914–1918 et le premier quart du XXe siècle* (Genève, 1981).

Meynier, O., 'La Guerre sainte des Senoussya en Afrique (1914– 1918)', *Revue militaire française*, 131 (mai 1932), 176–204; 138 (decembre 1932), 412–32; 139 (janvier 1933), 121–44; 140 (février 1933), 244–54; 148 (octobre 1933), 120–42; 149 (novembre 1933), 336–53; 152 (février 1934), 214–37; 153 (mars 1934), 399–426.

Michalka, Wolfgang, (ed.), *Der Erste Weltkrieg. Wirkung, Warnehmung, Analyse* (Munich, 1994).

Michel, Marc, *L'Appel à l'Afrique: contributions et réactions à l'effort de guerre en A.O.F. (1914– 1919)* (Paris, 1982).

Michel, Marc, *Gallieni* (Paris, 1989).

Michel, Marc, 'Le Cameroun allemand aurait-il pu rester unifié? Français et Britanniques dans la conquête du Cameroun (1914–1916)', *Guerres mondiales et conflits contemporains*, 168, (octobre 1992), 13–29.

Miller, Charles, *Battle for the Bundu: The First World War in East Africa* (London, 1974).

Miller, Geoffrey, *Superior Force: The Conspiracy behind the Escape of 'Goeben' and 'Breslau'* (Hull, 1996).

—— *Straits: British Policy towards the Ottoman Empire and the Origins of the Dardanelles Campaign* (Hull, 1997).

Millett, Allan R., and Williamson Murray (eds.), *Military Effectiveness*, vol. I, *The First World War* (Boston, 1988).

Ministère de la Guerre, État-Major de l'Armée—Service Historique, *Les Armées françaises dans la grande guerre*, 11 vols. (Paris, 1922–37).

Ministry of Munitions, *History of the Ministry of Munitions*, 12 vols. (London, 1922).

Miquel, Pierre, *La Grande Guerre* (Paris, 1983).

Mitchell, T. J., and G. M. Smith, *Medical Services: Casualties and Medical Statistics of the Great War* (London, 1997; first published 1931).

Moberly, F. J., *Military Operations: The Campaign in Mesopotamia*, 4 vols. (London, 1923–7).

—— *Military Operations: Togoland and the Cameroons 1914–1916* (London, 1931).

Le Monde, La Trés Grande Guerre (Paris, 1994).

Monson, Jamie, 'Relocating Maji Maji: the politics of alliance and authority in the southern highlands of Tanzania', *Journal of African History*, XXXIX (1998), 95–120.

Moreman, T. R., *The Army in India and the Development of Frontier Warfare, 1849–1947* (Basingstoke, 1998).

Morgan, Kenneth O., *Lloyd George* (London, 1974).

Mosley, Leonard, *Duel for Kilimanjaro: An Account of the East African Campaign 1914–1918* (London, 1963).

Moukbil bey, M., *Le Campagne de l'Irak 1914–1918: le siège de Kut-el-Amara* (Paris, 1933).

Moyse-Barlett, H., *The King's African Rifles: A Study in the Military History of East and Central Africa, 1890–1945* (Aldershot, 1956).

Mühlmann, Carl, *Deutschland und die Türkei 1913–1914. Die Berufung der deutschen Militärmission nach der Türkei 1913, das deutsch–türkische Bündnis 1914 und der Eintritt der Türkei in den Weltkrieg* (Berlin-Grunewald, 1929).

—— *Das deutsch–türkische Waffenbündnis im Weltkriege* (Leipzig, 1940).

Müller, Herbert Landolin, *Islam, Gihad ('Heiliger Krieg') und deutsches Reich. Ein Nachspiel zur wilhelminischen Weltpolitik im Maghreb 1914–1918* (Frankfurt am Main, 1991).

Murfett, Malcolm H. (ed.), *The First Sea Lords: From Fisher to Mountbatten* (Westport, Conn., 1995).

—— and John N. Miksic, Brian P. Farrell, Chiang Ming Shun, *Between two Oceans: A Military History of Singapore from the First Settlement to British Withdrawal* (Oxford, 1999).

Nasson, Bill, 'A great divide: popular responses to the Great War in South Africa', *War & Society*, XII (1994), 47–64.

—— 'War opinion in South Africa, 1914', *Journal of Imperial and Commonwealth History*, XXIII (1995), 248–76.

Neulen, Hans Werner, *Feldgrau in Jerusalem. Das Levantekorps des kaiserlichen Deutschland* (Munich, 1991).

Nevakivi, Jukka, *Britain, France and the Arab Middle East 1914–1920* (London, 1969).

Newbury, Colin, 'Spoils of war: sub-imperial collaboration in South West Africa and New Guinea', *Journal of Imperial and Commonwealth History*, XVI (1988), 86–106.

Newell, Jonathan Quentin Calvin, 'British military policy in Egypt and Palestine, August 1914–June 1917', London University Ph.D. thesis, 1989.

O'Brien, Phillips Payson, *British and American Naval Power: Politics and Policy, 1900–1936* (Westport, Conn., 1998).

—— (ed.) *Preparing for the Next War at Sea: Technology and Naval Combat in the Twentieth Century* (London, 2001).

Occleshaw, Michael, *Armour against Fate: Intelligence in the First World War* (London, 1989).

Oelhafen, Hans von, *Der Feldzug in Südwest* (Berlin, [1923]).

Offer, Avner, *The First World War: An Agrarian Interpretation* (Oxford, 1989).

Olson, William J., *Anglo-Iranian Relations during World War I* (London, 1984).

Omissi, David, *The Sepoy and the Raj: The Indian Army, 1860–1940* (Basingstoke, 1994).

Osuntokun, Akinjide, *Nigeria in the First World War*, London, 1979).

Overlack, Peter, 'Australian defence awareness and German naval planning in the Pacific 1900–1914', *War & Society*, X (1992), 37–51.

—— 'German interest in Australian defence, 1901–1914: new insights into a precarious position on the eve of war', *Australian Journal of Politics and History*, XL (1994), 36–51.

—— 'The force of circumstance: Graf Spee's options for the East Asia cruiser squadron in 1914', *Journal of Military History*, LX (1996), 657–82.

Overlack, Peter, 'Australasia and Germany: challenge and response before 1914', in David Stevens (ed.), *Maritime Power in the 20th Century: The Australian Experience* (St Leonards NSW, 1998).

—— 'Asia in German naval planning before the First World War: the strategic imperative', *War & Society*, XVII (1999), 1–23.

Overstraeten, R. von (ed.), *The War Diaries of Albert I, King of the Belgians* (London, 1954).

Overton, John, 'War and economic development: settlers in Kenya, 1914–1918', *Journal of African History*, XXVII (1986), 79–103.

Page, Melvin E., *The Chiwaya War: Malawians and the First World War* (Boulder, 2000).

—— 'The War of *Thangata*: Nyasaland and the East African campaign, 1914–1918', *Journal of African History*, XIX (1978), 87–100.

—— '"With Jannie in the jungle": European humour in an East African campaign, 1914–1918', *International Journal of African Historical Studies*, XIV (1981), 466–81.

—— (ed.), *Africa and the First World War* (London, 1987).

Pavlovich, N. B., *The Fleet in the First World War*, vol. 1, *Operations of the Russian fleet* (New Delhi, 1979; first published, Moscow, 1964).

Peattie, Mark R., *Nanyo: The Rise and Fall of the Japanese in Micronesia* (Honolulu, 1988).

Pélissier, René, 'Campagnes militaires au Sud-Angola (1885–1915), *Cahiers d'études africaines*, IX (1969), 54–123.

—— *Les Guerres grises: résistance et révoltes en Angola (1845–1941)* (Orgeval, 1977).

—— *Naissance du Mozambique: résistance et révoltes anticoloniales (1854–1918)*, 2 vols. (Orgeval, 1984).

Perham, Margery, *Lugard: The Years of Authority 1898–1945* (London, 1960).

Perkins, Kenneth J., *Tunisia: Crossroads of the Islamic and European Worlds* (Boulder, Col., 1986).

Pochhammer, Hans, *Before Jutland: Admiral von Spee's Last Voyage: Coronel and the Battle of the Falklands* (London, 1931).

Pokrowski, M. N. (ed.), *Die internationalen Beziehungen im Zeitalter des Imperialismus*, ed. Otto Hoetsch, series 1, ii (Berlin, 1933).

Pomiankowski, Joseph, *Der Zusammenbruch des Ottomanischen Reiches. Erinnerungen an die Türkei aus der Zeit des Weltkrieges* (Vienna, 1928).

Popplewell, Richard, 'British intelligence in Mesopotamia 1914–1916', *Intelligence and National Security*, V (1990), 139–72.

—— 'British intelligence and Indian subversion: the surveillance of Indian revolutionaries in India and abroad 1904–1920', Cambridge University Ph.D. thesis,

1988; published as *Intelligence and Imperial Defence: British Intelligence and the Defence of the Indian Empire, 1904–1924* (London, 1995).

Porch, Douglas, *The March to the Marne: The French Army 1871–1914* (Cambridge, 1981).

—— *The Conquest of the Sahara* (London, 1985; first published 1984).

—— *The Conquest of Morocco* (London, 1986; first published 1982).

Prasad, Yuvaraj Dera, *The Indian Muslims and World War I: A Phase of Disillusionment with British Rule 1914–1918* (New Delhi, 1985).

Pürschel, Herbert, *Die kaiserliche Schutztruppe für Kamerun. Gefüge und Aufgabe* (Berlin, 1936).

Quinn, Frederick, 'An African reaction to World War I: the Beti of Cameroon', *Cahiers d'études africaines*, XIII (1973), 722–31.

Ranger, T. O., 'Revolt in Portuguese east Africa: the Makombe rising of 1917', *St Antony's Papers*, 15 (1963), 54–80.

—— *Dance and Society in Eastern Africa, 1890–1970: The Beni 'Ngoma'* (London, 1975).

Rathbone, Richard, 'World War I and Africa: an introduction', *Journal of African History*, XIX (1978), 1–9.

Rathmann, Lothar, *Stossrichtung Nahost 1914–1918: zur Expansionpolitik des deutschen Imperialismus im ersten Weltkrieg* (Berlin, 1963).

Rayaud-Lacroze, E., *Méharistes au combat* (Paris, 1983).

Reichsarchiv, *Der Weltkrieg, 1914 bis 1918*, 14 vols. (Berlin, 1925–44).

Reitz, Denys, *Trekking On* (London, 1933).

Renouvin, Pierre, *La Crise européenne et la première guerre mondiale (1904–1918)*, 6th edn. (Paris, 1969).

Riezler, Kurt, *Kurt Riezler. Tagebücher, Aufsätze, Dokumente*, ed. Karl Dietrich Erdmann (Göttingen, 1972).

Ritter, Gerhard, *The Sword and the Sceptre: The Problem of Militarism in Germany*, 4 vols. (London, 1970–3).

Rivet, Daniel, *Lyautey et l'institution du protectorat français au Maroc 1912–1925*, 3 vols. (Paris, 1988).

Robbins, Keith, *The First World War* (Oxford, 1984).

Roberts, A. D. (ed.), *The Cambridge History of Africa*, vol. 7, *1905–1940* (Cambridge, 1986).

Roberts, Richard, *Schröders: Merchants and Bankers* (Basingstoke, 1992).

Robinson, Ronald, and John Gallagher, with Alice Denny, *Africa and the Victorians: The Official Mind of Imperialism* (London, 1961).

Rodger, N. A. M. (ed.), *Naval Power in the Twentieth Century* (Basingstoke, 1996).

Rohwer, Jürgen (ed.), *Neue Forschungen zum Ersten Weltkrieg* (Koblenz, 1985).

Rothwell, V. H., 'The British government and Japanese military assistance 1914–1918', *History*, LVI (1971), 35–45.

Rothwell, V. H., *British War Aims and Peace Diplomacy 1914–1918* (Oxford, 1971).

Rumbold, Algernon, *Watershed in India 1914–1922* (London, 1979).

Sanders, Michael, and Philip M. Taylor, *British Propaganda during the First World War 1914–18* (London, 1982).

Santorini, Alberto, 'The first Ultra secret: the British cryptanalysis in the naval operations of the First World War', *Revue internationale d'histoire militaire*, 63 (1985), 99–110.

Sareen, Tilan Raj, *Indian Revolutionary Movements Abroad (1905–1921)* (New Delhi, 1979).

Savage, Donald C., and J. Forbes Munro, 'Carrier corps recruitment in the British East Africa Protectorate 1914–1918', *Journal of African History*, VII (1966), 313–42.

Scham, Alan, *Lyautey in Morocco: Protectorate Administration, 1912–1925* (Berkeley, 1970).

Schencking, J. Charles, 'Bureaucratic politics, military budgets, and Japan's southern advance: the imperial navy's seizure of German Micronesia in World War I', *War in History*, V (1998), 308–26.

Schmidt-Richberg, Wiegand, 'Die Regierungszeit Wilhelms II', in Militärgeschichtliche Forschungsamt, *Handbuch zur deutschen Militärgeschichte*, vol. V (Frankfurt am Main, 1968).

Schnee, Heinrich, *Deutsch-Ostafrika im Weltkriege: wie wir lebten und kämpften* (Leipzig, 1919).

Schoen, Erich, *Geschichte des deutschen Feuerwerkswesens der Armee und Marine mit Einschluss des Zeugwesens* (Berlin, 1936).

Schulte, Bernd F., *Die deutsche Armee 1900–1914: zwischen beharren und verändern* (Dusseldorf, 1977).

—— *Vor dem Kriegsausbruch 1914. Deutschland, die Türkei und der Balkan* (Dusseldorf, 1980).

Schwarte, Max, (ed.), *Der Weltkampf um Ehre und Recht*, 10 vols. (Leipzig, 1921–33); first published as *Der grosse Krieg 1914/18* (Leipzig, 1921).

Scott, Ernest, *Australia during the War* (Sydney, 1940; first published 1936).

Scott, J. D., *Vickers: A History* (London, 1962).

Sebald, Peter, *Togo 1884–1914. Eine Geschichte der deutschen 'Musterkolonie' auf der Grundlage amtlichen Quellen* (Berlin, 1988).

Seitz, Theodor, *Südafrika im Weltkriege* (Berlin, 1920).

Self, Robert C. (ed.), *The Austen Chamberlain Diary Letters: The Correspondence of Sir Austen Chamberlain with his Sisters Hilda and Ida, 1916–1937* (Cambridge, 1995).

Semmel, Bernard, *Liberalism and Naval Strategy: Ideology, Interest, and Sea Power during the Pax Britannica* (Boston, 1986).

Sheffy, Yigal, *British Military Intelligence in the Palestine Campaign 1914–1918* (London, 1998).

Shepperson, George, and Thomas Price, *Independent African: John Chilembwe and the Origins, Setting and Significance of the Nyasaland Native Rising of 1915* (Edinburgh, 1958).

Simon, Rachel, *Libya between Ottomanism and Nationalism: The Ottoman Involvement in Libya during the War with Italy (1911–1919)* (Berlin, 1987).

Smith, C. Jay, jr, 'Great Britain and the 1914–1915 straits agreement with Russia: the British promise of November 1914', *American Historical Review*, LXX (1965), 1015–34.

—— *The Russian Struggle for Power, 1914–1917: A Study of Russian Foreign Policy during the First World War* (New York, 1969; first published 1956).

Smith, Paul, (ed.), *Government and the Armed Forces in Britain 1856–1990* (London, 1996).

Smith-Dorrien, Horace, *Memories of Forty-Eight Years' Service* (London, 1925).

Soames, Mary (ed.), *Speaking for themselves: The Personal Letters of Winston and Clementine Churchill* (London, 1998).

Soutou, Georges-Henri, *L'Or et le sang: les buts de guerre économiques de la première guerre mondiale* (Paris, 1989).

Spies, S. B., 'The outbreak of the First World War and the Botha government', *South African Historical Journal*, I (1969), 47–57.

Stanley, William R., 'Review of Turkish Asiatic railways to 1918: some political-military considerations', *Journal of Transport History*, VII (1966), 189–204.

Stegemann, Hermann, *Geschichte des Krieges*, 4 vols. (Stuttgart, 1918–21).

Stevenson, David, *French War Aims against Germany 1914–1919* (Oxford, 1982).

—— *The First World War and International Politics* (Oxford, 1988).

Stoecker, Helmuth (ed.), *German Imperialism: From the Beginnings until the Second World War* (London, 1986; first published 1977).

Stone, Jay, and Erwin A. Schmidl, *The Boer War and Military Reforms* (London, 1988).

Storz, Dieter, *Kriegsbild und Rüstung vor 1914. Europäische Landstreitkräfte vor dem Ersten Weltkrieg* (Herford, 1992).

Strachan, Hew, (ed.), *Oxford Illustrated History of the First World War* (Oxford, 1998).

—— *The First World War: A New Illustrated History* (London, 2003)

Stromberg, Roland N., *Redemption by War: The Intellectuals and 1914* (Lawrence, Kan., 1982).

Student, Erich, *Kameruns Kampf 1914–16* (Berlin, 1937).

Stuermer, H., *Two War Years in Constantinople* (London, 1917).

Summers, Anne, and R. W. Johnson, 'World War I conscription and social change in Guinea', *Journal of African History*, XIX (1978), 25–38.

Suren, Hans, *Kampf um Kamerun: Garua* (Berlin, 1934).

Swart, Sandra, '"A Boer and his gun and his wife are three things always together": republican masculinity and the 1914 rebellion', *Journal of Southern African Studies*, XXIV (1998), 737–51.

Swietochowski, Tamusz, *Russian Azerbaijan, 1905–1920: The Shaping of a National Identity in a Muslim Community* (Cambridge, 1985).

Sykes, Christopher, *Wassmuss: The German Lawrence* (London, 1936).

Tan, Tai-Yong, 'An imperial home-front: Punjab and the First World War', *Journal of Military History*, LXIV (2000), 371–410.

Taute, M., 'A German account of the medical side of the war in East Africa, 1914–1918', *Tanganyika Notes and Records*, 8 (Dec. 1939), 1–20.

Teixeira, Nuno Severiano, *L'Entrée du Portugal dans la Grande Guerre: objectifs nationaux et stratégies politiques* (Paris, 1998).

Thomas, Roger, 'Military recruitment in the Gold Coast during the First World War', *Cahiers d'études africaines*, XV (1975), 57–83.

—— 'The 1916 Bongo "riots" and their background: aspects of colonial administration and African response in eastern upper Ghana', *Journal of African History*, XXIV (1983), 57–75.

Thompson, Wayne C., *In the Eye of the Storm: Kurt Riezler and the Crises of Modern Germany* (Iowa City, 1980).

Ticktin, David, 'The war issue and the collapse of the South African Labour party 1914–15', *South African Historical Journal*, 1 (1969), 59–80.

Townsend, Mary Evelyn *The Rise and Fall of the Germany's Colonial Empire 1884–1918* (New York, 1930).

Trumpener, Ulrich, 'German military aid to Turkey in 1914: an historical re-evaluation', *Journal of Modern History*, XXXII (1960), 145–9.

—— 'Turkey's entry into World War I: an assessment of responsibilities', *Journal of Modern History*, XXXIV (1962), 369–80.

—— 'Liman von Sanders and the German–Ottoman alliance', *Journal of Contemporary History*, I (1966), 179–92.

—— *Germany and the Ottoman Empire 1914–1918* (Princeton, 1968).

Turner, John, *British Politics and the Great War: Coalition and Conflict 1915–1918* (New Haven, 1992).

—— (ed.), *Britain and the First World War* (London, 1988).

Usborne, C. V., *The Conquest of Morocco* (London, 1936).

Vincent-Smith, John, 'Britain, Portugal, and the First World War, 1914–1916', *European Studies Review*, IV (1974), 207–38.

Vogel, Renate, *Die Persien- und Afghanistanexpedition Oskar Ritter v. Niedermayers 1915/16* (Osnabrück, 1976).

Walker, Eric A., *A History of Southern Africa* (London, 1957).

Wallach, Jehuda L., *Anatomie einer Militärhilfe. Die preussisch–deutschen Militärmissionen in der Türkei 1835–1919* (Dusseldorf, 1976).

War Office, *Statistics of the Military Effort of the British Empire during the Great War* (London, 1922).

Warburg, Gabriel, *The Sudan under Wingate: Administration in the Anglo-Egyptian Sudan 1899–1916* (London, 1971).

Warhurst, P. R., 'Smuts and Africa: a study in sub-imperialism', *South African Historical Journal*, XVI (1984), 82–100.

Weber, Frank G., *Eagles on the Crescent: Germany, Austria, and the Diplomacy of the Turkish alliance 1914–1918* (Ithaca, NY, 1970).

Wegener, Wolfgang, *Die Seestrategie des Weltkrieges* (Berlin, 1929); English edn., *The Naval Strategy of the World War*, ed. Holger Herwig (Annapolis, 1989).

Wilcox, Craig, 'Relinquishing the past: John Mordike's *An Army for a Nation*', *Australian Journal of History and Politics*, XL (1994), 52–65.

Williams, Rhodri, *Defending the Empire: The Conservative Party and British Defence Policy 1899–1915* (New Haven, 1991).

Wilson, Jeremy, *Lawrence of Arabia: The Authorised Biography of T. E. Lawrence* (London, 1989).

Wilson, Keith, 'The British cabinet's decision for war, 2 August 1914', *British Journal of International Studies*, I (1975), 148–59.

—— 'The Foreign Office and the "education" of public opinion before the First World War', *Historical Journal*, XXVI (1983), 403–11.

—— *The Policy of the Entente: Essays on the Determinants of British Foreign Policy 1904–1914* (Cambridge, 1985).

—— 'Hankey's appendix: some Admiralty manoeuvres during and after the Agadir crisis', *War in History*, I (1994), 81–97.

—— 'Understanding the "misunderstanding" of 1 August 1914', *Historical Journal*, XXXVII (1994), 885–9.

—— (ed.), *The Rasp of War: The Letters of H. A. Gwynne to the Countess Bathurst 1914–1918* (London, 1988).

—— (ed.), *Decisions for War, 1914* (London, 1995).

Wilson, Trevor, *The Downfall of the Liberal Party 1914–1935* (London, 1966).

—— *The Myriad Faces of War: Britain and the Great War 1914–1918* (Cambridge, 1986).

Wingate, Ronald, *Wingate of the Sudan: The Life and Times of General Sir Reginald Wingate, Maker of the Anglo-Egyptian Sudan* (London, 1955).

Woodward, Llewellyn, *Great Britain and the War of 1914–1918* (London, 1967).

Yates, Keith, *Graf Spee's Raiders: Challenge to the Royal Navy, 1914–1915* (Annapolis, 1995).

Yearwood, Peter J., 'Great Britain and the repartition of Africa', *Journal of Imperial and Commonwealth History*, XVIII (1990), 316–41.

Yearwood, Peter J., ' "In a casual way with a blue pencil": British policy and the partition of Kamerun, 1914–1919', *Canadian Journal of African Studies*, XXVII (1993), 218–44.

—— 'The reunification of Borno, 1914–1919', *Borno Museum Society Newsletter*, xxv (1995), 25–44.

Yorke, Edmund James, 'A crisis of colonial control: war and authority in Northern Rhodesia, 1914–19', Cambridge University Ph.D. thesis, 1983.

Young, Francis Brett, *Marching on Tanga: With General Smuts in East Africa* (London, 1919; first published 1917).

Zirkel, Kirsten, 'Military power in German colonial policy: the *Schütztruppen* and their leaders in East and South-West Africa, 1888–1918', in David Killingray and David Omissi (eds.), *Guardians of Empire: The Armed Forces of the Colonial Powers c.1700–1964* (Manchester, 2000).

INDEX